Quiet Powers of the Possible

John D. Caputo, *series editor*

TAREK R. DIKA
and W. CHRIS HACKETT

Quiet Powers of the Possible

Interviews in Contemporary French Phenomenology

FORDHAM UNIVERSITY PRESS
New York ▪ 2016

Fordham University Press also publishes its books in a variety of electronic formats. Some content that appears in print may not be available in electronic books.
Visit us online at www.fordhampress.com.

Library of Congress Cataloging-in-Publication Data
Dika, Tarek R.
Quiet powers of the possible : interviews in contemporary French phenomenology / Tarek R. Dika and W. Chris Hackett. — First edition.
pages cm. — (Perspectives in Continental philosophy)
Includes bibliographical references and index.
ISBN 978-0-8232-6471-1 (cloth : alk. paper) — ISBN 978-0-8232-6472-8 (pbk. : alk. paper)
1. Phenomenology. 2. Philosophers—France—Interviews. I. Title.
B829.5.D55 2016
142′.70944—dc23

2015032364

Printed in the United States of America

18 17 16 5 4 3 2 1

First edition

Contents

Foreword by Richard Kearney ix

Introduction: Phenomenology and the Concept of Reason
Tarek R. Dika and W. Chris Hackett 1

French Phenomenology in Historical Context
Jean-François Courtine 24

The Phenomenology of Givenness
Jean-Luc Marion 40

The Fundamental Concepts of Phenomenology
Claude Romano 65

Contextualism, Realism, and the Limits of Intentionality
Jocelyn Benoist 97

Material Phenomenology
Michel Henry 117

The Phenomenology of Life
Renaud Barbaras 145

Phenomenology and Finitude
Françoise Dastur 176

Phenomenology and the Frontier
Jean-Yves Lacoste 188

The Collision of Phenomenology and Theology
Emmanuel Falque *211*

Attempting to Think Beyond Subjectivity
Jean-Louis Chrétien *228*

Acknowledgments ***239***

Bibliography ***241***

List of Contributors ***257***

Index ***259***

Foreword

RICHARD KEARNEY

The title of this work comes from a closing line in Heidegger's *Being and Time*. He is speaking of the future of phenomenology as a promise of things to come—a sentiment already anticipated in an opening claim of the book: "In phenomenology possibility stands higher than actuality."[1] For Heidegger this spelled a revolutionary reversal of the old metaphysical paradigm of being as presence, substance, and act and a radical openness to new kinds of questioning.

The first generation of French phenomenologists was deeply influenced by this opening. Or, to be more precise, by the momentous legacy of the three Hs: Hegel, Husserl, and Heidegger. Lévinas and Sartre were the first to translate the exciting philosophical messages arriving from Germany in the late twenties and early thirties. Ricoeur and Merleau-Ponty took up the running in the forties and fifties, with Derrida, Irigaray, and others refining and refashioning the legacy of the three Hs well into the sixties and seventies. If the first great wave of phenomenology was decidedly German, the second was ingeniously French. But the promise of phenomenology was far from exhausted by these two extraordinary generations. A third was soon to follow, as the current volume powerfully demonstrates. Covering an important span of thinking and writing from the 1980s to the present day, the authors interviewed in this volume show how phenomenology's "quiet power of the possible" had unsuspected strengths and resources that mobilized a whole new set of philosophical conversations. Surviving both the structuralist and poststructuralist challenges, this emerging generation of French thinkers, extending well into the third millennium, has managed to open doors to hitherto undeveloped areas of questioning—theological, anthropological, analytic, and aesthetic.

Jean-Yves Lacoste speaks of phenomenology as a form of "hospitality" and this volume certainly bears this out. There is a remarkable readiness in the interlocutors featured here to engage with what might be called "limit questions"—those of Life (Barbaras and Henry) and Death (Dastur), of God (Lacoste, Chrétien, Falque) and Gift (Marion), of Language (Benoist) and Being (Romano and Courtine). And to do so in new and interdisciplinary ways unwitnessed in previous generations, with the possible exception of Paul Ricoeur. This interdisciplinary character lends itself to a dialogical approach—not only between French and German voices over three generations of phenomenology but also between Continental and Anglo-American thought (Romano and Benoist), between hermeneutic ontology and the philosophy of language, and, more generally, between the claims of reason (phenomenology as science) and imagination (phenomenology as art). Indeed, one of the things that have distinguished contemporary French phenomenology since the 1980s has been a willingness to embrace a philosophy of problems rather than proper names. And this is yet a further indication of how the new generation of phenomenologists remains hospitable to the possible. Defying the restriction of metaphysical rationality to a priori normativity—of subjectivity or objectivity—those engaged in dialogue here keep the phenomenological conversation open to ever-new ways of hosting and responding to the "things themselves." This is phenomenology at the frontiers—that is, at its best.

Tarek Dika and Chris Hackett have done sterling service in bringing these novel developments and assessments of phenomenology to our attention. And in doing so in a manner less disputatious than conversational, less abstract than engaging, thus translating what are often highly complex, dense, and even imponderable speculations into the accessible language of question and answer. The editors have succeeded in making these remarkable French thinkers more available to an English-language readership in a timely and compelling fashion.

Note

1. Heidegger, *Being and Time*, 63.

Quiet Powers of the Possible

Introduction

Phenomenology and the Concept of Reason

TAREK R. DIKA AND W. CHRIS HACKETT

§1 New Developments and the Need for a Reassessment

The American reception of contemporary French phenomenology, however fecund, has been both selective and cloistered. For many, the "theological turn," an expression initially coined as an epithet by Dominique Janicaud (and that, like many epithets, has become something of a rallying cry this side of the Atlantic), unquestionably represents what, for better or worse, distinguishes phenomenology from other trends in contemporary philosophy, be they French or Anglo-American. No doubt, French phenomenology has demonstrated a remarkable capacity for describing phenomena hitherto deemed beyond the pale of reason. But according to what (or whose) concept of reason? Whether phenomenology has gone beyond the pale of rationality remains a matter of dispute within the French and, indeed, the broader phenomenological community.

In our view, the idea that phenomenology has somehow abandoned the commitment to reason is seriously mistaken. The interviews collected here make clear that, since the 1980s, French phenomenologists have, if anything, been engaged in a systematic re-evaluation of the history and forms of reason, both scholastic and modern. This evaluation has been made in light of a consistent problem about the limits and possibilities, historical and conceptual, of a distinctively *phenomenological* concept of reason. French phenomenology has been nothing if not committed to developing an expanded concept of reason, one according to which transcendental, ontological, and/or even historical conditions of experience do not and, indeed, cannot foreclose or rigidly determine, once and for all, the space of what can be described "within the limits of reason alone," to use the Kantian expression. Phenomenology, unlike a number of other trends in contemporary philosophy, neither rigidly identifies reason and normativity nor, for that matter, does it simply dissociate them. Rather, it fosters what may be termed an "empirical sensitivity" to phenomena whose modes of givenness can decisively affect (and need not, therefore, merely conform to) the norms that condition the possibility of experience. A norm that cannot be affected in this way—a norm wholly immune to events—is not a norm but an eternal law.

New developments have made a reassessment of the last three decades of French phenomenology not only desirable but necessary. What has come to be known, rightly or wrongly, as the "theological turn" represents but one dimension of French phenomenology (see §2, below). In the United States, other areas of phenomenological research have been occluded by the deserved but nevertheless partial emphasis on the "theological turn," a loaded term that needs to be used cautiously. For example, by taking positions on historical and contemporary issues in the analytic philosophy of mind, the philosophy of language, and metaphysics, Jocelyn Benoist and, more recently, Claude Romano have initiated what may very well be a new chapter in the history of French phenomenology. This aspect of contemporary phenomenology remains almost completely unknown in the United States. Its significance, however, should not be underestimated, not only because of the divergent ways in which these two figures have responded to the growth of analytic philosophy in their own country but also because their work may begin to affect debates taking place in the United States (see §4). Whether as an anodyne designation of the current state of French phenomenology or, conversely, an accusation of betrayal, the label "theological turn" simply cannot account for the broad range of projects that have informed French phenomenology since the 1980s.

In the United States, French philosophy (not only phenomenology) has been a familiar presence ever since the late 1960s,[1] a fact celebrated by some and deplored by others. More recently, the work of figures like Gilles Deleuze and Alain Badiou has come to be seen by many as alternatives to the allegedly linguistic orientation of French philosophy after Derrida. Although this way of identifying theoretical alternatives tends to be reductive and needlessly polemical, it does indicate, at the very least, that the intellectual mood has changed. The use of neuroscience, in philosophy but also, more recently, in anthropology and literary and political theory—much of it inspired by a certain reading of Deleuze and Henri Bergson—is one example of this. The change of mood can also be detected in phenomenology. Figures in twentieth-century philosophical biology—such as Hans Jonas, a student of Heidegger's—have come to exert a notable influence on contemporary French phenomenological theories of life, perception, knowledge, and action, particularly in the work of Renaud Barbaras and, somewhat differently, Claude Romano. Many phenomenologists, for whom phenomenology has too frequently (and oftentimes ignorantly) been derided for distancing itself from the sciences, have sought to deepen the foundations of phenomenology by grounding it in a conceptual horizon that can no longer be regarded as straightforwardly or dogmatically anti-naturalistic. To be sure, the phenomenological concept of life—a concept whose history can be traced back to Husserl's concept of *Erlebnis*, Heidegger's concept of "factical life," Michel Henry's "autoaffective life," and, most recently, Renaud Barbaras's "phenomenology of life"—has never been reductively naturalistic. Its contribution to contemporary debates about these matters, many of which have far too uncritically embraced the language of natural science, consists precisely in the ways it absorbs these trends without losing sight of the irreducibility of intentionality.

As this very brief catalog already makes clear, contemporary French phenomenology cannot be identified by tacking labels onto this or that figure or, worse, the whole batch of them. In his interview, Jean-François Courtine, who deals with the historiographical problems pertaining to the development of phenomenology in the 1980s and 1990s, stresses—correctly, in our estimation—that contemporary phenomenologists can be superficially schematized in any number of ways, none of which would capture the relevant differences or the underlying unity, if any, of contemporary phenomenological research. That unity can only be discerned, not by a providing a superficial classification of *positions* but rather by identifying the relevant *problems* to which phenomenologists have felt compelled to respond—each in their own way—since the 1980s. The contention behind this book is that a consistent problem regarding the status of reason is what most clearly defines the field of contemporary phenomenology.

§2 What Is Phenomenological Reason?

Dominique Janicaud coined the expression "theological turn" in order to characterize what he saw as French phenomenology's deviation from the phenomenological method in the 1980s and 1990s. For Janicaud, "phenomenology and theology make two,"[2] and the expansion of phenomenological research beyond the constraints of the phenomenological method laid down by Husserl in *Ideas I* leads phenomenology into regions of inquiry that are dogmatic in the Kantian and Husserlian senses of the term.[3]

This calls for two remarks, one historical and the other philosophical. According to Jean-Luc Marion, Janicaud did not take part in the weekly discussions held at the Archives Husserl de Paris of the École normale supérieure throughout the 1980s. Those discussions—which were attended by Michel Henry, Jacques Derrida, Gérard Granel, Jean-Luc Marion, Didier Franck, Jean-François Courtine, Françoise Dastur, Jean-Yves Lacoste, Jacques English, Jacques Colette, Jacques Garelli, Éliane Escoubas, Michel Haar, Jean Greisch, Jacques Taminiaux, Rudolf Bernet, Daniel Giovannangeli, and a host of others from the younger generation, including Jocelyn Benoist, Claude Romano, and Emmanuel Falque—had a decisive impact on the development of French phenomenology over the last thirty years, particularly when it comes to questions of methodology. One could argue (as Marion has) that the concept of method underlying Janicaud's criticism of the theological turn was narrowly defined and unexamined and had already undergone significant displacement and reconfiguration. In short, Janicaud conservatively misidentified a transformation in the phenomenological method as an assault on reason.

From a philosophical point of view, how French phenomenologists have scrutinized metaphysics and its history has as much to do with the character of phenomenology and its claim to reason as it does with the history of metaphysics. Ever since its Husserlian institution in 1900, the most basic ambition of phenomenology has been to describe phenomena as they themselves are given to consciousness, independently of all prior theoretical commitments that, in one way or another, prejudice the description without having proper phenomenological justification. The successive transformations of the phenomenological method after Husserl only make sense in relation to this ambitious and elusive requirement. For many contemporary French phenomenologists and historians of philosophy, metaphysics is not, as it was for Heidegger, to be identified with a single "history of Being" (*Seinsgeschichte*) but rather, as Jean-Françoise Courtine emphasizes:

> This [. . .] is a history of metaphysics [. . .] disassociated from the Heideggerian *Seinsgeschichte*, which also explains the possible (improbable?) collusion with Foucauldian archaeology and the attention given, if not to "discourses," at least to *minores*, to the effects of traditions, to commentarism, to the scholarly (Scholastic) and university institution [. . .].[4]

In phenomenology, "metaphysics" has become the name of a philosophical lexicon with a determinate or determinable history of concepts and institutions. More broadly, it has functioned as the name of a problem pertaining to the basic ambition of phenomenology itself, as defined above. In his interview, Marion offers a general characterization of metaphysics as any system of a priori norms that lay down prior constraints on the sense and possibilities of phenomena. From a traditionally transcendental point of view, that which, for whatever reason, does not conform to these norms cannot, strictly speaking, be an object of possible experience. But from a phenomenological point of view, questions as to why any such norms should determine the space of rationally permissible phenomena prior to or independently of the possibilities that phenomena themselves proffer can in principle always be raised. By definition, phenomena can exert considerable, even transformative pressure on the norms in terms of which they are or have been typically cognized and described. All such norms project a horizon of intelligibility whose screen remains permanently, if not chronically, exposed to the possibility of being punctured. Norms are much weaker than the events that destabilize.

In French phenomenology after Lévinas, an obvious trend can be discerned, one that has accorded a certain privilege to phenomena that do *not* conform to normative regimes on how they must be cognized and described. Taking off from Descartes's Third Meditation and Husserl's descriptions of transcendental intersubjectivity in *Cartesian Meditations*, Lévinas began a trend of identifying and describing, in painstaking detail, irreducible differences between the intentional relation to objects, on the one hand, and the "ethical relation" to other human beings, on the other. This is already clear from Lévinas's first major formulation of this irreducible difference in what has now become one of his most celebrated essays, "Is Ontology Fundamental?" (1951):

> Comprehension, as construed by Heidegger, rejoins the great tradition of Western philosophy wherein to comprehend the particular being is already to place oneself beyond the particular. It is to relate to the particular, which alone exists, by knowledge which is always knowledge of the universal. [. . .] Such is not the case, however, when it is a matter of my relation with the other. Here also, if one likes, I comprehend the being of the other, beyond his or her particularity as a being. The person with whom I am in relation I call being. But in so calling him or her, I call to him or her. [. . .] I have spoken to the other, that is to say, I have neglected the universal being that the

> other incarnates in order to remain with the particular being he or she is. Here the [Heideggerian] formulation "before being in relation with a being, I must first have comprehended it as being" loses its strict application [. . .].[5]

Lévinas's argument that the relation to the other cannot be described according to any prior condition of comprehension, including Heidegger's understanding of Being (*Seinsverständnis*), means that this relation cannot be described in a priori terms describing what and how the relation must be. As Hent de Vries has argued: "Absolute alterity, Levinas [*sic*] suggests, manifests itself, above all, in the countenance of another human being, to whom I am referred in a manner that is neither dialectical nor dialogical, neither conversational (i.e., in Habermas's idiom, interactive or communicational) nor reciprocal, but premised on a heteronomy that precedes my initiative and, Levinas says, 'invests' my freedom with a meaning and responsibility that it cannot [. . .] measure up to on its own."[6] Unlike Hegel, phenomena are not the mere incarnation or expression of an Idea. Unlike Heidegger and Habermas, the other does not (simply) appear under a prior condition of comprehension. The other appears, rather, as him- or herself, as a singular individual to whom I, together with all my expectations and conditions, however universal and binding, am essentially and ever *exposed*. Any and all norms and conditions of the relation to others are vulnerable to the structure of the ethical relation itself. This introduces a high degree of empirical sensitivity that transcendental, ontological, and Hegelian and neo-Hegelian accounts of the relation to others cannot accommodate, at least not on the interpretation Lévinas himself offers of these accounts.

As Jocelyn Benoist has argued in *L'idée de phénoménologie*,[7] Lévinas's descriptions of the ethical relation profoundly affected the development of French phenomenology from the 1960s on. What for Lévinas represented a decisive step beyond the constraints of Hegelian dialectics and Husserlian and Heideggerian phenomenology eventually became paradigmatic for an entire generation of French phenomenologists, especially during the revival of the 1980s to which many of the figures interviewed here regularly refer, some fondly, others (such as Benoist himself) less so. Phenomenology, armed with a new figure of phenomenality, began re-evaluating its methodological foundations in order to push Lévinas's "break" to its outermost limit, beyond the ethical relation and into hitherto uncharted territory. Among others, figures like Didier Franck, Jean-Luc Marion, Jean-Yves Lacoste, and Jean-Françoise Courtine, many of whom had studied under Emmanuel Lévinas, were now training a new generation of phenomenologists (Romano, Benoist, Falque) and began publishing new studies on Husserl and the relation between Husserlian and Heideggerian phenomenology, the history of scholastic and modern metaphysics, and theology. Many of their students followed suit, and the reconstruction of phenomenology, both in relation to its own history and the Western philosophical canon more generally, eventually became an institutional presence in French universities and publishing houses. Heidegger's account of the history of metaphysics (sobered up by historical acumen) and Lévinas's decisive extension of the descriptive possibilities of phenomenology together made for the revivification of a movement that had hitherto been considered stale or, worse, dead.

§3 The Hospitality of Phenomenological Reason: Marion, Lacoste, Falque

Strongly influenced by Didier Franck,[8] Jean-Luc Marion developed his phenomenology of givenness over a period of some twenty years, from the late 1980s to the early 2000s, singlehandedly making the problem of givenness the fulcrum of phenomenological debate in France, starting with the debate over the relation between signification and intuition in Husserl's phenomenology.[9] By zeroing in on how, for Husserl, signification (intuitively empty intentions) and intuition (both sensible and categorial) are but determinate modes in which objects can be given to consciousness and arguing that both can be subsumed under the broader concept of givenness, Marion successfully established givenness as the basic preoccupation of phenomenology ever since its Husserlian institution. The ambition to secure and describe what is given within the limits prescribed by the given, no more, no less—this ambition has always defined phenomenology. Following Lévinas, for Marion, this ambition means, above all, that the given alone decides the limits of description, not vice versa. Here again, empirical sensitivity—phenomenological empiricism—is the *mot d'ordre*. Marion canonizes this sensitivity with his concept of the saturated phenomenon, which formalizes and generalizes Lévinas's descriptive strategies by extending them to any phenomenon whose mode of givenness cannot be constrained by a priori conditions. Saturated phenomena contest the sense that has, as it were, been prepared for them. For Marion, the possibility of such phenomena must be admitted and it forces phenomenology to rethink the concept of the phenomenon informing its methodological foundation and descriptive horizons.

In *Being Given*, Marion, using a transcendental lexicon, argues that saturated phenomena are unconditioned by any regime of a priori conditions. What distinguishes Marion from contemporary neo-Kantianism is that, for Marion, the conditions of the possibility of the experience and its objects neither constrain nor exhaust the possibilities of givenness. Phenomena can be given that do not conform to any antecedent system of conditions, in which case such phenomena can no longer, strictly speaking, be referred to as "objects."[10] Phenomenology from Lévinas on is not compatible with the strategy pursued in the Transcendental Deduction of the *Critique of Pure Reason*.[11] Marion inverts the relation between the conditions of experience and its objects, on the one hand, and what they condition (the phenomena), on the other. He does not determine phenomena according to prior conditions but rather conditions according to phenomena. What Kant would have referred to as a posteriori ultimately becomes, for Marion, the decisive member of the distinction between a priori and a posteriori. This is why he refers to the phenomenology of givenness as a form of "radical empiricism." He writes:

> Phenomenology goes beyond metaphysics in the strict measure that it gets rid of any a priori principle in order to admit givenness, which is originary precisely insofar as it is a posteriori for the one who receives it. Phenomenology goes beyond metaphysics insofar as it gives up the transcendental project in order to allow the development of an empiricism that is finally radical [. . .].
>
> What the ego defines according to the limits of what it sees [*certus, cernere*] is replaced by the fact of the givenness of the phenomenon by itself, *according to its own requirements*.[12]

The requirements proper to a transcendental concept of reason are here declined in favor of the requirements specific to the phenomena themselves. For Marion, the fact that transcendental conditions, however broadly defined, do not exercise authority over givenness is the *sine qua non* of phenomenology. The only principle of phenomenology remains Husserl's famous "principle of principles," which, for Marion, hands the final word to givenness alone. This principle makes it possible for phenomenology to describe a broad range of phenomena, including, for example, the phenomenon of the revelation as described in the New Testament. Unlike Kant and Fichte, Marion does not evaluate the events described in scripture according to the requirements of practical reason (the moral law) but rather as they are given according to their own mode of givenness, simply as phenomenologically *possible* phenomena whose historicity phenomenology need not (indeed, cannot) determine. Although this has struck many, like Janicaud (but also many on this side of the Atlantic), as a departure from the basic principles of phenomenology or as a turn toward theology, for Marion, phenomenology becomes more, not less, phenomenological by describing such phenomena.

Jean-Yves Lacoste's work needs to be read along similar lines.[13] In his interview, Lacoste makes a strong case for what he calls the essentially "hospitable nature" of phenomenological reason:

> We must take note of the hospitable nature of phenomenology, such as it burst on the scene with Husserl. We are not dealing here with a bed of Procrustean theory, such that everything that is, and every way of being, would have to comply with its constraints on pain of losing the right to be. Husserl treats everything that appears as it appears, and as it appears from itself—a starting point that he never denied and that has a "realistic" character. Every phenomenon is a phenomenon. But "to every fundamental mode of objectity . . . there belongs a fundamental mode of evidence." What, then, is the fundamental mode of evidence of the phenomena we call "religious"? We are entitled to ask this question. We are entitled to ask it, especially, as a question capable of receiving a consistent answer, or answers. [. . .] Nothing is impossible for anyone exploring the "liturgical" or "religious" field in phenomenological terms. Phenomenology would collapse altogether if it only contained, in essence, one possible theological moment—an observation that does away with the critique of a "theological turn" [. . .]. The liturgical possibility is an "anthropological" possibility, *sit venia verbo*, whose phenomenological description is unrestrictedly possible in phenomenology.[14]

For Lacoste, the phenomena of the liturgical or religious field, no less than the phenomena of mathematics or perception, have definite modes of givenness that can be carefully and rigorously described, all in a way that need not presuppose dogmatics. On the contrary, dogmatics presupposes the very mode of givenness of the phenomena the phenomenologist undogmatically, even "scientifically," describes. What Lacoste refers to as the "liturgical possibility" (i.e., the possibility of a relation to God)[15] is a possibility that cannot be circumscribed in exclusively conceptual terms. To be sure, Lacoste accepts Hegel's critique of Schleiermacher. For Lacoste as for Hegel, the relation to God does not take place in the element of feeling or immediate knowledge. However, Lacoste does not accept Hegel's thesis that the relation to God is reducible to a fully developed knowledge of the self and of history: "The Hegelian theory betrays a consistent refusal to let the relation between man and God find its truth anywhere other than in the happiness of knowledge, in discursive knowledge, in a totally logical, nonaffective mode," realizing itself exclusively "in the element of social existence."[16] For Lacoste, the relation to God is cognitive but not exclusively or even primarily so, and the element of affectivity cannot be ignored or overcome but requires a phenomenological hermeneutic of its own.

What Lacoste refers to as the "hospitality" of phenomenological reason has become the backdrop to the kind of research undertaken by figures like Emmanuel Falque. For Falque, the history of metaphysics, as debated by Marion and his generation, has become a more or less established, uncontroversial field of research. However, it would be something of an exaggeration to argue that Falque is terribly interested in the problem of overcoming metaphysics. For Falque, the language of metaphysics is here to stay, like it or not. In his interview, Falque argues that Marion and his generation "remained highly dependent on the idea of overcoming metaphysics—an idea that has itself been overcome these days." He continues:

> Nothing is more inconsequential to this new generation [of phenomenologists] than knowing whether or not their discourse remains within metaphysics or so-called onto-theology. [. . .] Whether one is inside or outside of metaphysics is not all that important. All that counts is the validity of the concepts forged to deal with what is being considered, whether those concepts have to do with language, the body, experience, literature, etc.[17]

For Falque, it is not obvious what "overcoming" metaphysics could even mean. This becomes very clear in his interpretation of figures like Augustine. In *Dieu, la chair, et l'autre*, Falque demonstrates that Augustine elevates the traditional metaphysical category of "relation" over that of "substance" as first category, rendering the latter relative to the former in order to think through a distinctively Christian concept of a Triune God, effectively modifying the order of the categories of first philosophy bequeathed to Augustine by Aristotle:

> The exit from metaphysics—the detachment and then reattachment of the category of "relation" to the pair substance/accident—operates paradoxically *within* metaphysics itself, at least when it passes through the filter of medieval philosophy. Similar to the ruse of the hedge-

> hog (in Grimm's fairy tale) placing at the finish his hedgehog wife and passing himself off as "already there" wherever the hare runs, metaphysics is therefore "always there" when theology is tried within it—but the difference is that the second totally modifies the first (primacy of relation over substance in St. Augustine), all the while serving it (modification of the concept of "being" in Aristotle to the "act of being" in Aquinas). The metaphysical categories "are transformed (*mutantur*) when applied to God."[18] Theology does not destroy them in order to pass to another order, but only works from within them in order to attempt to render them adequate, as far as possible, to the novelty of the object studied: the Triune God and therefore here relational (*ad aliquid*).[19]

Clearly, the idea of overcoming metaphysics finds no clear footing here. On the contrary, the emphasis on transformation betrays an acknowledgment of the irreducible historicity of metaphysics. Falque's sentiment that the idea of overcoming metaphysics is no longer the primary concern of contemporary phenomenology is shared by a number of the figures interviewed in this volume, particularly Benoist and Romano, both of whom, while sympathetic to what motivates the concerns of Marion and his generation, do not define their research in the same terms.

§4 Contemporary Phenomenology and the Analytic Philosophy of Mind and Language

Throughout the 1990s, largely through the work of Jocelyn Benoist, new questions regarding the possibility of phenomenology were posed from a philosophical idiom that had hitherto barely affected the culture of French phenomenology: Anglo-American or "analytic" philosophy. This would not have been possible were it not for the fact that analytic philosophy had already begun to make its presence felt in France through the work of figures like Jacques Bouveresse, Vincent Descombes, and Claude Imbert. Jocelyn Benoist and Claude Romano stand out as the two contemporary French philosophers who have undertaken to systematically re-examine the history and conceptual foundations of phenomenology in relation to historical and contemporary debates in analytic philosophy, particularly in the analytic philosophy of mind and language. Whereas Benoist, more than any other figure in contemporary French intellectual life, has subjected Husserlian phenomenology and nearly every aspect of contemporary French phenomenology to exacting critique, Romano has undertaken the most sustained, systematic, and impressive defense of phenomenology (and, more specifically, a phenomenological concept of reason) in recent history. The rise of analytic philosophy in European universities, universities in which the phenomenological movement first took root, has compelled these figures to position themselves vis-à-vis thinkers like Ludwig Wittgenstein, John Austin, Wilfrid Sellars, Hilary Putnam, Stanley Cavell, Robert Brandom, and John McDowell. Benoist and Romano represent two opposing poles in an ongoing exchange with analytic philosophy, an exchange the full implications of which have not yet been decided.

A perennial problem for analytically trained scholars of phenomenology in the United States has been their inability or unwillingness (the distinction between the two has never been altogether clear) to deal with phenomenology in the entirety of its tradition. Many analytically trained readers of Heidegger, for example, tend to focus exclusively on his early work, dismissing the later work as misguided mysticism. Phenomenology frequently gets confused with or presented as a form of pragmatism or philosophical anthropology. Meanwhile, many American continental phenomenologists have shown a similar inability and/or unwillingness to deal with the challenges posed by developments taking place in contemporary analytic philosophy. This should no longer be considered acceptable. Benoist and Romano have the unique advantage of bringing the full force of the phenomenological tradition to bear on a serious, well-read exchange with the analytic tradition. This distinguishes them from many of their French and American contemporaries.

For Benoist, the basic problem of phenomenology—the problem of intentionality—cannot be successfully treated within the parameters of Husserlian and Heideggerian phenomenology. Sense, he argues, is constituted in the efficacy of speech, an efficacy in which worldly contexts play an essential part. As he shows in his conclusion to *Les limites de l'intentionalité* (2005)—his first foray beyond Husserlian phenomenology and into what he now, with the publication of *Éléments de philosophie réaliste* (2011), refers to as "intentional realism"—the basic error of Husserlian idealism consists in its "autonomisation of sense in relation to being and in making it precede/determine being. Realism, by contrast, is the philosophical posture that consists in privileging being over sense and regarding the former as determining the latter, which never has complete autonomy in relation to being."[20] Husserl's epistemological reflections in and around 1906–1907, which culminated in the publication of *Ideas I* in 1913, constrained him to determine the sense of any given intentional object (and, more broadly, the world as a correlate of consciousness and its acts) independently of any thesis regarding the world's existence. Sense had to be constituted in and by a transcendental consciousness alone, access to which is made epistemologically secure by the phenomenological reductions. All regional ontologies are, in Husserlian phenomenology, ultimately referred back to transcendentally pure "acts" that constitute the sense of any given region of objects beforehand. Within the parameters of an epistemologically motivated phenomenology of constitution, then, the relation between sense and the world cannot be one in which the latter plays any constitutive role.

This, however, does not lead Benoist to embrace Heidegger's hermeneutics of sense. On the contrary, for Benoist, the hermeneutical concept of sense, for all its ontological sensitivity, remains no less committed to the prior availability of a sense that, having already been constituted in the understanding of Being, has merely to be explicated after the fact. For Heidegger, we already know what Being means, if only in an average, vague manner, and if we did not already know what Being means (and, by extension, what any given region of being means), we could not so much as relate to the being in question. The same precedence and/or prior determination of sense, here of any given being by *Dasein*'s understanding of Being (*Seinsverständnis*), prohibits, according to Benoist, Heideggerian hermeneutics from articulating a concept of sense that takes into account its essentially effective, contextual constitution. Benoist's emphasis on the efficacy of language betrays the influence of Wittgenstein, Austin, and, more recently, Charles Travis and marks him off from both Husserl's idealistic theory of signification and Heidegger's hermeneutics of the understanding:

> A "theory of signification" as I found it all ready-made in Husserl, far from constituting the philosophy of language in action [*en acte*] (taking into account *what speaking is*) I was looking for, was on the contrary a major obstacle on the path of such an elucidation. To understand what it is to speak, one needs first of all to be interested in the efficacy of speech [. . .] and, above all, to place speech back in context, to apprehend it in its constitutive relation [. . .] to what is not linguistic. What I needed was a non-hermeneutic (thus non-Heideggerian) theory of context, for which meaning is not "always already given" but rather always constructs itself with its limitations in an effective relation to what is not linguistic—beginning with what is given in perception.[21]

For Benoist, contextualism alone can properly describe the relation between language, intentionality, and ontology. As he argues in *Éléments de philosophie réaliste*:

What is intentionality [. . .] and in what sense is it irreducible?

Intentionality is the simple fact that whenever the question regarding what there is is posed, the response that can be given to this question is indissociable from a certain point of view. If, for example, one places a certain object in front of me, in certain circumstances it will be normal to respond that it is a book; in others, a parallelepiped. There is no response to the question regarding what "there is" that is not thus *qualified*. A realism is "intentional" starting from the moment that it integrates this logical constraint of intentionality.[22]

There is no question, here, of grounding sense on a phenomenologically prior, autonomous logic of the sensible, as one finds in Husserl and, more recently, Claude Romano. Romano has forcefully criticized the so-called linguistic turn (in which he understands Wittgenstein, Sellars, and McDowell, among others, to be implicated) and given the most sustained defense of a phenomenology that takes what he refers to as the "immanent logic of the sensible"—a logic that owes nothing to the linguistic and conceptual capacities of the human animal—as the object of its descriptions. Romano too has defended a certain brand of realism, a realism of Husserlian inspiration, according to which the logic of phenomena (e.g., the relations between colors or the relations between sounds) cannot be understood on the basis of linguistic convention but rather solely on the basis of the material necessities immanent to the phenomena themselves as given in the antepredicative, pre-conceptual experience of sensible subjects.

Romano's defense of what he calls the "phenomenological thesis" could not have been further removed from Benoist's line of questioning. For Romano, the origin and singularity of phenomenology can only be understood in relation to a concept of givenness introduced and elaborated by Husserl in opposition to both empiricism and neo-Kantianism: "I call the 'phenomenological thesis' the thesis that the pre-linguistic order of our experience presents necessary structures and intelligible outlines that are autonomous with respect to the forms of our conceptual thought and the linguistic schemes that underlie them."[23] Drawing on his work in the phenomenology of color, he continues:

To take an elementary example, certain laws that govern the domain of colors or sounds are not simply contingent regularities that would be the consequence of an inductive generalization of the Humean type: they are *necessary* in a strong sense. This necessity is not of a conventional nature, it is not the pure product of a linguistic conceptualization that we apply to colors or to sounds, it is not derived

> from "the arbitrary nature of grammar." It is rooted in experience itself, which possesses here an order, an immanent "reason." It is this idea that Husserl expressed by the formula of a "*logos* of the aesthetic world," which phenomenology aims to bring to light, thus deepening—by completely different means—the Kantian idea of the autonomy of the "aesthetic" with respect to the "transcendental logic," consequently forging the program of a *phenomenological* transcendental aesthetic that must necessarily precede the investigation of "superior" forms of thought and of judgment, to the extent that they presuppose it.[24]

Romano denies that the only kind of necessity is logical or conceptual necessity. The necessities governing the relations between colors and sounds are not conceptual or "grammatical," as they must be for Benoist, but rather *phenomenological*, pertaining as they do to the phenomena themselves. They are given in and with experience prior to the logical and/or linguistic norms governing the relations between concepts and judgments. Thus, for Romano, there does indeed exist a domain that constitutes the proper object of phenomenology, a domain defined by a givenness that does not hark back to the brute causal impact of impressions on the sensory apparatus of a perceiver. Romano does not feel obliged to choose between an empiricist myth for which the given is but a throng of impressions that is somehow supposed to justify belief, and an idealism for which there is, in the end, no real difference between concepts and what is given in intuition. The concept of givenness to which he refers is not identical to the empiricist concept of givenness criticized as mythical by Wilfrid Sellars. Unlike McDowell, he does not see in sensibility nothing more than the prior activity of the spontaneity of the understanding but rather, with Husserl, an autonomous order governed by a priori material necessities.

Benoist's and Romano's verdicts on the phenomenological concept of reason are diametrically opposed. Whereas the former sees in phenomenology an obstacle to understanding the effective constitution of sense, the latter sees in it the possibility of overturning the so-called linguistic turn and, more recently, the rise of neo-Kantianism and neo-Hegelianism. The difference between Benoist and Romano indicates the extent to which French phenomenology has developed and responded to positions it previously did not feel compelled to take very seriously. Now that it has done so, there is more room for debate among phenomenologists and those trained in phenomenology as well as between the latter and philosophers working in the analytic idiom.

§5 Phenomenology and the Concept of Life

Lauded in France as a pioneer in phenomenology, Michel Henry's magnum opus, *L'essence de la manifestation* (1963), barely affected mainstream German or American phenomenology. One reason for this no doubt stems from his radical position on the foundations of phenomenology. For Henry, the phenomenological reduction in all of its forms (Husserlian, Heideggerian, and, most recently, that of Marion) errs in defining phenomenality according to the concept of transcendence (i.e., of being other than or beyond consciousness). Henry questions whether being affected by something transcendent to consciousness is phenomenologically primitive. Historical evidence for Henry's thesis can be found in *Ideas I*, §85, where Husserl introduces a distinction between sensile matter (*hylê*) and intentional form (*morphê*). For Husserl, only the latter has properly to do with transcendence. But Henry uses this passage to draw attention to the fact that Husserl himself discusses the possibility of a "hyletic phenomenology."

> *The stream of phenomenological being has a twofold bed: a material and a noetic.*
>
> Phenomenological reflections and analyses which specially concern the material may be called *hyletically phenomenological*, as, on the other side, those that relate to noetic phases may be referred to as *noetically phenomenological*. The incomparably more important and fruitful analyses belong to the noetical side.[25]

Henry reverses Husserl's position on the relation between these two sides of phenomenology. He writes: "Material phenomenology, as I conceive it, results from a radical reduction of every transcendence, which yields the hyletic or impressional component as the underlying essence of subjectivity."[26] For Henry, the hyletic or purely affective life of the subject conditions the possibility of intentionality. This purely affective dimension renders possible intentional informings of sense. Immanence without horizon and without intentionality, it remains prior to representation. Although Husserl already separated the purely impressional component of the *hylé*, he failed to consider it in and for itself (i.e., apart from its role in the transcendence established by intentional *morphé*). Henry's material phenomenology investigates this autonomous impressional component. Husserlian phenomenology, as a transcendental phenomenology, ignores what Henry calls the "arch-givenness" of this material *Ur-impression* by reducing it to an inert *hylé* waiting to be informed by intentionality, effectively resigning itself to the description of the "second givenness" characteristic of the intentional relation.[27]

Although Henry applauds Marion for his development of Husserl's principle of givenness, he differs from Marion on a fundamental point. For Henry, Marion is not sufficiently faithful to this principle: the concept of givenness Marion deploys remains determined by an "ecstatic" horizon, a horizon in which givenness is defined as givenness to consciousness of something other than consciousness. By contrast, Henry identifies the impressional component of givenness with what he refers to as the priority of "auto-affection" (i.e., an affection of the self by itself).[28] Henry's concept of auto-affection is grounded in his phenomenological concept of life. Life, for Henry, is not an object of consciousness, does not affect consciousness as something other than consciousness, but rather:

> Life senses itself, undergoes itself [. . .] that is its essence: the pure feeling of self, the fact of sensing itself. The essence of life resides in auto-affection. [. . .] Life, in its first affection, is in no way affected by something other than itself. [. . .] It senses itself without the intermediary of a sense. [. . .] Everything that affects and touches us in the world, everything that comes to us can only do so insofar as this coming is first the coming of life in itself. [. . .] What we sense, determine each time by that which affects us, finds itself overdetermined by the effectivity of life in us.[29]

For Henry, the possibility of subjectivity, prior to the intentional relation to objects, resides in a concept of life thoroughly determined by the concept of auto-affection. Understanding this requires carrying the phenomenological reduction so far as to reduce intentionality itself. Material phenomenology, according to Henry, penetrates deeper into subjectivity than most phenomenologies have been willing to go. Despite the fact that Henry locates the proper object of phenomenology below or before intentionality and its acts (therefore, before the most elementary dimension of rationality), this does not amount to an abandonment of the phenomenological concept of reason. On the contrary, Henry's phenomenology seeks to embed reason in auto-affection:

> Whatever freedom one may recognize in noetic acts of sense-bestowal, a freedom with respect to which the "same material complex can undergo a diversity of mutually discrete and shifting construings," this freedom remains bound to a more profound necessity that is rooted in the subjectivity to which the reduction returns. This is precisely

the lawfulness that is immanent to hyletic contents and according to which the constitution of a coherent and meaningful universe becomes possible.[30]

It is here that Barbaras distinguishes himself from Henry by introducing an element of negation into his ontology. For Barbaras, consciousness is only possible as a limitation, restriction, and/or negation of pre-intentional, affective life. Intentionality emerges from this negation:

> For Michel Henry, consciousness—understood in the pure immanence of auto-affection and its incessant variations—gives itself as a *production* of a life that it reveals. Consciousness is in immediate contact with life, a pure expression of life. In short, it is Life itself in its subjective or phenomenal dimension. There is no trace here of negativity: we are in the fullness of an embrace in which no gap, no limitation, and no negation can ever arise. [. . .] For my part, I have wanted to show that, if consciousness indeed bears witness to life, this is not so much in the mode of a saturating presence but that of a negation. [. . .] This is why it only gives itself in consciousness as what consciousness has always returned and what consciousness limits. Life subtracts itself from consciousness more than it gives itself.[31]

What this means can only be understood on the basis of the broader aims of Barbaras's phenomenology and his anthropology in particular. For Barbaras, the history of philosophical anthropology has been plagued by a problem regarding the status of those predicates that distinguish the human being from other beings, be they the "attributes" of a mental substance as conceived in a present-at-hand ontology of the subject, the "I" of transcendental philosophy, or the existentials of *Dasein*. In each case, according to Barbaras, these predicates distinguish the human being only by rendering its relation to life ambiguous. Even Merleau-Ponty, who responded to this dilemma by grounding the possibility of intentionality on corporeality, did not, according to Barbaras, manage to deal with this problem:

> In Merleau-Ponty's eyes, the dimension of the subject's belonging to the world is straightaway thought in terms of corporeality: to say that the subject is of the world is to recognize that it has a body. However, insofar as reference to the subject's own body functions to account for perception, [. . .] Merleau-Ponty does not raise the question regarding the ontological meaning of the body. In his work, the body is given more as a solution than as the index of a problem. The consequence is clear: the body is inevitably compromised as a

body (*Körper*), that is, as a fragment of matter, which is supposed to found the belonging of the subject to the world. Subjectivity is forced into corporeality rather than corporeality being reintegrated into existence. Another consequence: in order to understand the body as one's own—that is, in its difference from other bodies—Merleau-Ponty has no other solution than to make consciousness intervene, such that the body is now nothing more than its "vehicle" or "mediator." Hence, subjectivity and belonging are merely juxtaposed rather than genuinely articulated.[32]

The concept of life functions for Barbaras to both differentiate and ground the human animal in its vital existence. Its two senses (*leben* and *erleben*, "living" and "experiencing" or, better, "undergoing") articulate both the ground of the subject in the world (as a living being among other living beings) and the "transitive" dimension of its intentional relation to objects: "While transitive living (*erleben*) is another name for phenomenalization, intransitive living (*leben*) corresponds to belonging (a living that would not be a part of the world, involved in exchanges with it . . .)."[33]

Barbaras's determination of the difference between human and nonhuman modes of being rests on an ontological position that is essentially continuist, influenced by Hans Jonas:

> To say that the being of the subject [. . .] must be defined as life is to recognize that the phenomenological correlation—that is, phenomenalization—pertains to every living thing. I thus place myself in a resolutely continuist perspective (I admit that on this point I have been influenced by Hans Jonas) and I hence refuse to make the human subject an ontological exception. But with this approach—starting with life—I was faced with the necessity of accounting for the difference of the human subject, a difference that we name with the help of the notion of consciousness.[34]

For Barbaras, "consciousness" does not name an additional, positive attribute that other living beings lack. If it did, it would give rise to a metaphysical duality that his phenomenology seeks to avoid. Distinguishing human beings by rationality leaves open the question regarding "how an animal can be rational [. . .] how consciousness or reason can belong to a living thing." The solution to this problem, according to Barbaras, consists in thinking the emergence of consciousness as a negation or limitation of life, one that opens the possibility of an intentional relation: "Man becomes consciousness and the worldly totality becomes objective reality only by virtue of an interruption of the living engagement within the world, by a sort of contraction and withdrawal or recoiling within pure vital activity."[35]

Whereas Barbaras has sought to rethink the foundations of phenomenology on the basis of the concept of life, Françoise Dastur, following Heidegger, has, in addition to her enormous output of historical scholarship, focused primarily on the role played by concepts of time and finitude in the history of phenomenology. The phenomenological tradition from Husserl on has accorded pride of place to time in relation to its most basic problems. Dastur's own work on time has sought to determine more fully the scope and significance of Heidegger's philosophical and historical investigations into the relation between mortality, finitude, and human existence. In her interview, she emphasizes the idea that phenomenology is not "a 'doctrine' or a philosophical position, it is not a 'science of phenomena' that one could oppose, for example, to the 'science of being' (ontology), but [. . .] a concept of method." The method of phenomenology is "neither speculative nor explanatory but rather simply disclosive [*monstrative*]. [. . .] Work in phenomenology consists in 'saving the phenomena,' snatching them from the dissimulation to which our preconceived ideas and habits of thought relegate them."[36] It is not difficult to find this disclosive procedure at work in Dastur's texts.

Her work on mortality and finitude is both historical and philosophical. Historically, Dastur sees in Greek metaphysics (Plato) a denial of mortality that anchors the Platonic concept of truth in the immortality of the soul after death, which alone delivers knowledge of the supersensible. The religions of the book, too, deny the possibility of a genuine encounter with mortality, promising, rather, to overcome it. Indeed, for Dastur, a modern philosopher like Hegel, no less than Plato and the religions of the book, also denies mortality by making mortality (or, more specifically, the risk of one's own death) a necessary moment in the development of a free self-consciousness, a moment that must likewise be overcome for mutual recognition between two self-consciousnesses (and, therefore, self-consciousness itself) to be possible:

> If—as expressed by what are no doubt the most celebrated passages of the *Phenomenology of Spirit*, namely, those dealing with the dialectic of the master and slave—access to humanity is as such only possible in the confrontation with death, the "absolute master," this involves the capacity of man to elevate himself above simple animal life, to put the entirety of his life at risk in order to accede to self-consciousness as a free being.[37]

As Dastur notes, the negation of life is purely spiritual for Hegel: it has the form of an "*Aufhebung* that conserves the very life it negates."[38] For Dastur, this means that Hegel remains inscribed within the tradition of metaphysics, which, from Plato on, deals with mortality only in order to go beyond and negate it. In short, the mode in which death is originally given does not and cannot appear as such in metaphysics. This, however, does not mean that its mode of givenness cannot be described. Here as elsewhere, what cannot appear in metaphysics can appear in phenomenology. The hospitality of phenomenological reason can be exhibited here no less than in the description of the phenomena of religion. Phenomenology, Dastur argues, "uniquely proposes to *describe* the manner in which the human being relates to its own death. [. . .] This phenomenology of the mortal condition of the human being requires the reduction of every thesis, whatever its origin, regarding death, in order to place us before the 'pure phenomenon' of mortality."[39] This sharply contrasts Dastur's methodological atheism from Falque's concept of the metamorphosis of finitude, in which the concept of resurrection plays a fundamental role.[40]

As a coda to this collection, we include a translation of a recent interview with a philosopher who, perhaps even more than others in this volume, refuses to be circumscribed by any definition: Jean-Louis Chrétien. Well-known to readers in the English-speaking world through translations of a significant but nevertheless minor sample of his works, Chrétien is an author whose thought is deeply indebted to phenomenology and whose writing portrays a phenomenological sensibility of the highest order.[41] As his interview makes clear, what appears as Chrétien's broad eclecticism (which involves a retrieval and juxtaposition of concepts from the breadth of the Western theological, philosophical, and literary tradition) is in reality a product of his acute sensitivity to layers of experience that can only be brought to light by means of this assembled chorus, which, when properly arranged, is given a stronger voice to perform a philosophical task (to utilize two key images from Chrétien's *oeuvre*). This sensitivity is doubtlessly phenomenological in practice. The influence of Chrétien's phenomenology of the call and response is well known and has functioned as a model for describing relations between self and other in a broad variety of domains. In his interview, Chrétien discusses the genealogy of interiority as a phenomenon in Christian spirituality and the modern European novel, the principle subject of his book, *Conscience et roman*. The narrative techniques deployed by the modern novel, especially in figures like Balzac and James, appropriate a number of Christian motifs and practices, such as "the equal dignity of every human person, the importance of quotidian life, within which my salvation or ruin is decided, the examination of conscience and the scrutinization of my deepest intentions." "The novel," he continues, "takes possession of this unlimited depth of interiority, obtained or constituted by centuries of doctrines and practices, and, in the strict sense of the word, renders it *profane* by eliminating its center and source, God himself. This profanation becomes the site of a new sacrality, that of subjectivity."[42] Phenomenology, religion and theology, and literature are all archives from which Chrétien draws in order to describe historically emergent forms of self-knowledge. Chrétien acutely raises the endlessly debatable but fruitful question regarding the definition of phenomenology, as well as the question of *which* phenomenology we are to assign a normative or regulative role, two questions that, in preparing this volume, we have left as wide open as possible. Chrétien's interview provides the English-speaking world with a better picture of the synthetic breadth of his own thought than previously available. Its inclusion in this volume allows for a wider and therefore clearer sense of the range and diversity of phenomenology in France today.

In addition to providing the most systematic English-language survey of contemporary French phenomenology to date, the interviews collected here contain a fair amount of intellectual history and biography. Taken together, they shed light on significant aspects of the pedagogical, cultural, and institutional history of contemporary French phenomenology.

Notes

1. See Macksey and Donato, *The Structuralist Controversy.*

2. See Janicaud, "The Theological Turn of French Phenomenology," in Janicaud et al., *Phenomenology and the "Theological Turn."*

3. Ibid.

4. See Courtine's interview in this volume.

5. Lévinas, "Is Ontology Fundamental?," 124–25.

6. See Vries, *Minimal Theologies*, 348.

7. See Benoist, *L'idée de phénoménologie*, 1–45.

8. See Franck, *Chair et corps.*

9. See Marion, *Reduction and Givenness*, 4–40.

10. See Marion's inversion of Kant's Transcendental Deduction in *Being Given*, 212–21.

11. This is perhaps one of the most promising ways of distinguishing between French phenomenology and contemporary neo-Kantian and neo-Hegelian analytic philosophy of mind. The very fact that these two traditions can be distinguished in this way (i.e., vis-à-vis a common text) indicates the extent to which the historical situation of philosophy has significantly changed over the past thirty years.

12. See Marion, "Metaphysics and Phenomenology," 582–83. Translation modified. Emphasis added.

13. Interestingly, Janicaud himself, though for reasons far removed from the logic of our argument, exonerated Lacoste from any association with the theological turn. See Janicaud et al., *Phenomenology and the "Theological Turn,"* 100n23.

14. See Lacoste's interview in this volume.

15. Lacoste, *Experience and the Absolute*, 22.

16. Ibid., 91.

17. See Falque's interview in this volume.

18. Boethius, *The Theological Tractates*, 17.

19. Falque, *Dieu, la chair, et l'autre*, 81.

20. Benoist, *Les limites de l'intentionalité*, 271.

21. See Benoist's interview in this volume.

22. Benoist, *Éléments de philosophie réaliste*, 54.

23. See Romano's interview in this volume.

24. Ibid.

25. Husserl, *Ideas I*, 207.

26. Henry, *Material Phenomenology*, 9. Translation modified.

27. "Everything that is given to us is given, so to speak, two times. The first givenness, the *Empfindung*, is mysterious. It is the type of givenness and given in which the mode of givenness is itself the given. It is the transcendental in a radical and autonomous sense. And then, this first given, which is always already given and presupposed, is given a second time in and through intentionality, as a transcendent and irreal thing, as its 'vis-à-vis.'" Ibid., 17.

28. See Henry, *De la phénoménolgie*, 77–105. Needless to say, the concept of autoaffection is not original with Henry; Kant argues that time, because it is an a priori intuition, is a form of autoaffection.

29. Ibid., 49–52.

30. Ibid., 20.

31. See Barbaras's interview in this volume.

32. Ibid.

33. Ibid.

34. Ibid.

35. Ibid.

36. See Dastur's interview in this volume.

37. See Dastur, *La mort*, 89–90.

38. Ibid., 93.

39. Ibid.

40. See Falque, *The Metamorphosis of Finitude*.

41. See Derrida's engaging discussion of Chrétien in Derrida, *On Touching*.

42. See Chrétien's interview in this volume.

French Phenomenology in Historical Context

JEAN-FRANÇOIS COURTINE

For over twenty years (1987–2009), you were director of the Archives Husserl de Paris at the École normale supérieure, which has historically been an important center of phenomenological research in France. From this position, you have a unique vantage point on the present state of French phenomenology and its future. Are there certain pertinent moments to the story of phenomenology in France that stand out to you over the course of these last three decades?

The Archives Husserl de Paris, a research center at the Centre national de la recherche scientifique (CNRS), was in fact "refounded," so to speak, at the École normale supérieure in 1986. We—Didier Franck and myself—refounded it together, and this is something I want to stress, since I never would have undertaken to do it alone, even if afterward I directed the Center by myself for many long years, probably too long. I use the term "refounded" because in 1986, the Archives Husserl de Paris already had a rich history behind it. I tried to tell this history in 1994, in a book edited by Michel Espagne, *L'école normale supérieure et l'Allemagne*.[1] A proto-foundation can be identified as early as 1944–48 in the initiatives of Jean Cavaillès, Maurice Merleau-Ponty, and the very young Tran Duc Thao.[2] A team of researchers, led by Paul Ricoeur, was officially established at the Sorbonne in 1958 under the title Centre Husserl. After Ricoeur's retirement in 1980 there followed a period in which the center had no director, so Didier Franck and I sought to revive or, if you like, refound it by linking it to the École normale supérieure with the support of the CNRS.

It might be helpful to recall the context in which the center was refounded. There is an edited volume from 1984, *Phénoménologie et métaphysique*,[3] with contributions by Didier Franck, Rémi Brague,[4] Dominique Janicaud, Rudolf Bernet, myself, and others. The volume opens with a preface by Jean-Luc Marion, who notes:

> Obviously, since metaphysics has found its end, either as an accomplishment with Hegel, or as a twilight with Nietzsche, it has been possible to continue only under the form of phenomenology. . . . [Husserl] claims very early on (from 1907, in the Göttingen Lectures) that phenomenology as a science (soon after, in 1910, he called it "rigorous") undertakes the tasks of metaphysics by other means: "A new science here begins to take flight. . . . The possibility of a metaphysics, a science of being in its absolute and total sense manifestly depends on the good fortune of this science."[5]

Marion continues: "The late evolution of Husserl—as we know so clearly now—will ceaselessly accentuate phenomenology's strange imitation of metaphysics. Phenomenology, fascinated by its most intimately foreign other, only strives to do away with it in order to claim its legacy." And later, at the end of this thoroughly Heideggerian diagnosis, he says:

> The incongruity, as awkward as it is fascinating, is that the Husserlian institution wishes, in its radical powerlessness, to take up a position against the essence of metaphysics. Husserl establishes phenomenology as such and, in the same gesture, misjudges it, for he misjudges its essential relation to the essence of metaphysics. This is an ignorance that causes the establishment to drift into a restoration and causes the rupture with metaphysics within the legacy of metaphysics.[6]

I wanted to give you this rather long quotation because it is so representative of a perspective that a certain number of us held at the time: first, the idea—straight from Heidegger—of an "accomplishment" of metaphysics, of the exhaustion of the possibilities inaugurated with Plato and Aristotle, and, second, the idea that Heidegger's radicalization of phenomenology was capable of defining, or at least of approaching, the "non-metaphysical" essence (the *Wesen*) of metaphysics, and of taking it over. Today, it is hardly necessary for me to clarify that I no longer recognize myself in any of these ideas: "the" metaphysics, perceiving its "essence," the originary founding ("first beginning"), the "Husserlian restoration," and so forth.

Didier Franck's contribution to the same collection of essays significantly begins with a long quotation from the end of Heidegger's 1963 contribution to a volume in honor of Niemeyer:

> And today? The age of phenomenological philosophy seems to be over. It is already taken as something past which is only recorded historically along with other schools of philosophy. It is the possibility of thinking, at times changing and only thus persisting, of corresponding to the claim of what is to be thought [*dem Anspruch des zu Denkenden zu entsprechen*]. If phenomenology is thus experienced and retained, it can disappear as a designation in favor of the matter of thinking whose manifestness remains a mystery.[7]

It is still important to remember that the upshot of Didier Franck's contribution, far from unreservedly adhering to this late claim to heritage, was to reaffirm, prior to any attempt at an "overcoming," the necessity of a "proper determination, a determination of what is proper to transcendental and constitutive [Husserlian] phenomenology."[8] To characterize this "return to Husserl" more adequately, it is equally important to recall Franck's *Chair et corps. Sur la phénoménologie de Husserl.* This text played an absolutely decisive role. Franck, who had already translated an important classic by Eugen Fink,[9] did not come from the "school" of Jean Beaufret. (My impression is that he was closer to Derrida at the time.) He posed a number of decisive questions about Husserl's work, in a way renewing some of the problems already present in Merleau-Ponty and Michel Henry. It is also important to remember the fact that the first issue of the journal *Philosophie* (founded by Franck and coedited with Pierre Guenancia) opened "symbolically" with one of Husserl's late texts, which also played a large role in the reception of Merleau-Ponty, Tran Duc Thao, and Derrida. I am referring to Husserl's "L'archie-originaire Terre ne se meut pas." In the second and third issues of the same journal (in 1984), there can also be found the first version of a long contribution by Jean-Luc Marion that would eventually become the principal and opening chapter of *Réduction et donation*.

Jocelyn Benoist, a member of the younger generation and still a student at the École normale supérieure at the time of the "refoundation," cast a very interesting light on the intellectual situation of the late eighties. I am referring to his "Sur l'état présent de la phénoménologie."[10] What I retain most of all from this study (which is characterized by a slight, assumed impertinence) is the emphasis on the paradox that the "return" to Husserl of the eighties was in part the work of former Heideggerians, even former students (direct or indirect) of Jean Beaufret. This observation appears to me to be quite relevant, despite the relative fragmentation and dispersion of the French scene toward the end of the eighties. To gauge this diversity, it suffices to mention some of the colleagues who regularly participated in the activities of the Husserl Archives: Jacques English, Françoise Dastur, Jacques Colette, Jacques Garelli, Éliane Escoubas, Dominique Janicaud, Michel Haar, Jean Greisch, and, in Belgium, Jacques Taminiaux, Rudolf Bernet, and Daniel Giovannangeli. And let us not forget the generation of the thirties, active in the background, especially Jacques Derrida and Gérard Granel.

Bernhard Waldenfels's excellent study *Phänomenologie in Frankreich*, published in 1983, stops before the period that interests you. I don't think we can say that Hans-Dieter Gondek and László Tengelyi's recent book, *Neue Phänomenologie in Frankreich*, carries the torch of Waldenfels's inquiry. In fact, it presents a succession of particular studies that is a little arbitrary, and its general perspective, divided between Marc Richir[11] on one side and Jean-Luc Marion on the other, does not seem to me to give an adequate account of the French situation in the eighties or nineties beyond giving the "theological turn" invented by Janicaud a disproportionate role. Gondek and Tengelyi's massive book also contains a rather long introduction, more than thirty pages, that tries not only to carve out and define its object (chronologically, for the most part) but also, and above all, to determine what properly characterizes (*das Eigentümliche*) the so-called new phenomenology. In the introduction we find clearly formulated principles that are going to guide their endeavor, which they also present as a review or inventory (*Bestandsaufnahme*). In French we would more naturally speak of a *panorama* of the new phenomenology since the early eighties. Yet this is not exactly what the book offers. It does not claim to be exhaustive, and it pays no attention to institutional descriptions or analyses of university sociology, descriptions attentive to places of power, what is being wagered through terminological decisions, editorial practices and politics, and above all translations. These aspects—involvement in academic life and its conflicts, the play of forces between different currents or traditions—weren't within their purview. When it comes to editing and publication history, however, the book suffers from more than a lacuna, the result of running quickly through the thirty years under consideration. This is perfectly comprehensible from the other side of the Rhine, but it isn't inconsequential when it comes to appreciating a real or supposed "return to Husserl," or when it comes to characterizing the renewal of French phenomenology as post-Heideggerian.

How would you take these factors into consideration?

Well, it would have been interesting, it seems to me, to raise questions starting from some simple observations on the nature and rhythm of the translations of Husserl's texts or of those of the first phenomenologists, even the republications, on the effects—here we are within the logic of transfer and countertransfer—of the publication of the volumes of *Husserliana* and also—perhaps above all—those of Heidegger's *Gesamtausgabe*. To put the matter somewhat brutally, the authors of the large volume tend to insularize the "new phenomenology in France."

As is well known, Heidegger's *Gesamtausgabe* begins in 1975 with the publication of *Die Grundprobleme der Phänomenologie*, which was very quickly translated into French. Toward the end of the seventies, it was followed by Heidegger's lecture-course, *Prolegomena zur Geschichte des Zeitbegriffs* (which contains a very long immanent critique of the Husserlian enterprise from *Logische Untersuchungen to Ideen I*), then by *Logik. Die Frage nach der Wahrheit* and the first courses he gave in Freiburg (starting from 1919). It seems to me that the texts of the so-called early Heidegger (up to 1927 or *Die Grundbegriffe der Metaphysik* of 1929/30)[12] can help clarify what interests the two authors more directly—the transformation of the concept of the phenomenon that a certain number of post-Heideggerian phenomenologists have carried out in France. The observation that the return to Husserl that took shape in the eighties was made by authors who had first traversed Heidegger's work is totally accurate. But—for us here in France—what beckoned that return was access to Heidegger's early Freiburg and Marburg courses.

This is why it is probably easier to detect this turn by focusing on the concept of the phenomenon ("Wandel im Begriff des Phänomens" is the title of the first part of *Neue Phänomenologie in Frankreich*) and easier to read this transformation by starting with Jean-Luc Marion's phenomenology of givenness (to which Gondek and Tengelyi devote the third chapter) than with Henry's phenomenology of life or Richir's symbolic institution (the first two chapters, meant to illustrate the "Wandel im Begriff des Phänomens").

In order to capture with subtlety the "moment" of French phenomenology they are analyzing—always in relation to bodies of work, to transfers and appropriations, as partial or as wild as they may be—it would also have been desirable to consider some parallel and simultaneous phenomena. I'll only mention two, but they could be supplemented and multiplied. Here again I am trying to be prudent. The two authors of the volume are both excellent colleagues and friends. Everything that I invoke here so quickly under the banner of a French contextualization, of the history of translations and related modes and loci of reception (the Marburg School, the so-called Southwest School,[13] the followers of Brentano, "realist" phenomenology, the publication of a growing number of Merleau-Ponty's manuscripts) is much more difficult to understand, even to perceive from the outside. The same thing is acutely true of our knowledge and ignorance of—and our relation to—neo-Kantianism, the significance of which was self-evident in Germany but not at all in France, not until the last twenty years. We now have a clearer idea of what was at stake in the debates between Husserl and Natorp, Heidegger and Emil Lask, Patočka and Husserl and Heidegger, and so forth. No doubt everything I'm saying here can come off as merely historicist or anecdotal, but it bears witness to what one could characterize as differentiated or crossed and stratified temporalities that entail one other, as one says about certain drugs that have "delayed effects" or "prolonged release." The other example, which I won't develop here, is the "discovery" or rediscovery of "Austrian philosophy."[14]

These two examples teach us about the difficulties involved in every purely generational, chronological division of subject matter. Nothing is less linear than the temporality of intellectual work, and characterizing it requires more than a succession of monographs; it requires more of a sense of verticality, recoveries, repetitions, and transmutations, of which a staggering literary illustration can be found, for example, in the work of Claude Simon.[15]

I know that it's tempting and almost necessary to mark the strong accents in the scansion: the premature death of Merleau-Ponty, which put an end to a first phase of French phenomenology, the end of structuralism and poststructuralism in the late seventies, and so forth. But such a division of things leaves questions raised by other chronologies intact: Merleau-Ponty's *Le visible et l'invisible* was published by Claude Lefort in 1964, the first edition of Lévinas's *Totalité et infini* dates from 1961, though, with the quite notable exception of Derrida's study, "Violence et métaphysique" in 1964, the reception of *Totalité et infini* was remarkably delayed. Likewise, Michel Henry's *L'essence de la manifestation* dates from 1963, but we had to wait until 1990 for a reissue.

I'll leave aside for the moment the main quasi-methodological difficulties involved in characterizing a philosophical "moment" in order to make a second remark about *Neue Phänomenologie in Frankreich*. Maybe it was inevitable—because of the audience to whom the book is addressed—but I still wonder about the pertinence of opening the work with the "theological turn" of Janicaud's *Tournant théologique de la phénoménologie française*, which dates from 1991.[16] Janicaud's little book has—perhaps productively—provoked many debates and spilled much ink, which I don't at all intend to rehash here. I simply wonder about the structuring effect, the kind of perspective it induces in the reader at the beginning of the book. Indeed, Gondek and Tengelyi themselves seem quite uncomfortable with the very terms of Janicaud's "diagnostic" and his proposed alternative: "minimalist" phenomenology vs. attention given to extreme phenomena or to anything that exceeds so-called ordinary phenomenality. This makes my question all the more important. Parenthetically, on this point, recourse to the Heideggerian syntagm of the phenomenology of the inapparent (*Unscheinbares*)—a syntagm attributed (wrongly, it seems to me), to the later Heidegger, risks being a *lucus a non lucendo*, given the extraordinary polysemy of this word *inapparent*, already implicit in the famous §7 of *Sein und Zeit*.[17] But beyond this point, I simply want to highlight the incompatibility between the terms of Janicaud's diagnosis and the view the two authors take from two of Jocelyn Benoist's remarkable studies, collected in 2001 for *L'idée de la phénoménologie* ("Sur l'état présent de la phénoménologie" and "Qu'est-ce qui est donné?").

You mean his emphasis on givenness as an "event"?

Yes, it is from the second study I mentioned, it seems to me, that the idea and expression of the "event-character" [*caractère événementiel*] (*ereignishaft*) of the phenomenon or of the given is drawn. This amounts to naming the true, no doubt central, difficulty, since almost all of the differences between the multiple versions of this "new French phenomenology" hinge on how concepts like the given, pure givenness, the event, or, even more, the *Ereignis* are to be defined. This is what Jocelyn Benoist tried to settle in a presentation given at the ENS in 1995 by highlighting ideas such as "*survenance*" [occurrence] or "singularization" and also of subjectivation and the pluralized regime in the world's occurring, or of that which makes the world [*régime pluralisé dan's l'avoir du monde ou de ce qui fait monde*] (with the lovely formula, "la poussière du monde" [dust of the world]). Here, perhaps, you have an example that would have allowed for another systematization (through the confrontation of analyses and descriptions) than the one we find in the conclusion to Gondek and Tengelyi's book (I am referring to the beautiful and very famous foreword later added by Merleau-Ponty to his *Phénoménologie de la perception*—the guiding thread of their conclusion). I entirely agree with Françoise Dastur, who observed in 1999 during another exchange between French and German phenomenology,[18] that Merleau-Ponty's foreword presents a "charter" for phenomenology. But again, I am not so sure that the five themes that Gondek and Tengelyi retain from it—analytic description, intentional correlation, the eidetic, *epochê* and reduction, transcendental constitution—can today truly serve as the touchstone to characterize and distribute positions in the context of the new phenomenology in France. Put differently, it seems to me that it is the program itself that has radically changed since Merleau-Ponty's 1945 text, and that it would have been necessary to provide another "complex of questions and responses." My only question here—again, regarding the grounds of the investigation—is to know if it is possible (which I do not believe to be the case) to hold together these two perspectives, that of Dominique Janicaud and of Jocelyn Benoist.

Janicaud's opuscule still appears to me to completely dominate the concluding (and most systematic) part of their book, in which something like a typology or topology is proposed, a logic of the positions proper to a certain number of the protagonists of the work, namely: *post-metaphysical religion* (Lévinas, Henry, Marion, Chrétien, without knowing at all how to classify Paul Ricoeur, but this goes for almost the entire work—perhaps Ricoeur is unclassifiable?); "*quasi-theology without religion*," where we find, a little haphazardly, the later Merleau-Ponty but also Derrida and Marc Richir. I am not sure they make very good bedfellows! Then there are Didier Franck and Françoise Dastur (or Eliane Escoubas), who are rather unclassifiable as well! And if we were to extend the investigation—which, again, is not meant to be exhaustive—what to do with Gérard Granel, Henri Maldiney, or Jacques Garelli? Unless these categories, "post-metaphysical religion," quasi-theology without religion," are simply ineffective catchalls? As for the third position or third way, it is taken from or pioneered by Jocelyn Benoist alone: *non-metaphysical atheism*—a formula that only has clear meaning in relation to Marion's analyses in *L'idole et la distance*.

So much for the conclusion to Gondek and Tengelyi's book, a conclusion that is no doubt a little playful, and I do not want to take it too seriously. I only want to observe that if, obviously, we are all in one way or another in fact confronted with the death of God, I am not at all sure that this way of dividing things up à la Janicaud is illuminating or pertinent.

In the introduction to the volume Phénoménologie et théologie (1992), *you outline some of the key elements of an encounter between German Idealism and phenomenology, specifically concerning the philosophy of religion, taking note of the fundamental determinations made by Hegel and Schelling of some of its most basic concepts, such as revelation, manifestation, and phenomenon—concepts that saturate much recent phenomenology. How do you understand your work to have related to theology and religion?*

This volume corresponds to the brief final meeting of a seminar held in 1990–1991 and 1991–1992, after many seminars dealing with "phenomenology and . . . ," all of which sought to bring phenomenology into contact with different figures of heterogeneity: psychiatry, the work of art and its ontological status, logic, etc. It is wrong to see in my introduction a "program" or "answer" to Janicaud's opuscule. I will not enter into the deeply biased debate that followed. I have a resolutely deflationist reading of this little volume whose relative success seems to me completely short-term. In order to respond more precisely to your question, if in the introduction to the volume I made reference to a certain number of major concepts of German post-Kantian philosophy (*Offenbarung*, *Manifestation*, *Erscheinung*, *Schein*, *Phänomen*), it was not with the intention of mashing together Idealist philosophy of religion and post-Husserlian, post-Heideggerian phenomenology but rather to acknowledge the differences, to do exactly what the Michel Henry of *L'essence de la manifestation* sought to do in his own way.

My "project" has never been centered on the question of phenomenology *and* theology or on the rather vain and ideological denunciation of a theological "turn." I belong to a generation (born at the end of the war and therefore completely closed to insufferable debates: Christian-communist, existentialism, post-humanism, etc.) formed in a context (end of the sixties, beginning of the seventies) in which "structuralism" triumphed and Althusserian neo-Marxism was already losing steam. A number of us rediscovered, with or without a confessional stance—that is not the point—the rich tradition of medieval (largely theological) and patristic philosophy (thanks especially to the admirable series, Sources Chrétiennes).[19] We became apprentices in what the great scholar Harry Austryn Wolfson termed "the philosophy of the Church Fathers,"[20] and we considered the exclusion of this philosophy by the great majority of university institutions (setting aside very specific sectors like l'École pratique des hautes études—a section for the study of the religious sciences) to have been deeply harmful to "properly" philosophical research (but it was also this "properly" that was in question). The works of Jean-Luc Marion (I am thinking here of his *Sur la théologie blanche de Descartes*) or even, among many others, those of Emmanuel Martineau dealing with the *De Consideratione* of Saint Bernard, those of Alain de Libera dedicated to Rhineland mysticism *and* medieval logic, my own work on Francisco Suàrez,[21] all bear witness to an attempt to reintegrate into university research those themes or authors the study of whom had been scandalously confined to the "*grands séminaires*"[22] or to the religious orders. I remember what my dissertation advisor, the very liberal and magnanimous Pierre Aubenque, the great Aristotelian, told me when I revealed to him my project for the *thèse d'État*: "What you are doing with an author like Suàrez is not acceptable in the university system, leave it to the Jesuits!" I think that when it comes to matters like this, my generation, or at least a part of it (we were probably a small minority), will have in the end made a contribution toward redefining the boundaries.

In any case, to return to your question about Idealism, the very same concern animates the great collective enterprise for which my colleague Jean-François Marquet and myself have assumed responsibility: the translation of Schelling's late philosophy (*pure rational philosophy*, *philosophy of revelation*). This (again, collective) project has never been militant and even less "confessional"! We were simply taking cognizance of the fact that a large part of German post-Kantian philosophy, from Fichte, Schelling, and Hegel up to Rosenzweig in particular, remains for the most part unintelligible, or in any case gravely mutilated, if the background, or even—in order to propose another image that is probably more pertinent—these thinkers' own, properly theological fertile soil is not seriously taken into consideration. One ought to be excused for having to recall such truisms! Whether this amounts to who knows what kind of turn, in line or not with a "return of religion," is preferably left to journalistic *cacographie*[23] and has no rigorous meaning. It is as if someone were to think that a religious or irrationalist swerve in the work of Alexandre Koyré could be discerned on the grounds that he devoted a great book to Jacob Böhme!

Speaking particularly as a historian of modern philosophy, what is the substance of your interest in phenomenology?

Let me make a clarification before responding: traditionally in France, remember that "modern philosophy" corresponds to the classical era and the Enlightenment. After Kant, we speak instead of "contemporary philosophy." Whatever there is to say about this non-innocent way of dividing things up, my response is not completely straightforward: my interest in the history of philosophy, or better, my practice of the history of philosophy—attentive, over the long term, to the transformation of defined problematizations, with its slidings, repetitions, but also its "epochal" or "*historiales*"[24] turns and ruptures—is very much indebted to the Heideggerian staging of a history of metaphysics and its ontological orientation. But the way I do the history of metaphysics is always disassociated from the Heideggerian *Seinsgeschichte*, which also explains the possible (improbable?) collusion with Foucauldian archaeology and the attention given, if not to "discourses," at least to *minores*, to the effects of traditions, to commentarism, to the scholarly (Scholastic) and university institution, but also—and I recognize here a certain naiveté that perhaps has not been without fecundity—to the idea that it is possible to continue the efforts of the young Heidegger (say, from the time of *Sein und Zeit*), his readings or phenomenological critiques of the great authors (as is well known, Heidegger attempted this magisterially with Aristotle, Kant, Leibniz, etc., even Nietzsche). Put differently, it is the idea of research engaged less in the reconstruction of doctrines and in the order of rationality that supports them than in the questions, the "things themselves" with which the great authors were involved (I think here, for example, of Rémi Brague's great work, *Aristote et la question du monde*).

The work of revision on this point will have been double: on the one hand, a better account of the breadth and impact of Heidegger's debate with Husserlian phenomenology, taking full advantage of the publication of the first volumes of the *Gesamtausgabe* starting in 1975; on the other hand, a progressive appropriation of the Husserlian corpus. As I mentioned, Jocelyn Benoist very fittingly noted in *L'idée de phénoménologie* in a rather ironic, if not polemical tone, that, curiously, it was the "Heideggerians" or the "post-Heideggerian" generation that had largely contributed to or at least initiated the "return to Husserl" in the eighties. In the present context this analysis seems to me to be again pertinent, and it is doubtlessly this phenomenon that allows us to account for the fact that it was during the very same years that the "post-Heideggerians" (in order to pick up a quick but convenient expression) were also able to take renewed interest in the works of Lévinas or Michel Henry (in the first place I intend here—besides the two volumes that appeared immediately after the war, Lévinas's *Le temps et l'autre* and *De l'existence à l'existant*—the two great books of 1961 and 1974 [*Totalité et infini* and *Autrement qu'être ou au-dela de l'essence*] or, in 1963, Henry's *L'essence de la manifestation*).

What, in your conception, is the specific philosophical fruit that historical research bears? For example—and we intentionally put this provocatively, even crudely—is the history of philosophy simply a "handmaiden" to the serious business of philosophizing, or does it contribute to constructive philosophical work? How do you understand their relation?

This kind of question is a veritable *pons asinorum*: purely antiquarian or erudite historical research—if it exists in a pure state, which I do not believe for an instant—does not enter into consideration here. We could learn Greek "for the love of Greek," but this very passion confronts us straight away with a thousand different questions, access to which is found radically renewed when it becomes a question of citizenship, virtue, the sacred, friendship, etc., and which force us to consider—to speak like Foucault—other modes of problematization. It is well known that philosophy "*en train de se faire*" [in the act of being accomplished] maintains an intrinsic and intimate relation to its history, which is constantly revisited and reinterrogated. It is merely in the context of a vain and sterile polemic that one opposes the "culture of commentary" to the "practice of argumentation."

Following Collingwood, an author like Alain de Libera, for example—in the field of medieval studies but also far beyond it (I am thinking especially of his monumental and ongoing *Archéologie du sujet*)—has contributed significantly to restoring the reputation of what he calls "question-answer" complexes, to reconstructing the history of the constitution of these complexes, which, if we integrate (as is necessary) a dimension that is not only textual but also institutional in the large sense, are not so far at all from what Foucault called "problematization." The historiography of philosophy has taken into account the writing of history for some time, whether it be a matter of the lessons learned from Michel de Certeau, or even better, in order to continue the reference to proper names, Carlo Ginzburg (*Occhiacci di legno. Nove riflessioni sulla distanza*).

From a slightly different vantage point, how would you respond to critics who see the singular focus on the transgression of the onto-theology as obfuscating the basic tasks of phenomenology or even as the rise of a new "historicism" in philosophy? One thinks, again, of Jocelyn Benoist's critiques of the "theological turn" of phenomenology . . .

Concerning what Heidegger called the "onto-theological constitution of metaphysics," there are some among us in France—against Heidegger's own teaching or its reification into a school and a tiresome "orthodoxy"—who are all tied up in historicizing it. Playing only a little on words, it would be a matter precisely of deconstructing the supposed "constitution" (*Verfassung*) in order to retrace the complex history and genesis of a definite "structure," the heuristic function of which is found, by the same token, singularly limited. I do not think that the history of metaphysics à la Heidegger, when it is elaborated as "*Seinsgeschichte*" in a staunchly destinal way, stands guard over fecund reserves for thought or, more simply, for reflection, and even less so when phenomenology is concerned. But if what Heidegger called "*Ereignis*" is understood in a "non-Greek" way (and we should admit this without trouble!) as beckoning toward a co-belonging to being or to the meaning of "to be," which identifies in its own way the humanity of man—something like a new way of interrogating the *zoon logon ekhon*—then yes, without a doubt this history of being harbors meaning for philosophy today. But I am not sure that those whom Merleau-Ponty called the "orthodox Heideggerians" understand it in this way.

As for metaphysics, if it is a matter of reviving some classically metaphysical questions (like the questions of the status of universals, personal identity, accidentality, substance, modalities, etc.), then we can only rejoice at its "return." One would have to be very naive to think that the work of "deconstruction" undertaken for decades was, as far as such questions go, for the sole purpose of returning to the store goods that have been made definitively obsolete. Beyond a certain vulgar understanding of "deconstruction," doubtlessly dominant in the United States (once Derrida said to me, half-seriously, half-ironically: "Deconstruction is America!"), I don't think the "lesson" he could bequeath to phenomenology is a general critique of philosophizing as such and of its exigencies, or even concerning its descriptive rigor. We must not re-elaborate these themes totally ignorant of the history that has been traversed, its stratifications and crystallizations.

Vis-à-vis Benoist, I no longer think that the historicization (if you will permit the expression) of the supposed onto-theological constitution of metaphysics has to do directly or indirectly with the commonly and all-too-hastily termed "theological turn" of French phenomenology, except in order to imagine—which would perhaps be the intention of my friend Jean-Luc Marion—a philosophizing "after metaphysics" or even a post-metaphysical theology.[25]

Given your now classic work on the Baroque Jesuit philosopher Francisco Suàrez and your work on the history of metaphysics more broadly, metaphysics as transcendental philosophy has a specific, determinable ancestry in the history of Western thought, particularly in its complicated relation to theology.

It is possible, in fact, and completely legitimate in my opinion (but this is a point thoroughly studied by Ludger Honnefelder and Jan A. Aertsen), to retrace a long and differentiated history of the transcendental problematic that emphasizes specific medieval bifurcations (notably Duns Scotus) without accentuating the theological dimension of the transcendental problematic. It would be instead—and allow me to be allusive here—precisely the contrary: the emphasis that Duns Scotus puts on the transcendental aim of metaphysics (at least the *quoad nos*) presupposes a strongly philosophical decision that shattered a certain number of great theologoumena—for example, the ones that structure the "Proem" of Thomas Aquinas's *Commentary on Aristotle's* Metaphysics.

It has never been a question for me of retracing a calamitous history of the univocalization of being or of its meaning, and even less to do with who knows what secret origin of a modernity that would make appear an unprecedented figure of subjectivity in its self-presence. I am interested in what I called the *inventio analogiae* precisely in order to retrace the archaeology of what only becomes a stabilized "doctrine" in the schools [*scolarisée*] very late, after Thomas Aquinas. This archaeology also tries to bring into view the transformations of the categorial problematic over a long period, like those of the triptych, homonymy, synonymy, and paronymy. How can we articulate the birth of modernity, rising up out of post-Cartesian subjectivity, and the univocity of the meaning of being, or, better, of the "*conceptus entis*"? For me this remains in part an enigma, or more moderately a problematic knot to disentangle: we would doubtlessly have to turn to the neutrality and indifference of being and, I have to say, to Ignatian spirituality as well, though the work remains to be done. *Ars longa, vita brevis* . . .

One thing is sure in any case: as far as "the invention of analogy" or "the constitution of the system of metaphysics" goes, I have never seen anything there that resembles a history of being, with its epochal scansions that are more or less necessary and uniformly unfolding in decline. The attention given to the long term—which has nothing to do with a taste for the great epic sagas supposed to deliver a global intelligibility—in my mind, goes together not only with a micrological scrupulousness for which I could be reproached but also with a concern for the "regional" and "local"—that which precisely focuses on the always provisional and contingent development of problematic lines that draw forth a network or come to crystallize in one before disappearing or, in any case, ceasing to be "in good health," which does not exclude later resurgences and distortions. If the term "historial" happens to be used (a felicitous rediscovery of an old forgotten French word by Henry Corbin), it is less in order to mark an adherence to the Heideggerian scenario of a *Seinsgeschichte* that would at the same time be a *Seinsgeschick* than it is to distance myself from every linear history, be it progressive or desperately declining. There is nothing stopping you, if you insist, from characterizing this approach as historicist or relativist . . .

Theological problematics cannot be "deconstructed" in the same way as philosophical problematizations. This does not mean that it is impossible to discover the philosophemes that have been able to "contaminate" or more radically structure certain theological questions (let us think, to return to an already ancient debate, about the "Platonism of the Fathers," not to mention the conciliar decisions related to the hypostatic union that have contributed to the reformulation of the concepts of substance, essence, hypostasis, person, unity, etc.), but in the last analysis many different essentials ought to be emphasized: the first is that these theological problematics also or at first lead us back to a "dogmatic" content and we ought not become—as philosophers—historians or exegetes of "dogmas" or conciliar decisions; the second is that theology—Heidegger insisted on this in his Marburg lecture, "Phenomenology and Theology"—pertains to a content of faith that is certainly capable of being rationally clarified for those who adhere to this content of faith (this is the great tradition of *fides quaerens intellectum*), which considers the *positum* as *revelatum* and in fact *revelabile*. But it is clearly pointless to claim to "refute" it from the outside. This is something completely different than attempting—in philosophy—to account for some return effects of theological problematics on philosophical questioning.

Translated by W. Chris Hackett

Notes

1. See Espagne, *L'école normale supérieure et l'Allemagne*, 157–70.

2. Tran Duc Thao was a Vietnamese philosopher whose development of a materialist theory of consciousness was highly influential in Paris during the 1950s and '60s. See Thao, *Phenomenology and Dialectical Materialism*. For a recent appraisal of his influence on French phenomenology, see Benoist and Espagne, *L'itinéraire de Tran Duc Thao*.

3. Marion and Planty-Bonjour, *Phénoménologie et métaphysique*.

4. Rémi Brague is a French historian of philosophy, specializing in Jewish, Christian, and Arabic philosophy of the Middle Ages; professor emeritus of Arabic and religious philosophy at the University of Paris 1 Panthéon–Sorbonne; and author of, among others, *The Wisdom of the World*, *Aristote et la question du monde*, and *The Legend of the Middle Ages*.

5. Marion, "Avant-Propos," 11–12. (Authors' translation.)

6. Ibid. The passages from Husserl to which Marion refers can be found in Husserl, *Husserliana*, 2:32, and in Husserl, *The Idea of Phenomenology*, 25.

7. See Franck, "La chair et le problem de la constitution temporelle," 175. Franck's quotation from Heidegger can be found in *On Time and Being*, 82.

8. Franck, "La chair et le problem de la constitution temporelle," 126.

9. Fink, *De la phénoménologie*.

10. Benoist, "Sur l'état présent de la phénoménologie," in *L'idée de phénoménologie*, 123–59.

11. Marc Richir is a Belgian phenomenologist, a professor of philosophy at the Free University of Brussels, and the author of *Phénomènes, temps, et être I. Ontologie et phénoménologie*, *Recherches phénoménologiques I, II, III, IV, V*, and *Le Rien et son apparence*.

12. Heidegger, *Gesamtausgabe*, 29/30.

13. Also termed the Baden School, after the state in Southwest Germany, represented by Wilhelm Windelband, Heinrich Rickert, Ernst Troeltsch, and others.

14. Represented by figures like Franz Brentano, Alexis Meinong, and Bernard Bolzano. See Benoist, *Représentations sans objet.*

15. Claude Simon is a French novelist and 1985 Nobel laureate in literature and the author of *Leçon de choses.*

16. See also Janicaud, *La phénoménologie dans tous ses états.*

17. Heidegger, *Gesamtausgabe,* 2: 27–39.

18. Janicaud, Dastur, and Escoubas, "Entretien," 187.

19. The series Sources Chrétiennes is published by Éditions du Cerf.

20. Wolfson, *The Philosophy of the Church Fathers.*

21. See Martineau, "Prudence et consideration;" Libera, *La Mystique rhénane* and *La Référence vide*; and Courtine, *Suarez et le système de la métaphysique.*

22. In France, the "grand séminaire" is a seminary properly speaking—an institution of higher education for the formation of priests—whereas the "petit séminaire" is a secondary school that educates both laypersons and future seminarians.

23. The French *cacographie* does not carry the same sense as the English "cacography," which is typically understood as a deliberately humorous misuse of words or style. The French term most often concerns a horrendously bad and erroneous style of writing.

24. Contemporary French phenomenologists use the term "historial[e]" in a specific way, which, as Courtine observes, recovers an obsolete French word first reintroduced into the language by Henry Corbin. Note that in the Martineau translation of *Sein und Zeit* "historialité" is used to translate the German *geschichtlich,* which in the Macquarrie English translation is rendered as "historicality" and the Stambaugh translation as "historicity." Historicity, however, in French, is more commonly simply "historicité," the state of having a historical character. *Historial*[*e*] is meant to indicate, then, to quote the relevant passage from *Being and Time,* the existential and temporal conditions of the possibility of history: "To lay bare the *structure of historizing* [*Geschehens-struktur*], and the existential-temporal conditions of its possibility, signifies that one has achieved an *ontological* understanding of *historicity* [*Geschichtlichkeit*]" (Heidegger, *Being and Time,* trans. Macquarrie and Robinson, 427). As Martineau says in the French translation of *Being and Time,* historicity is that which is "antérieure à ce que l'on appelle histoire . . . L'historialité désigne la constitution d'être du 'provenir' du *Dasein* comme tel . . . [*L'historialité* means the constitution of being of the 'arising' of *Dasein* as such]." See *Être et temps,* 37.

25. Among many others, we could recall Marion's very sane study, "Métaphysique et phénoménologie."

The Phenomenology of Givenness

JEAN-LUC MARION

Did you begin studying phenomenology (as a student) immediately?

Not at all.

What brought you to phenomenology?

I was studying history, French literature, Latin, Greek, and so on in the *classe préparatoire* for the École normale supérieure's compulsory admissions exam. At that time, my "major," so to speak, was, in fact, French literature. So when I was admitted to the École Normale my initial plan was to study literature. And for two years—I was very fortunate but not aware of how fortunate I was—I had Jean Beaufret as my teacher, one of Heidegger's closest friends. He was very good at the history of philosophy but spoke, in fact, *very rarely* of Heidegger. At the same time—and, again, we were not aware of this—he taught us the Heideggerian view of the history of philosophy as metaphysics, the "history of Being," and so on. It was very illuminating. It was the first time I got into the habit of writing sentences in Greek, next to which, for example, you would have a sentence from Kant in German, with him telling us that they say exactly the same thing! That way of teaching Heidegger was, for me, key. I switched to philosophy because I was pushed by some close friends of mine at the very beginning of my stay at the École Normale, like Rémi Brague,[1] who told me: "You cannot *not* do philosophy! There's nothing more interesting than philosophy, everything else is boring." I found that he was right, and so I made the switch.

At the École Normale, I started with a twofold formation, partly at the Sorbonne (where I went to complete my regular classes). I decided to start off by studying the history of philosophy. As far as teachers go, Ferdinand Alquié[2] was undoubtedly one of the best. So, with some friends, including Jean-Robert Armogathe,[3] I started studying the history of philosophy in the classical style under the stewardship of Alquié. We took classes on Spinoza, Malebranche, Kant, seminars on Descartes, and so on. Alquié taught me how to work in the workshop. And, together with my regular tutors, at the École Normale we had people like Althusser and Derrida. I gave them papers, they graded them. We had a student-teacher relationship. I was not, to be sure, a disciple of Althusser (being in no way Marxist), but I had very good personal relations with him. The same goes for my relation to Derrida, from whom I learned to start reading Heidegger seriously . . .

This was when exactly?

Fall of '67 and '68. I spent my time studying the history of philosophy (at least when there was no turmoil) and reading Aristotle in Greek and Heidegger's *Sein und Zeit* in German, even though I wasn't all that good in either language (it was my way of improving). I spent very fruitful but demanding years at the École Normale doing that kind of very solitary work, although not without many friends and discussions. It was a very good generation: Bernard-Henri Lévy (who was not a great philosopher but a very smart guy), Emmanuel Martineau, who later translated *Sein und Zeit* (in his way a genius, very learned and very brilliant), Rémi Brague, Pierre Manent, the political philosopher, and Alain Renaut, who was in those days a very strong Heidegger scholar and hard-line believer.[4]

There were also visiting professors, a whole bunch of them: Lacan, Michel Serres (teaching Leibniz), Deleuze, Stanislas Breton (teaching Neoplatonism).[5] Even Paul Celan, teaching a German crash course for math students. He was a very bad teacher [*laughs*]. And we weren't aware that he *was* Paul Celan.

Really?

He was a very shy, modest man.

He never announced himself?

No, no. I don't think he was very well known at the time. He had published a few things, but he wasn't—not yet—very popular in poetry. Indeed, he *wasn't* known. And we didn't discover that he was Paul Celan until after he had committed suicide, not until *Die Niemandsrose* was published for the first time. There were a lot of real people at the École Normale during that time. I spent three or four years there. After that I got the *agrégation*.[6] I was very fortunate because I got a position at the Sorbonne only one year later. I was twenty-six, and I was already an assistant professor. I was very lucky.

So, backtracking a bit, would it be fair to say that, in some sense, you were a Heideggerian before you knew it?

As far as my overall view of the history of philosophy goes—yes. But that is probably also why I was *never* a Heideggerian. I was very close to Beaufret and the circle of "strong believers," so to speak, like François Fédier, Claude Roëls, François Vezin,[7] and a few others. And very quickly, despite my good relations with them and very good relations with Beaufret (who became a friend toward the end), it was very clear that I was not a "part of the team," for a number of different reasons, the first being that I was openly Catholic in an increasingly anti-Christian environment. The second being that I refrained from being personally introduced to Heidegger.

Interesting.

I don't know why.

But you had the opportunity . . .

Yes, indeed. I sent Heidegger my first book, *Sur l'ontologie grise de Descartes*, through Beaufret in the summer of '75, and Heidegger, according to Beaufret's report, was interested (he read and taught Descartes's *Regulae ad directionem ingenii*, and he too was involved in reading it in relation to Aristotle). His response was very positive, so I was very glad. But I refrained. I refrained from being baptized into the church, from having *that* kind of fascination—personal fascination. I didn't want to be part of a special chapel.

Were you afraid of being absorbed in his personality to such a degree that you would not be able to take the required philosophical distance?

Yes, exactly. It was a very difficult time in France: the temptation was to be part of a team, be it political or ideological or philosophical—and I wouldn't. I refrained from all that. In hindsight, I made the right decision. I was not "registered" as an official Heideggerian. We were told that when Althusser saw people like Brague, Renaut, myself, and Martineau first come to the École Normale, the joke was: "Beware—here come the new Heideggerians. They have the following four characteristics: they don't sit in class, they read the great books in the original language, they know a lot, and they *never* talk about Heidegger!"

During that period, I had only written and published a few papers in theological journals, very small ones. I was studying a lot with friends, studies in patristics and theology. I started teaching the history of philosophy and the philosophy of science as an assistant professor at the Sorbonne under the authority of Alquié. I taught there for seven years, and during that period I had, first, to write my dissertation, because at that time you could get a position without having written a dissertation yet.

The good old days.

The good old days. So they told me that I had three years left to finish my PhD. I wrote my dissertation in less than a year—during vacation, in fact, because I had no time (once you start teaching, it's quite a burden). In any case, during my vacation I wrote *Sur l'ontologie grise* in addition to an annotated French translation of the *Regulae*, together with one of the first computer indexes ever made in philosophy, in Italy (I'm very proud of it). It was the whole thing, a computer index, in Latin, of the *Regulae*: every word, every page. It was quite an innovation: we are talking about the early seventies here. Anyway, I finished all that in '74, and Alquié retired in '75 or '76. Together with Geneviève Rodis-Lewis, who was a great specialist on the history of Descartes and the Cartesian movement (not deeply creative but a great scholar), I established the Centre d'études cartésiennes at the Sorbonne (Paris IV).

As it became increasingly difficult for me to be ruled by a professor, even the best, I decided to become a professor as soon as possible. In 1980, I finished my *doctorat*, the *doctorat d'état*, *Sur la théologie blanche de Descartes*. I was very fortunate: exactly one year after my doctorate, I was given a position as full professor at the University of Poitiers, the only university from which Descartes earned a degree, in law. I was only thirty-five. In any case, it was very quick, I was fortunate (I was able to work quickly), and it was only at that time, in fact, that I decided not to remain a historian of philosophy for the rest of my life.

How did that decision come about?

Because it was obvious. In one of my classes at Poitiers, I started teaching Husserl (I taught Husserl from the start to finish), Heidegger, and so on. So I got a double specialization during my years in Poitiers.

It was four years after you started teaching at Poitiers that you published the article that would become the first chapter of Réduction et donation.

Yes, exactly. It was published in 1984. It was the first result of my teaching. I was becoming a phenomenologist, while keeping my eye on the history of philosophy. There remained a third interest: theology. I started with *L'idole et la distance* (1977). I was pretty tricky and diplomatic: I decided to publish a regular university book first, *Sur l'ontologie grise* (1975), which allowed me to have something more public and more daring with *L'idole et la distance*. I did the same thing—it was intended—with *Dieu sans l'être* (1982), publishing it only after I got my position and after having published *Sur la théologie blanche de Descartes* (1982).

In Dieu sans l'être, *you say that it occurred to you at that point that if you were rigorously to think through the possibility of revelation, it would require a complete restructuring of the transcendental conditions of manifestation as phenomenology had understood them until that point. Immediately after* Dieu sans l'être, *you discovered what you felt needed to be done in phenomenology.*

The question of the *Es gibt* was already asked, many things were already there—a clear link. But it was only a sketch.

And so the first chapter was published in 1984. By that time, did you already have a premonition of where you were going?

No. There was some controversy surrounding Husserl's *Logical Investigations*, with Derrida, but also Heidegger and others. So I decided to work my way through that open issue, but I was not at that time aware of the other chapters of *Réduction et donation*; it was only a first attempt to enter the debate. The second issue concerned the relation between Husserl and Descartes, so the book started to build itself quickly.

At what point, exactly, did the thematization of givenness came about for you? In the first chapter it's clear that you're moving in a direction that nobody had quite moved in yet. Derrida had assigned givenness to . . .

Intuition.

Intuition alone.

Very important for the broader understanding of givenness was a book by Didier Franck, *Chair et corps*. I found myself struck by his insistence that *Selbstgegebenheit* (self-givenness), or *Leiblichkeit* (bodily presence), was on both sides of the distinction between consciousness and the world, that both were expressed by Husserl as given. Franck insisted on the term *Leibhaftig* (presence in the flesh), but in the texts we find not only *Leibhaftig* but also *Gegebenheit* (givenness). It was a very important moment: after all, *Gegebenheit* has a far broader meaning in Husserl than Derrida noticed, even Heidegger, and even, in another way, Franck himself. In another way, the question of the given and the gift was already of interest to me for similar reasons, but, *pace* Dominique Janicaud, there was as yet no connection between the two questions. It was all in his imagination. (Janicaud was until the end a close friend. He first invited me to Nice to lecture on *L'idole et la distance* soon after its publication and gave a good review of the book. But the core of the debate—the status of givenness—was not already in question.)

To tell the concrete story of phenomenology: in the early eighties, I supported, as far as I could, Didier Franck. Through Derrida, he got an assistant professorship at the École Normale, and, with Courtine, we reestablished the Archives Husserl de Paris, which was first initiated by Ricoeur in the fifties but was truly decaying.

Out of date?

Yes, digested by the CNRS and diluted by the administration. And when Ricoeur retired from Nanterre and left for Chicago, the archives were, in fact, in something like a coma. The idea was to revive them at the CNRS and the École Normale, which we did. During the eighties, I would say that things were very much alive: we had large Saturday seminars on a weekly basis, all day, crowded and with everyone coming: Derrida, Michel Henry, the new generation. It was very creative and had a great impact on everyone there. It was also the first time that Husserl and Heidegger scholars actually met and worked together and, more important, the first time that the same people were scholars in both Husserl *and* Heidegger, which was absolutely not the case before. The scholarship on Husserl in France was primarily on the side of the philosophy of science, philosophy of knowledge (you would say philosophy of mind now), which was determined by the kinds of questions people like Cavaillès and Jean-Toussaint Desanti were asking.[8] It was Beaufret who was dealing with Heidegger, who was more "leftish" at that moment, more radical—politically speaking—and with apparently no position on science, the philosophy of science, and so on. The opposition was very strong. The Husserl specialists were admitted into the university but not so much those who worked on Heidegger. By the eighties—our generation—the same scholars were specialists in both fields and were also university professors, which really opened up the institutions. During that same period, a shift in the publishing business had also taken place: Courtine was at Vrin, Franck had his own series at Les Éditions de Minuit, and I had taken over Epiméthée of Presses Universitaires de France, so we could publish. And we did.

You could affect the culture very strongly . . .

Yes. We had the weapons—and we used them.

We'd like to ask you some questions about Réduction et donation. *In the preface, you raise the following question: "Can the conditions of presence be extended to the point that all beings reach it, beyond the limits fixed by previous states of metaphysics, or even by any metaphysics at all? Can the givenness in presence of each thing be realized without any condition or restriction?"*[9] *The question of time seems to permeate your work without ever becoming an explicit theme, or, at any rate, not one to which you give a sustained amount of attention. This distinguishes you from other figures in the history of phenomenology, both German and French: Heidegger, of course (the question of time was central for Heidegger from the very beginning), and Derrida (also from the very beginning). One could even say that, in a certain sense, the question of time was* the *question for Derrida. The opening chapter of* Réduction et donation—*your first foray into the phenomenology of givenness—takes the form of a debate with Derrida on his reading of Husserl in* La voix et le phénomène. *You preliminarily define givenness as "a mode of presence that is still undetermined and that, for this very reason, might not be defined exactly by the word 'presence.'"*[10] *A very intriguing line, given the history of phenomenol-*

ogy and the person with whom you're debating. In rereading La voix et le phénomène, *we were struck by the fact that in neither* Réduction et donation, *nor yet in Étant donné do you discuss Derrida's reading of Husserl's* Phenomenology of Internal Time-Consciousness, *which would, it seems to us, be the more important part of Derrida's book. Derrida, as you know, questions the very integrity of the phenomenological concept of the present, together with the concept of the phenomenon and the concept of intuition, concepts that you have yourself sought to reconstruct on the basis of the phenomenology of givenness. This seems to mark a very strong difference here between your work and that of Derrida. How do you understand Derrida's reading of Husserl's* Phenomenology of Internal Time-Consciousness *in relation to the work that you've done on the phenomenology of givenness? To put the matter in somewhat stronger terms, do you think that Derrida's position on the* Phenomenology of Internal Time-Consciousness *and particularly his deconstruction of the distinction between intuition and non-intuition complicates or in any way problematizes the concept of givenness as you've developed it?*

Frankly, to tell you my position, I think that taking the question of time seriously requires that we not take up the debate on the constitution of time in Husserlian terms. We really should not. With *Sein und Zeit* (and some texts of Husserl's on time, which are controversial, because they were not completely written by Husserl himself—we don't exactly know what Husserl's doctrine was), we were given a renewed understanding of the relation between time and Being. This allowed us to reread Kant's aesthetics of time. Thinking the experience of time, not, indeed, by the subject but by *Dasein*, played a crucial role in Heidegger's definition of the modes of being. But that was only Heidegger's first step. The *real* breakthrough made by Heidegger was to suggest that time pertains first to Being and *not* to *Dasein*. The real point, in other words, was to include time itself *within* the *Es gibt*, within the *Ereignis*, as Heidegger was to make clear in "Zeit und Sein." *That's* the point. When he discovered that time and Being were related not *through* the *Gemüt* of Kant, or even through *Dasein*, but through something far more radical: the *Ereignis* or, in my language, the *Es gibt* (I think the *Ereignis* is a bad nickname for the original phenomenon, which is, in fact, the *Es gibt* according to Heidegger himself). It's more radical to question how time is a function of the *Es gibt* than to consider the "inner" consciousness of time. Time is not a question of consciousness: it is a question of givenness. That's why I never focused on time as the primary feature of consciousness. Even Derrida remained trapped in a certain Husserlian conception, because when discussing the relation between "intention," "retention," and so on, he's just deconstructing . . .

Husserl's discourse.

Yes. We have a very good argument in support of the view that, even in Husserl, the main problem was not "protension" and "retention"—it was, rather, the meaning of *Urphänomen*, *Urimpression*. In fact, that the question of time is the question of *Urimpression* means that consciousness is an *effect* of time and not the place where time is constituted. Franck was very clear about this, as was Michel Henry. I think it's obvious. Time first happens as an unconscious, preconscious *event*. The *Urphänomen* is not constituted. So the question of presence is not a question of intuition. You can deconstruct intuition, and to a certain extent Derrida's argument against Husserl is very classical: already in Augustine you find that there is no intuition of the present.

The threefold ekstasis *of the present, you mean, in Book XI of* The Confessions . . .

Yes. You cannot—by intuition—reach something you could call "the present." In fact, time is an event prior to the distinction between present, past, and future—prior to consciousness. So, very early, the question of time was, for me, an effect of the general issue of givenness. I did not avoid or dodge anything but rather pointed it out.

And, as an additional confirmation (which I was not aware of at the time of *Réduction et donation*), we have Claude Romano's work. He has demonstrated that, in *Sein und Zeit*, for instance, Heidegger had no approach to the concept of the event, and the event is precisely what in time cannot be reconducted to consciousness. Romano's critical reading of *Sein und Zeit* also confirms that time is not about consciousness.[11]

To a certain degree one could claim that, on Derrida's reading, really, the "trace" is, of course, not a question of consciousness either: it does not, properly speaking, belong to consciousness.

Yes . . .

In a sense, Derrida would be in agreement with you on this question: time does not "as such" belong to consciousness—consciousness is an effect of the movement of the trace, rather than the other way around . . .

But you would agree that that's not the main theme of *La voix et le phénomène*. It's not obvious in his interpretation of Husserl. It emerges in Derrida's later work.

It's interesting that you say, for example, that time must be thought from givenness when, at the same time, "givenness" has a certain time-determination: the present, no?

No. I was already very much aware of Heidegger's "criticism," so to speak, of the present, of the reduction of *presence* (*Anwesenheit*) to the *present* (*Gegenwärt*). We have his criticism of the interpretation of *Gegenwärt* as "persistence." So the distinction between "the present" and "presence" is crucial. That said, I could not *not* be struck by the fact that there is a *third* meaning of "present," namely, "gift." The concept of the gift again led me to the question of givenness, and with this came the idea that the whole process of giving, receiving, and so on, might be the right way to get into the aporia of time. With the concept of the gift, you have the much more fundamental structure of the call and the response, which cannot be described according to time or, if it can, then only according to a very paradoxical time: traditionally, the call is supposed to come *first*, to be already past in relation to the response, which is supposed to happen in the present. In fact, the response makes the call heard for the first time. We can reverse and upset the order with a much more intricate structure of time if we interpret the question of time, not as a *flux* or a *stream*, but rather as the structure of givenness. Givenness can be seen in the structure called "response," and already, just with that, you have a more complicated scheme than that of protension, retention, and so on. So: I agree that I did not pay attention to the "inner" consciousness of time, but I think I was more serious about the real issue of time.[12]

One more point to explain how I connect my interest in theology to this. For instance—and there is no "turn," no confusion here—if you know a few things about theology as enacted in liturgy, you have a very complex structure of time. You have a *very* strong and complex understanding of all the *ekstases* of time, which is not a mere succession in metaphysical time. I was driven by this responsive performance of time *par excellence* in the Eucharistic liturgy (as achieved in Catholic style).

What do you say to the classical Husserlian who says that those are merely "empirical" formations dependent upon a more originary constitution of time by consciousness?

That begs the question. The problem is that *if* consciousness is the most a priori region of time, then how is consciousness itself constituted? The idea of an "inner" consciousness of time is based on the primacy of the transcendental subject.

Your understanding of the phenomenology of givenness as a "post-metaphysical" philosophical enterprise seems to depend rather crucially on a certain circumscription of the territory covered by the highly contentious term "metaphysics"—a term that has received as many determinations in the history of philosophy as there have been attempts to "overcome" metaphysics itself. Your historical work on Descartes has focused almost entirely on developing a rigorous, systematic concept of modern metaphysics, and your constructive and reconstructive work in theology and phenomenology has had as its primary ambition the creation of a conceptual space irreducible to metaphysics. What, then, are the conditions under which a philosophical discourse can be said to be "metaphysical" and what ultimately justifies both your use of the term and your claim to the effect that only phenomenology can exceed whatever that term designates? To what does phenomenology (and the phenomenology of givenness in particular) open access that we could not have access to before?

It is all too clear that "metaphysics" is a very equivocal concept. I've studied the history of the word. In every tradition, you have some people claiming to be "for" metaphysics and some people claiming to be "against" it. Even analytical philosophy was once "against" metaphysics and now it's standing "for" metaphysics, so the situation has completely changed—it's very strange.

Same with phenomenology. There is a very long history to this reversal of roles. This is perhaps one of the reasons why the last generation—my generation—reached a balanced point of view on the matter. Two results came out of this, which to some extent now overlap, at least partly. The first was a very strong theoretical determination of metaphysics by Heidegger: metaphysics as "onto-theology," which, in fact, remains one of the very few real and rigorous concepts of "metaphysics," one that becomes very useful for interpreting many authors. You can disagree with Heidegger's understanding of onto-theology, but the fact is that it existed for a certain, determinable period of time. Its conceptuality can be mapped out, and you can adjust that map—some authors partly fit, some fit completely, and some do not.

The second result was a careful study of the history of the constitution of metaphysics in the philosophical texts themselves, which formed a part of my intellectual life. For ten years, in fact, I worked very closely with Jean-François Courtine, while he was studying Francisco Suárez. We worked roughly on the same thing for many years, and with Breton and others (in the seminar of Pierre Aubenque)[13] we renewed interest in the late medieval period. When we started reading Suárez in the late seventies, there weren't a lot of people doing that. Now you have scholars like Jacob Schmutz, who knows everything there is to know about Suárez. To be able to make the distinction between Vasquez and Suárez[14]—in the late seventies there were not a lot of people who could do that. Today, it is more or less taken for granted.

In any case, we now have a precise historical determination of the concept. The word "metaphysics" emerges in the early fourteenth century. It was not yet really established even in Thomas Aquinas. And it went on, say, to Nietzsche, who was clearly very aware of the fact that he was deconstructing it. We can say that metaphysics, historically speaking, has been documented from Duns Scotus to Nietzsche. With a historically determinate concept, there is no metaphorical, arbitrary use of the word "metaphysics." Before Scotus, "metaphysics" was an interpretation of philosophy. After Nietzsche, it became a polemical word.

Same thing with "ontology," for instance. "Ontology" is used in a polemical way now. It was metaphorical in Aristotle, who had no concept of "ontology." Same thing with "analogy," "analogy of being," and many other expressions. I think we can agree that metaphysics has a lifetime of about five centuries, a birth in the texts, and a death. And we have concepts to make sense of that period. It is, roughly speaking, a documented lexicon—the *lexicon metaphysicon* (as Clauberg used to say): the true metaphysics of the second scholastic period to Kant—that is the lexicon of metaphysics, we can document it. We have texts and a lexicon.[15] And we have an interpretation of that lexicon and history with Heidegger, an interpretation that to some extent fits Hegel's interpretation.

The first point to keep in mind when it comes to "metaphysics" is that not just any kind of philosophy amounts to metaphysics; there are some determinations of metaphysics that cannot be found in other kinds of philosophy.

What are these determinations?

To sum it up very briefly, I think "metaphysics" means, first, that Being amounts to beings insofar as beings are present. To be present is to persist, to be self-identical (principle of identity), to be in time, that is, to be is to be as long as you can: the *conatus essendi* as perseveration *in suo esse*.[16] The principle of identity leads to persistence and persistence may be achieved in the best possible way when no indetermination is left. The best case of this is that of the "object." The object can be exhaustively produced, any indetermination being rejected from its definition, from the essence of the object. It can be reproduced so as to be present.

The second characteristic is that presence is made real so long as it has a reason. That reason can either be the essence itself, in which case the thing is *causa sui*, or the reason comes from outside, in which case we speak of a foundation. And you have *causa sui*—foundation—with the principle of sufficient reason. I think you can articulate metaphysics with these two concepts, I mean both *metaphysica generalis* and *metaphysica specialis*. If these features cannot be found, then we are not unambiguously dealing with metaphysics. You can argue that Kierkegaard does not belong to metaphysics (Nietzsche perhaps to some extent). I think Husserl does not belong to metaphysics because eventually he had to give up any dream of an absolute foundation.

That's a very strong claim . . .

The final foundation is to come, it is teleological.

But that could be assigned to the most classical of metaphysical concepts, no?

You can at least raise the question as to whether Husserl belongs to metaphysics or not. You can argue—perhaps it is an illusion, but you *can* argue, and some have argued in that way. You can raise the question with regard to Bergson and you should ask the question even with regard to Aristotle. The very fact that there is no unity between the two sides in Aristotle (between "theology" and "ontology")—a very old, classical problem in the interpretation of Aristotle—shows that the question remains open. You cannot doubt it with Descartes, Spinoza, Leibniz, and Kant. So we can have a not too imprecise and controversial concept of metaphysics and we can stick to that. It is very difficult to explain this to people who have an ideological definition, an assumption about metaphysics. In some deconstructionist rhetoric, for example, you are a metaphysician as soon as you begin to speak! And, they add, metaphysics is *very bad*. On the other hand, according to some neo-Thomists, you have to be a metaphysician if you want to be a Christian—they cannot imagine the possibility of there being another way. I know this use of "metaphysics" from experience. But basically, as a historian of philosophy, I think we have reasonable grounds to admit a certain univocal and historically documented, limited, and finite concept of metaphysics, and I stick to that.

By the way, this explains why I did not repent in my interpretation of Thomas Aquinas (no matter what my critics say) in the second edition of *Dieu sans l'être*:[17] I simply applied my historical understanding of what metaphysics is and found that it did not fit Thomas Aquinas, and I think my critics agreed with me. But in that case, how could they agree with me on this and disagree with my concept of metaphysics? My concept of metaphysics should be correct to some extent, if I can find Thomas Aquinas to be "not guilty," as it were, of metaphysics. So I did not modify my standards by writing that chapter. The conflict surrounded the strict understanding of Heidegger as sustained by Beaufret and Fédier. That was the call, the origin of *Dieu sans l'être*. There was a private conference held in Paris, in 1980, and organized by Richard Kearney (now at Boston College) and Joseph O'Leary (a Jesuit now teaching in Tokyo).[18] The origin of the debate came from the publication of *L'idole et la distance*. Lévinas, Beaufret, Breton, Fédier, Greisch,[19] Kearney, O'Leary, Ricoeur, and I were all there. It was after my paper for this conference (against the reading of my book by Beaufret and Fédier), that I decided to follow up *L'idole et la distance* with *Dieu sans l'être*, which was concerned with questions of Heidegger (the question of God, of method, the question of Being). That was the crucial point. So, *Dieu sans l'être* was written with and against someone—against Heidegger, at least according to his leading interpretation of that time.

Why is phenomenology alone in a position to exceed whatever is designated by the term "metaphysics"? What does phenomenology open access to that metaphysics prohibits us from—supposing it to be a question of access, which is already a phenomenological question.

There are two answers. The quick answer would be that, to my knowledge, until now, only phenomenology has made an attempt to overcome metaphysics because the question regarding the "end of metaphysics" was first raised by phenomenologists. This question is not, for instance, steadily assumed by the analytical tradition, in which you can find any number of possible positions. It is not a key point for the analytical tradition. Indeed, they have no real concept of metaphysics. In the current philosophical situation, it was under the banner of phenomenology that the question was raised.

But there is a more demanding response to your question: we have to admit that some phenomenologies remain submitted to the question as to how far they still pertain to metaphysics. In Husserl's case it is very clear, even Derrida, even Heidegger in the analytic of *Dasein*. There was a moment when it was not so clear. With the analytic of *Dasein*, Heidegger assumed a concept of metaphysics (for a certain period). For Lévinas, even Heidegger did not escape metaphysics. The rift had to be drawn within phenomenology itself. But in phenomenology, at least we explicitly raised the question. I think that phenomenology has a special capacity to understand and pose the question correctly.

If I understand phenomenology correctly, there is no phenomenology without the reduction. There are those who might disagree, but I insist that without the reduction there is no phenomenology. Why do we have the reduction, for what reason? To expand givenness everywhere and all the time: that's the final goal of the reduction. What you see does not immediately amount to the given, and the given may perhaps extend far beyond what you imagine or stop short of. It most certainly leads you somewhere other than you initially expected. So, the reduction is about givenness: we test by reduction whether what appears matches the given.

What does this mean? It means that if there is a method in phenomenology, it is a counter-method. The reduction does away with the a priori, against metaphysics, which aims to establish the a priori in a number of different ways. Metaphysics means: establishing conditions or principles. And phenomenology, thus understood, does away with the a priori, the principles. Husserl's "principle of principles" consists in the paradox that there is no principle other than the given (with or without intuition—even that distinction is dismissed).[20] That's why there is a strong connection between phenomenology and deconstruction (or better destruction, *Destruktion*, *Abbau*). Understood in this way, phenomenology seeks to achieve a non-constitutive philosophy, which should not be debased as a form of empiricism, because the ordinary empiricist view assumes not only the existence of sense-data, but also that the mind, however passive it may be, awaits them as a silent pre-condition. That was my point about *l'adonné* in *Étant donné*: its characteristic feature consists in that it does not expect the given beforehand but discovers itself as given at the very same moment as the given itself. The one undergoing the reception has to be received and does not precede the given in the reception of the given. Givenness overrules both the given and the givee in the very same event. So there is no a priori, not even the passive a priori, nor that of the transcendental "I," nor yet that of the empirical self. This is a very strong move. I think I made this point with givenness. One may argue from time to time that the structure of passivity in Lévinas or Michel Henry remains a kind of a priori (you can, at least, raise the question). I hope that I am moving to a position where we have left the a priori entirely behind. That is why the most original saturated phenomenon is the event. The event achieves the destruction of the a priori. It happens as the only self-imposing a priori, so that everything else happens through it. To happen is to happen a posteriori by definition. The only correct a priori lies in the universal a posteriori of the event.

In one essay, "The Phenomenological Origins of the Concept of Givenness," you outline the history of the concept of givenness, even before phenomenology, as in, for example, the late logical debates of the nineteenth century . . .

Yes, the Marburg school . . .

Yes. You say there, right from the beginning, that the concept of givenness (in your usage) has nothing to do with the assumption of the non-constituted, non-conceptual given. By that it seems that you did not mean that it has everything to do with a constituted concept of the given. You meant to be ruling out the concept of something's being given prior to any and all signification: absolutely pure intuition with no signification whatsoever. This seems to be an ambiguous question in your work. To what degree can we talk about the given . . .

If there is only one saturated phenomenon, I am saved . . .

. . . without talking about concepts in some sense. We can talk about concepts in many ways. Surely we do not need to return to the paradigm of "the object" (in the Kantian or Husserlian sense) to talk about concepts and perhaps you do indeed have a concept of the concept based on the excess of intuition in the saturated phenomenon. This is certainly not a concept of the concept that would "anticipate" the form of the phenomenon; rather it would be a function of the phenomenon (although it remains to a certain extent unclear what this really amounts to). You use this concept of conceptual deferral quite freely in Étant donné, *in connection with the saturated phenomenon. To what extent, if at all, do you feel there to be some irreducibility of the concept in your work? For example, you say that without a phenomenological horizon in the Husserlian sense, nothing would appear, but even so, that does not mean that* with *the horizon* everything *appears.*

There is the question here of what a concept is, a question recently raised by Jocelyn Benoist. I have my own view of concepts, which is not the same as that of the others. Is there a concept of "givenness," strictly speaking? We can discuss that. I use "concept" in a very empirical way. One has a concept of something when there is the possibility of seeing. That is what a concept is. You can understand "concept" in two ways. Very basically, I think the concept is what one has conceived, what one has grasped. In that case, it is the same thing as *intuitus*, strangely, because *intuitus* is *tueor* and *tueor* means "to guard," to have a look upon. What is "to guard"? That which you keep, which you watch, by seeing it. But a concept is also the "newborn," *c'est qui était conçu* (*comme on dit en français*), the child.

The conceived . . .

The conceived is what "comes out." Here, we have another meaning of "concept." *C'est qui est conçu, visible.* In that case, the concept, as what makes visible, is a phenomenon.

But then the important thing to distinguish is the difference between the empiricist concept of the given as a pure "sense-datum," which has no conceptual dimension whatsoever, and a phenomenological concept of the given. I guess the question hinges on whether you entertain a minimal relation to classical empiricism (be it implicit or explicit).

First, I agree with the criticism made by both Husserl and Heidegger and, indeed, all phenomenologists that there is no such thing as a pure "sense-datum." So I wouldn't get into the discussion about how far a pure apprehension of the given might be possible, because there is no pure "sense-datum." What we experience at the basic experiential level is already signification.

I see phenomenology as a means to opening possibility, to let the phenomenon go by itself, to free the phenomenon. There is an excess. If you open the door for one phenomenon to escape, eventually all the others will follow. If you understand the phenomenon in terms of self-givenness, you cannot avoid the saturated phenomenon. If there is no a priori, there is no limit. The sky is the limit, not even the sky.

Speaking of the sky, we think this the appropriate time to raise the question of revelation. Now your decision to include the description of revelation in an explicitly phenomenological context was very controversial. You defended the phenomenological legitimacy of this decision by claiming, and we quote at some length here:

Here, I am not broaching revelation in its theological pretention to truth, something faith alone can dare to do. I am outlining it as a possibility—in fact the ultimate possibility, the paradox of paradoxes—of phenomenality, such that it is carried out in a possible saturated phenomenon. The hypothesis that there was historically no such revelation would change nothing in the phenomenological task of offering an account of the fact, itself incontestable, that it has been thinkable, discussible, and even describable. This description does not make an exception to the principle of the reduction to immanence. Here it is perhaps a case of something like the phenomena that Husserl thought could only be described by imaginative variations—imaginary or not, they appear, and their mere possibility merits an analysis and *Sinngebung*.[21]

Elsewhere, in Being Given, *you claim that the "transcendental conditions of the possibilities of manifestation"*[22] *must themselves be redefined in order to make room for the possibility of the phenomenon of revelation, as though, if there were even one phenomenon that would exceed these possibilities (and we have a responsibility to account for this phenomenon qua phenomenologists), then we have to rethink these conditions altogether. That is a very powerful claim.*

May I comment on that?

Yes, please.

The idea is that if objectivity (in the sense of *Gegenständlichkeit*) is not the standard definition of the phenomenon, if the phenomenon, according to Heidegger, is "that which gives itself from itself," well then, in that case, we are led to the possibility of the saturated phenomenon. This possibility is documented in the descriptions of some saturated phenomena by a number of philosophers: the flesh as the living body (Merleau-Ponty, Henry), the face of the Other (Lévinas), the excess of intuition (which is negatively Derrida's horizon), and the event (Romano). We have some phenomena that demand a combination of these four figures. In many cases, we have to face the possibility of such a combination, we need to combine two or three kinds of saturated phenomena just to account for what the writer is describing. This is obvious if you read Joyce, James, or Proust, and the same goes for poetry. We also have some other texts, and I am referring here especially, but not exclusively, to biblical texts, which obviously need all four figures. Anything less and you cannot interpret the text completely, cannot do justice to all the obvious aspects of the phenomenon described. This combination, the possible combination of the four types, enforces what I suggest we call the *phenomenon of revelation*. This is a possibility in phenomenological description, period. We need it. That is all I said. We have to yield to the claims of the possible.

As phenomenologists.

As phenomenologists. And I've just read a very good, short book by Emmanuel Housset, *Husserl et l'idée de Dieu*. He investigates Husserl's claim to try "to reach God without God." In so doing, Housset explains that the reduction of the transcendent God in fact clears the way for a description of God. Here, the saturated phenomenon is a theologically saturated phenomenon: not yet given, given as not yet given, infinitely remote, and so on. Thus, you have a description. It is a very fair description of the greatest accomplishment of man (theologically speaking), and its name is "God": the ultimate accomplishment of rationality. This makes perfect sense. It is the phenomenon of revelation, completely neutral. This is exactly what I referred to.

Now another question: When you assume the historical fact of the revelation of God, as some theologians do in our century (Karl Barth, Hans Urs von Balthasar, and some others), but which is not the case with Karl Rahner . . .

How strange: If you are to do theology, how can you do it without assuming the fact of revelation? If you want to be a theologian . . .

Well, you have transcendental Thomists who stick to a transcendental interpretation. It is strange, but it is a fact. Everything is possible, including deep inconsistency, and deep inconsistency, fully thought through, becomes a system. What I am saying is that the *Selbstoffenbarung* of God, if it should be studied by phenomenology, will be a special case of the phenomenon of revelation. That is all. You can disagree with this in two very weak ways. The first is Janicaud's objection: we simply should not study the phenomenon of revelation. Why? In fact, there is no answer.

In his critique he does not seem to give a genuine phenomenological justification for the exclusion.

No. The fact of the matter is that Dominique Janicaud was not by formation a phenomenologist but a Hegel scholar, and very well trained, through Beaufret, in Heidegger. But the phenomenological method, the reduction—this is very typical—he did not understand, or at least operate. He had no deep familiarity with Husserl's operations and so had a literal, rather narrow, orthodox reading of the evolution of phenomenology. He just saw things from the outside. He did not consider that, in fact, not only Henry, Lévinas, Chrétien, and Ricoeur—and now we know that to some extent Husserl and obviously the best of Derrida (it was the reason why we were having so many discussions)—were all asking the same questions, about "the impossible," for example, and so on. This was our daily bread. It was absolutely not the daily bread of Janicaud. He was seeing things as an outsider, without mastering the new rules of the game, like a Frenchman watching baseball! "What are they doing?" I asked the first time I watched a ball game. It took me years to understand that they were, in fact, doing something very subtle. Now I understand better. You always have to learn the rules.

We should take care and avoid excessively simple oppositions and admit that the phenomena in the end impose new distinctions, new concepts on us. But I think that today, at least in Rome, Paris, and the United States, the real theologians are starting to get the point that perhaps what they need is an adapted methodology that reaches far beyond a mere readaptation of what they call metaphysics or philosophy. They need to use a phenomenological strategy.

This raises questions about the importance of the phenomenological method to theology in general. It seems that you would prefer as a far better approach in contemporary theology . . .

I gave a lecture at the Gregorian University in Rome in October 2010. It was the opening lecture of a series of lectures at the Gregorianum on phenomenology and theology.[23] The fact that the Gregorian in Rome organized this series of lectures was an event in itself. I explained what is at issue—givenness, the concept of the saturated phenomenon, etc., and I brought these concepts into conversation with some critical texts in the New Testament. As an example, in the Synoptics, we repeatedly encounter the same formulation: "Nothing is covered up that will not be revealed, and nothing hidden that will not become known."[24] As if the role of Christ would have been (and still is) to open, to make visible everything that remains hidden, invisible. This looks like a typical phenomenological way of understanding the issue of manifestation. And you can, indeed should, read these texts as performing a phenomenological opening as well. Revelation is not such a theological concept after all. Historically, it is a philosophical concept. So how should we translate "revelation" back into the Greek text of the Bible? I think we should use *apokalypsis*, which means to make visible, to dis-cover, *Abbau*. Or even a substitute for *aletheia*, un-covering.

That seems deeply related to the Heideggerian concept of truth, no?

You know, there is a book, written by a young and brilliant philosopher, among my former students, Jean Vioulac, *L'époque de la technique. Marx, Heidegger et l'accomplissement de la métaphysique*. He has published papers on the concept of *apokalypsis* and has compared it to *aletheia*, and it makes perfect sense. That is the future.

Another thing on this question of philosophy and theology. I have written a paper that points out an obvious, well-known fact, namely that the entire question regarding "philosophy and theology" is not, in fact, all that old.[25] It is with Abelard and Thomas Aquinas that the distinction was first made. It was unknown to the Church Fathers; they were not doing "theology." "Theology" was a *pagan* word. They claimed, in their way, to be doing mere philosophy. This is very clear, assumed in Augustine and in all the others.

It is interesting that they did not understand "philosophy" to be a pagan word.

No, "theology" was a pagan word, but for *them* "philosophy" was *a Christian* word. *Philosophia christiana* was understood to mean the monastic life: the Christian philosopher was a monk because philosophy was his way of life (think of Pierre Hadot). Erasmus was still living *philosophia christiana* in that way. And there is historical ground for this: you cannot oppose philosophy to theology without having a self-sustaining interpretation of reason, that is, the possibility of developing an independent science, ruling all the others. This was, in fact, first a requirement of the theologians themselves: they had to have a *quadrivium* and a *trivium* in order to prepare people for the study of theology. So it was theology that created philosophy as an independent science. After that, the balance was upset and philosophers started claiming to be the only bearers of rationality. It followed that revelation became irrational, outside of reason, and "mystical." But such a distinction implies that there is a definition of reason set by philosophy, which ends with the transcendental definition of philosophy.

The Kantian determination is rooted here?

Which is metaphysics.

And then there is Fichte's determination of revelation.

Absolutely. And then with Hegel and Schelling you have an attempt to reverse the situation, albeit within the same context, assuming the fundamental determinations of metaphysics (concept versus faith, reason versus revelation, and so on), which are the real problem. But now, after them and beyond their context, we can say that the distinction between philosophy and theology is *not* a distinction of method or rationality. Instead, the distinction concerns the *datum* of inquiry. Perhaps we ought to say that the difference consists in the fact that philosophy does not take as its field the texts of the so-called revelation. That's a real distinction, but it is not a distinction of method. We should admit a method (or non-method) that could reach every kind of phenomenon, including the non-objective ones, which may nevertheless appear as well as objects do.

A distinction of object and not of method.

Yes, of field, not of method, because no philosopher, to my knowledge (or only the most old-fashioned), claims to be in a position to provide a transcendental definition of reason. We are in the period of nihilism. If you are a Wittgensteinian (and it was the case for Wittgenstein indeed) and you consider the moral, ethical, or religious field to be something completely unknowable—by this you are only deconstructing the transcendental conception of reason.

But the question of revelation in your work has had one particular phenomenological issue, which is the claim that it constitutes "the last possibility," the highest possibility—because, as you mentioned, it combines all of the other figures of saturation. Nevertheless, it would seem that, given your concept of phenomenology, you are also committed to refusing any such "last possibility," to refusing any foreclosure of or on the possibilities of phenomenality.

This was an objection raised by Kathryn Tanner[26] and since assumed by some French theologians. I responded by saying that this possibility has been the last possibility up to now, but it remains a possibility, not a principle, and possibility remains open by definition. So if there is possibility other than that last possibility, it too remains a possibility. I am not imposing a new kind of a priori. The possible is by definition the last. And givenness, coming as an event, after and against any a priori, cannot be itself an a priori, or the a posteriori as the last a priori.

What does it mean, exactly, to say that it is "the last"?

Everything that will come, will come: this amounts to a definition of the possible. If we have started to overcome metaphysics a bit, it means that we are not in quest of a new foundation: any new foundation will no longer be accepted. What we need is a new possibility, possibility as such, which is novelty itself, the event. We must recognize this. And this is why we are digging toward the minimum, the *khôra* (according to Derrida), which is impossible. And one of the characteristics of the possible is that you cannot distinguish it from the impossible. And it is absolutely consistent to say that. For us the possible and the impossible are the same. And to do metaphysics is exactly to make and sustain this distinction, which is expressed as the distinction between the possible and the impossible.

Determined by a certain a priori principle or foundation . . .

Exactly.

So, of course, in phenomenology, we no longer have an a priori principle delimiting the domain of the possible and distinguishing it from the domain of the impossible in advance: we have an a posteriori concept of the possible.

Exactly. And that is why I now focus on this formulation: the impossibility of impossibility. In *Certitudes négatives* and *Le phénomène érotique*, I focus on that. That is in fact the new frontier.

Two questions about your new frontier. The question about the banality of the saturated phenomenon and your recent course on Heidegger's concept of the thing at the Sorbonne. It appears that you have been pushing the saturated phenomenon from the domain of exception to that of the rule, to something like the rule itself . . .

Yes, indeed. One of the last chapters of *Certitudes négatives* concerns itself with the distinction between object and event in all phenomena. The *core*, the rule, lies in the event; the object is just a neutralization of the character of the event, of the phenomenon.

Would it be fair to say, then, that what is important to you in revelation is just this very character?

Yes, the event opens the main characteristic of any phenomenon that is given.

What possibility, or perhaps impossibility, does the concept of a negative certitude name and what prompted you to develop this concept?

Certitudes négatives is a move toward Kant. The fact that we can have a certitude without foundation, that foundation is not the condition of certitude.

Are there conditions of certitude?

For Descartes, yes: he said certitude was just about conditions. Yet, we have certitudes that are not based on the knowledge of the principle or the cause, objectivity, and the mastery of the known. In fact, sometimes *not* to know the cause can *lead you* to a certitude. There are certitudes *ohne warum*. And to some extent the greatest certitudes bear the characteristics of the *ohne warum*. I would even argue that our deepest certitudes have no reason.

In that, you would be in deep agreement with Wittgenstein, in fact.

Yes, yes, more and more . . .

Notes

1. Rémi Brague is a professor emeritus of Arabic and religious philosophy at the University of Paris 1 Panthéon–Sorbonne and author of, among others, *The Wisdom of the World*, *Aristote et la question du monde*, and *The Legend of the Middle Ages*.

2. Ferdinand Alquié was a historian of modern philosophy at the University of Paris 1 Panthéon–Sorbonne and is the author of *La découverte métaphysique de l'homme chez Descartes*, *La critique kantienne de la métaphysique*, *Le rationalisme de Spinoza*, and *Qu'est que comprendre un philosophe*.

3. Jean-Robert Armogathe is the cofounder of the Catholic journal *Communio*, a priest, a scholar, and the author of *Theologia cartesiana* and *La nature du monde*.

4. Bernard-Henri Lévy is a French public intellectual and author who coined the term "*les nouveaux philosophes*" in the 1970s to characterize a current of thought opposed to that of French Marxism. Pierre Manent is a professor of political philosophy at the École des hautes études en sciences sociales. Alain Renaut is a professor of philosophy at the University of Paris IV.

5. Stanislas Breton was a French philosopher and theologian and a professor at the Institut Catholique de Paris and the École normale supérieure.

6. A civil service competitive exam for positions in the French educational system.

7. François Fédier is a prominent Heideggerian and former professor of philosophy at the Lycée Louis Pasteur (Neuilly-sur-Seine). Claude Roëls is a French translator of Heidegger. François Vezin is a former professor of philosophy at Lycée Honoré-de-Balzac de Paris and a translator of Heidegger. All three men, together with Jean Beaufret, attended Heidegger's "Thor Seminars" in Le Thor, France (1966–1969). See Heidegger, *Four Seminars*.

8. Jean Cavaillès was a French philosopher of science and a member of the French resistance and is the author of *Méthode axiomatique et formalisme*, *Transfini et continu*, and *Sur la logique et la théorie de la science*. Jean-Toussaint Desanti was

a philosopher of mathematics and a student of Cavaillès and is the author of *Les Idéalités mathématiques* and *La philosophie silencieuse ou critique des philosophies de la science*.

9. See Marion, *Réduction et donation*, 1.

10. Ibid., 29.

11. See Romano, *L'aventure temporelle*, 43–87.

12. See Marion, *Being Given*, 295.

13. Pierre Aubenque is an Aristotle scholar and a professor emeritus at the University of Paris IV.

14. Gabriel Vasquéz was a Spanish Jesuit theologian and philosopher. Francisco Suárez was also a Spanish Jesuit theologian and philosopher and is the author of the historically influential *Disputationes metaphysicae* (1597).

15. Johannes Clauberg was a German Cartesian theologian and philosopher.

16. See Spinoza, *A Spinoza Reader*, 159: "Each thing, as far as it can by its own power, strives to persevere in its being [*Unaquæque res, quantum in se est, in suo esse perseverare conatur*]."

17. See Marion, *Dieu sans l'être*, xxix–1.

18. For the conference proceedings, see Kearney and O'Leary, *Heidegger et la question de Dieu*.

19. Jean Greisch is a professor of philosophy at the Institut Catholique de Paris and the author of *Ontologie et Temporalité*.

20. See Husserl, *Ideas I*, 83: "No theory we can conceive can mislead us in regard to the *principle of all principles*: that *every primordial dator intuition is a source of authority* [*Rechtsquelle*] *for knowledge*, that *whatever presents itself in 'intuition' in primordial form* (as it were in its bodily reality), *is simply to be accepted as it gives itself out to be*, though *only within the limits in which it then presents itself*."

21. See Marion, *Being Given*, 5.

22. Ibid., 336.

23. See Marion, "Remarques sur l'utilité en théologie de la phénoménologie."

24. See Luke 12:2–3; Matthew 10:26.

25. See Marion, "De fondement de la distinction entre théologie et philosophie."

26. See Tanner, "Theology at the Limits of Phenomenology."

The Fundamental Concepts of Phenomenology

CLAUDE ROMANO

In Au cœur de la raison, *you reconstruct, both historically and systematically, the basic concepts of phenomenology from Husserl to Heidegger to Merleau-Ponty. What developments in contemporary philosophy are you responding to?*

It seems to me that one could diagnose a current crisis in philosophy that echoes Husserl's statement at the beginning of the last century. On one side, the positivist paradigm that prevailed for a long time in the Anglophone philosophy of language, in the wake of a certain reading of the *Tractatus* and the work of the Vienna Circle, has reached exhaustion: not only the idea of a philosophy that carries out a progressively abandoned scientific model, but also, more generally, the style of thinking that prevailed in the "analytic" current, and that turned away from the great traditional philosophical problems, does not seem to be able to satisfy the vital interests to which classical philosophy was supposed to respond. Even when it revives certain traditional problems, as is the case, for example, with analytic metaphysics, it at best only offers us a pastiche of what had been the great tradition of first philosophy. This philosophy no longer speaks to us, and, moreover, its best representatives have drawn their conclusions by moving away more and more resolutely from the initial positivist paradigm. On the other side, the philosophy that is called "continental," and of which phenomenology (including its hermeneutic and deconstructionist continuations) is undoubtedly the best representative, has developed as an autonomous tradition, but it had a tendency to withdraw into and isolate itself; it lost something of the demand for rational justification that has defined philosophy from the beginning, to the point of sometimes sinking into a jargon that makes it opaque and idiosyncratic. From there, it is as if we only have a choice between a technical philosophy cut off from our vital questions and a philosophy more concerned about continuity with the grand ancient ideal but that no longer manages to raise itself to the level of universality that we have the right to expect from it because it neglects the demand for argumentation and justification that "analytic" philosophy almost exclusively emphasizes.

Naturally, this way of painting a picture of our present is still very crude and simplistic. For philosophy evolved greatly on both sides of the Atlantic and the English Channel over the course of the last forty years. The problems that it formulates in both places have come together little by little: we have only to think of the question of interpretation that is as central and decisive for Donald Davidson as it is for Gadamer, of the refusal of the dichotomy between facts and values, of the resurgence of pragmatism in American philosophy, and of the anti-positivism that triumphs in both the post-Wittgensteinian current and in hermeneutics. A new order seems to be emerging that for the first time makes a dialogue possible between these traditions, a dialogue that is no longer about the misunderstandings each has of the other. But for such a dialogue to be meaningful, it is necessary to go back to the historical sources of the two traditions and to bring to light their respective presuppositions, which often go unnoticed—or the importance of which remains at least insufficiently evaluated—by their principal representatives. It is notably this "genealogical" work that I undertook to accomplish in this book. I tend to think that the present philosophical field resembles a game of chess in which each of the players ignores certain possible moves and obsessively continues to make the same gambits. I am trying to suggest that the game would be more interesting if we were to become aware of the possibility that these moves were, in fact, played in the past, but we forgot about them.

Take an example that is central to my mind. One of the dominant paradigms in analytic philosophy, even all the way up to John McDowell, seems to me to be a mix of empiricism and "nominalism" (in a specifically post-Wittgensteinian sense of the term): on the one hand, experience is understood in an atomist manner as the causal impact that the physical world exercises on our sensibility, a chaos of impressions in themselves deprived of any necessary structure and of any immanent laws; on the other, whatever order and law that is introduced into experience can only come from our conceptual resources, which is to say from linguistic occurrences (for, in the wake of Wittgenstein, the possession of concepts is identified as the capacity to employ words), and consequently it is of an order exterior to sensibility. In order to be ordered and structured, McDowell tells us, experience must be conceptual, and it is only on this condition that a "true" empiricism that integrates the contribution of experience into the "logical space of reasons" and justifications becomes possible, overcoming the "myth" of a brute given as the foundation of knowledge [*connaissance*].[1] But this position is only justified by the presuppositions that underlie it, and it re-enacts the great debate between empiricism and neo-Kantianism at the beginning of the twentieth century without even realizing it (the critique of the myth of the given being precisely one of the centerpieces of the objections addressed by Natorp or Cohen[2] to both empiricism and the nascent phenomenology equally). In reality, the alternative between an amorphous experience, an experience of brute givens, directly observable, as a point of departure for all knowledge, and an experience that is conceptual "all the way out," could only be a false alternative that from the beginning fails to recognize that another concept of experience is possible, a concept advanced by Husserl early on and precisely in order to refuse both Humean empiricism and Kantianism. This concept is of an experience that is governed by laws that are necessary and a priori, which do not come from the projection of conceptual and linguistic schemes on simple amorphous sensations. Far from having been made null and void by the criticisms of the Vienna Circle, this idea seems to me to remain viable today.

For example, it allows us to take into consideration everything that, in our discursive intelligence, is rooted in a more vast intelligence, one that emerges from the level of our sensibility and from the ways that we are in touch with the world in our corporeal existence. The mistake of philosophy that claims to follow the "linguistic turn" was to remove the means of thinking about these bonds between our linguistic competence and a sensible intelligence that is both its base and resource. By shutting itself away in language and claiming to resolve the traditional problems of philosophy by analysis of language, it became disinterested in the very pre-linguistic dimension without which an understanding of language is doomed to fail.

Throughout the book, you defend what you call the "phenomenological thesis"—what is the phenomenological thesis and to what extent do you understand it to determine the specificity of phenomenology?

I call the "phenomenological thesis" the thesis that the pre-linguistic order of our experience presents necessary structures and intelligible outlines that are autonomous with respect to the forms of our conceptual thought and the linguistic schemes that underlie them. In a word: the structures of experience are not projections of our conceptual and linguistic schemes, although these schemes can of course *influence* the manner in which we experience the world, ourselves, and others.

To take an elementary example, certain laws that govern the domain of colors or sounds are not simply contingent regularities that would be the consequence of an inductive generalization of the Humean type: they are *necessary* in a strong sense. This necessity is not of a conventional nature, it is not the pure product of a linguistic conceptualization that we would apply to colors or to sounds, it is not derived from "the arbitrary nature of grammar." It is rooted in experience itself, which possesses here an order, an immanent "reason." It is this idea that Husserl expressed by the formula of a "*logos* of the aesthetic world,"[3] which phenomenology aims to bring to light, thus deepening—by completely different means—the Kantian idea of the autonomy of the "aesthetic" with respect to "transcendental logic," consequently forging the program of a *phenomenological* transcendental aesthetic that must necessarily precede the investigation of "superior" forms of thought and judgment, to the extent that they presuppose it.

This thesis is as simple in its formulation as it is difficult to apprehend in all of its ramifications. It seems to me to be *the* fundamental thesis that is shared among the ensemble of work that claims to be "phenomenology." Of course, it is implicit for many authors who are regularly placed in this current and who do not always try to make the presuppositions that underlie their method clear.

Most certainly, this thesis is open to debate, and I discuss it extensively. One could, in fact, be tempted to think that a proposition such as "Brown is an unsaturated and dark yellow (or orange or red)," even though it describes an apparently necessary feature of this color as we find in experience, still possesses a necessity that is not different than that of an empirical proposition of the type: "Under the earth's normal pressure conditions, water boils at 100°C." In both cases, this necessity would be based on an inductive generalization. The problem is that, while we can easily imagine an experience that would invalidate the physical proposition that I mentioned (it would suffice for us to measure the temperature of boiling water in the same conditions of pressure at 200°C) it is very difficult for us to conceive of an experience that would invalidate the proposition about brown. It seems that to be an unsaturated and dark yellow (or orange or red) pertains to the *essence* of brown: anything that does not appear to us in this way simply cannot be brown. Not only can we not imagine a brown that does not possess this characteristic, but if, despite everything, we were asked to try anyway, we would not even know *what* to imagine. What matters here is not a simple subjective inability, as if we were asked to imagine a thousand sheep, but an objective impossibility that holds of the nature of the color in question: since, in the case of sheep, we would know perfectly well what to imagine (if we were capable).

It is this situation that gave birth to an opposite temptation. After all, if such a proposition is not empirical, isn't it a simple rule of "grammar" and thus conventional? The characteristic expressed here would not belong to the brown as phenomenon but to the way that we apply the word "brown" to *our* concept of brown. This assertion of course contains something true. But the question remains whether our concept of brown is free from all anchoring in what Husserl would call "material necessities," that is to say, the *necessities of our experience as such*. Those who followed Wittgenstein rightly recall what he qualified as the "arbitrariness of grammar,"[4] that is to say, the fact that grammar, from which derives every necessity in the strong sense, "is not beholden to any reality"—that this "arbitrariness," therefore, does not exclude that grammar could depend *in another sense* on "certain natural and very general facts" (as he calls them in his *Philosophical Investigations*);[5] it depends on them, not in the sense that they would *justify* it (in which case, these very general facts that are supposed to justify it would be *presupposed* in order to be grammatical formulations and could not therefore *justify* it), but in the sense that grammar is adapted to our needs, fit to our practices, inseparable from our "forms of life." To learn a language, in this sense, is not solely to master a body of rules, it is to become initiated into common forms of life. What Wittgenstein here calls, in a rather obscure manner, "natural and very general facts" seem therefore to cover both biological or physical facts and anthropological facts: that is to say, in all cases, *contingent* facts. The only sense in which grammar is "not arbitrary" (or related to the non-arbitrary) is when it depends on contingent facts, without thereby receiving its justification from them. Put differently, there is something the perspective that takes shape beginning with Wittgenstein obstinately refuses: the idea of necessities that are not conventional (be they *pure* conventions or conventions depending on "very general facts") but that hold for the nature of our *experience* itself. One can contextualize the notions of language games and of grammar as much as one likes, one can insist as much as one likes on the "naturalness of conventions" (as Stanley Cavell says)—this will not get one out of what is indeed a philosophical *thesis* in the strong sense and that underlies all of Wittgenstein's thought, from the *Tractatus* to his last philosophy: namely, that "there is only logical necessity" (or, later, grammatical). Now phenomenology starts from the diametrically opposed thesis: there is a *Weltlogik*, a "logic of the world"—a logic of the world *as phenomenal world*—and the unconditioned necessities in which this "logic" is rooted are anterior to all the conventions that we can adopt about them. Our "grammar" depends not only on generally contingent facts but on the necessary and a priori states of affairs whose necessity does not derive from our linguistic conventions. This is the furrow phenomenology seeks to plough.

I believe that the fact that this avenue went unrecognized by an entire segment of contemporary philosophy (referred to as "analytic," which has become so diverse and fragmented) is linked to the considerable role played by classical empiricism (that of Hume in particular) in the genesis of that tradition. This influence even runs through Wittgenstein and post-Wittgensteinians, who are nevertheless persuaded that their philosophical practice is strictly "therapeutic" and thus immune to all substantial presuppositions. In fact, Wittgenstein did not at all *reject* the idea that our experience could contain necessities in a strong sense, necessities that, not being simple empirical regularities, need not be reduced to the rules of logic (or of grammar). He did not reject this possibility for the simple reason that he never envisaged it! And one could say the same thing of more recent attempts that, in the manner of McDowell, endeavor to overcome certain impasses of traditional empiricism by "importing" from the outside the necessities that govern the conceptual order into experience itself: again, the idea on which all this rests is that all order and all structure that one could discover in experience necessarily comes to it from elsewhere. That experience can contain its own immanent order, an order that is *necessary* and that underlies all conceptual creation, is something that the enormous weight of the empiricist tradition has made inconceivable, to the point that the "analytic" tradition is victim to a perpetual oscillation that is perhaps no less serious than that diagnosed by McDowell: it does not stop oscillating between a brute empiricism that claims to reconstruct knowledge "from below," starting from the data of sensation and statements of observation, and a more "refined" empiricism that is only a new version of neo-Kantianism, and that seeks to remedy the insufficiencies of the former by structuring experience "from on high" by means of our conceptual schemes (even expanded to the "symbolic forms" of Cassirer).[6] A simplistic empiricism is then opposed to a caricatured neo-Kantianism (which is also a form of intellectualism, as Merleau-Ponty said), which itself shares something essential with this empiricism: namely, the idea that experience is in itself amorphous and that to assume that it does possess a structure is to assume that this structure must derive from the conceptual order. Husserl—and all the phenomenology that followed in his wake—never stopped resisting this double temptation: he refused empiricism but also—and, it should be said, *at the same time*—what he calls "the transcendental constructions that come from on high" of neo-Kantianism. He maintained what, I believe, could serve as the watchword for phenomenology as a whole: "experience with its demands precedes conceptual thinking and its demands."[7] And, of course, this statement does not at all amount to an empiricist profession of faith, since it is no longer a matter of "experience" in the empiricist sense at all!

The force of your thesis is wide reaching. You claim that any concept of intentionality based on linguistic or conceptual or propositional criteria alone can neither remain faithful to the actual phenomenology of perception nor account for the possibility of a genuine intentional relation to the world. What, to your mind, are the fundamental limitations of the "conceptualist" approach?

Let me clarify what constitutes, to my mind, the force of Husserl's position and, I believe, nearly all phenomenologists after him. The problem of the current debate over the conceptual/non-conceptual, propositional/non-propositional content of perception seems to me not about choosing between one or the other of the two camps but rather about understanding the very terms of the debate. For Husserl, for example, the assertion that the content of perception could be "propositional" would not be false; it would, I believe, be absolutely unintelligible. Since when does the fact that the content of a perception can be expressed under the form of a proposition entail that this content is "propositional"? This makes no sense. The problem is that one relies here on a very questionable notion introduced by Russell in another context, that of a "propositional attitude." But Husserl would categorically refuse to think of intentionality in general, and the intentionality of perception in particular, in terms of propositional attitudes. The two idioms are not only different here but, it seems to me, incommensurable.

Of course, the assertion that perception possesses propositional content does not mean that its content is a proposition or that the content contains a sort of silent assertion. However, even if one supports Searle when he says that the claim that perception possesses propositional content simply means that there is a proposition that specifies the "conditions of satisfaction" of perception, which is to say the conditions in which a perception is "veridical," it must be recognized that this formulation is not much clearer. If a perception must be able to be veridical, it must also be able to be false—but what would it mean for our experience to "lie to us"? However intelligible it is to say that a *proposition* possesses conditions of satisfaction, which is to say states of affairs that, if they're fulfilled, make it true, the idea of "conditions of satisfaction" of perception (and, moreover, perception *as propositional*) remains for me enigmatic, and I wonder whether it isn't the consequence of a dubious analogy. And this, not only because perception essentially opens onto the world and, therefore, is necessarily true *as perception* (contrary to the proposition, which can always be false) but, as I just said, for another, deeper reason, which is that it is impossible to say *which* proposition specifies the conditions of satisfaction of a perception: for any given perception, they are infinite in number. As Husserl pointed out in the *Logical Investigations*, a perception can be expressed in infinitely different ways. That is what makes the assertion that perception has the same content as a proposition, namely "that things are such and such," extremely enigmatic. Besides, even supposing that it is intelligible, what then differentiates perception from judgment? McDowell, who defends this thesis, gets entangled in a series of pictures, some of which are less convincing than others: in perception facts are "imprinted" on our sensibility (the seal in the wax!). But how are facts, the notable characteristic of which is that they cannot be identified independently of their expression, "imprinted" on us through our senses? And if, as McDowell says elsewhere, the difference between conceptual perceptive content and the same content just considered at the level of judgment is the difference between passivity and spontaneity, how is the difference thinkable, how is the passivity of perception, in particular, thinkable, since perception, according to this perspective, has for its content a *fact* and a fact is something that cannot be conceived in abstraction from our faculty of expressing it, from our faculty of judgment and of "spontaneity"? All of this is far from being clear.

But the principal reasons that make it possible to doubt the well-foundedness of the conceptualist position are (1) the necessity of accounting for the acquisition of new concepts from experience and (2) the problem of relativism. I will restrict myself to the second problem. If all perception is conceptually (indeed, propositionally) structured, it follows that it depends on conceptual and linguistic schemes that are *particular*, differing from one culture to another. And since our experience is conceptually structured *all the way out*, the result is that representatives of two given cultures, endowed with heterogeneous conceptual repertoires, do not perceptively relate to the same world. To put it differently, two subjects of perception relate to a shared world only on the condition that they possess a shared conceptual repertoire. This condition is extremely restrictive and, translation always being a partial and imperfect transposition, it is not easy to see how to escape from the relativist conclusion.

Do you identify with those who defend the possibility of "non-conceptual content" in the Anglophone tradition?

Even though I surely feel closer to the position of those in favor of "non-conceptual content," like Gareth Evans or Christopher Peacocke, it seems to me that, for the most part, the conceptuality in which this entire discussion has been carried out for about twenty years is not the best. One regrets that the phenomenological tradition remains too marginalized in these debates (and, when it is present, reduced to vague references). At times, the advocates of non-conceptual content simply seem to repackage old ideas [*retrouver des vieilles lunes*] without even noticing it. Just one example: when Gareth Evans insists on the "belief-independence" of perception, he is really only rediscovering the thesis of Carl Stumpf, Husserl's teacher, who held that a judgment "exercises no force on the content judged."[8] One could of course take this idea much further back, even all the way to Aristotle, but the cleanest formulation belonged to Stumpf.

The whole analytic school of non-conceptual content appears to me to be singularly lacking in an awareness of theoretical alternatives to the dominant tradition of empiricism. Phenomenology allows us to make out such alternatives. For example, it allows us to critique the very notion of *sensation* that the majority of these theoreticians take as obvious; phenomenology, notably that of Merleau-Ponty (but also of Erwin Straus, Viktor von Weizsäcker, F. J. J. Buytendijk, Kurt Goldstein),[9] strongly insists that the idea of sensation was an *abstraction* endowed with explanatory pertinence when used to analyze neuropsychological phenomena but whose *descriptive* range is very slim and may induce error if we believe that all perception is *constituted* by sensations. The non-conceptual character of the experience affirmed by analytic and phenomenological authors is not, therefore, the same: in the phenomenological tradition it is an experience structured by the material a priori from the outset, as I already emphasized. It is also a *meaningful* experience from the outset, in the sense of the Husserlian *Sinn* and not the linguistic *Bedeutung*. Finally, the question of the world appears totally neglected in analytic debates and the notion of "horizon" hardly touched . . .

It should be added that when phenomenology thinks, in Husserl's wake, about the *pre*-conceptual (rather than non-conceptual) character of "perceptual" experience, it does so with extremely rich descriptive material (one need only think of all the diverse examples formulated in Merleau-Ponty's *Phenomenology of Perception*), while the debates over these questions in the Anglo-Saxon world turn exclusively on one or two examples, such as the famous "fine-grainedness" of experience, which always seemed to me to be a rather unfortunate expression. The "one-sided diet" of examples that Wittgenstein denounced seems, in this domain, to be more on the side of Anglo-Saxon philosophy than "continental" philosophy! More generally, it seems to me that the phenomenological tradition approaches these problems by tracing an authentic perspective: it is not only a matter of "rehabilitating" everything that comes under sensibility, affection, spontaneous behavior, habits, etc., everything that could be reduced to an "infrarational level," but the point is rather to elevate these different dimensions of experience and intelligibility to the rank of constitutive elements fully integrated into what must very well be called human "reason." Phenomenology thus takes over a movement that begins with Kant, romanticism, German idealism, the advent of modern aesthetics, Nietzsche, existentialism, and even Wittgenstein in many respects, in order to "expand" the concept of reason beyond the forms of logical, scientific, and instrumental rationality. On the contrary, I am struck by the fact that the whole debate over conceptual/non-conceptual content in the Anglo-Saxon world turns nearly exclusively on questions of *epistemology*, which is really to say on philosophy of knowledge [*connaissance*] (what one would call *Erkenntnistheorie* in Germany); there again, we are not so far from neo-Kantianism, which saw in this *Erkenntnistheorie* the royal road for philosophy in general and for its reappropriation of Kant in particular.

The problem of intentionality occupies a central place in your work. In Au cœur de la raison, *you develop a concept of intentionality based what you call a "holistic" concept of experience. You criticize Husserl and Heidegger for failing to appreciate the full implications of the phenomenological concept of the "horizon" of experience. How do you understand the problem of intentionality and how does your "holistic" concept of experience address this problem?*

The concept of intentionality seems to me to be both what made the "breakthrough" that gave birth to phenomenology possible and that which constitutes a stumbling block for it. That which enabled the "breakthrough" is also an obstacle for it, which is not exactly an accident if one takes the trouble to consider all the unresolved tensions of which the concept of intentionality is in some way or other the origin.

What is intentionality? It is worth saying a word about the historical origin of this notion. Intentionality is, at the end of the day, fundamentally two contradictory things: it is first of all the idea formulated by Aristotle in *De Anima* according to which *hè psykhè to onta pôs esti panta*, "the soul is in some way all that is," where the important word is, of course, *pôs*, "in a certain way," "so to speak," "as it were" [*en quelque sorte*].[10] "As it were"—why? Because the soul clearly cannot *be* everything in the sense of *being identical* to everything, otherwise it would destroy the very distinction that defines the soul by way of opposition to everything it is not—"everything," precisely. But an "everything" that the soul nonetheless *is* in a paradoxical way. "Being" must instead be understood here in the sense of being present, exerting presence, making present [*faire act de présence*]. In making present, the soul "is" all things in this very particular sense of "being," according to which the soul gives things the possibility of making themselves present, *being* at once for the soul and in themselves. All in all, this "definition" of the soul is a paradox because it sets out to describe a paradoxical presence: the soul is everything that is, while at the same time it differs from everything on pain of destroying itself (in its difference from everything) and, therewith, all things. Thus, the soul is—*in a certain way* [*en quelque sorte*]—nothing but this unresolved tension between its opening onto things that constitute it as such—as a soul—and constituting them as such—"things," beings. Here you have what Heidegger will recover with the notion of *In-der-Welt-sein*.

Intentionality, I said, is two contradictory things. We saw the first: it is the fact that the soul is nothing but its opening onto things. Here is the second: when medieval thinkers forged the concept of "intentionality," they always had an eye on Aristotle's text and were always in the process of giving a commentary on it. Only, in commenting, they no longer emphasized the soul's being open to things but rather the presence of things to the soul in the mode of their *inherence in it*. The *esse intentionale* is being *in* the soul (as the seal is imprinted *in* the wax). It is presence by delegation or by proxy in the soul, it is therefore the re-presentation, as opposed to the real presence of the thing *ad extra*, or *esse reale*. The concept of intentionality becomes the key element for a doctrine of mental representation that was entirely absent in Aristotle's thought, something the conceptual apparatus of *De Anima* even aimed to rule out. How can one and the same concept serve such different ends?

A new difficulty can be added the moment interiority is reinterpreted in Cartesian terms, where it is understood in light of the difference between a sphere of absolute certainty, that of "ideas" in us, and a sphere submitted to doubt, the exterior world. This last step was accomplished by Brentano in his *Psychology from an Empirical Standpoint*. From then on, intentionality becomes the foundation of the distinction between psychic phenomena on one side and physical phenomena on the other, the first being intentional and the second not. Intentional phenomena are the mark of the mental defined by evidence beyond doubt.

Inheriting a polysemous concept whose meaning continued to oscillate in the course of time until it gave rise to incompatible theories, Husserl endeavored to give it a new coherence. But, in spite of his efforts, this coherence remains fragile and threatened. We have to, in a way, unify the different exegetical and historical strata that belong to the constitution of the concept without giving up any of them: Aristotelian, medieval, and Cartesian. The consequence is that intentionality has a tendency to mean one thing and its contrary. Intentionality is supposed to make possible the thought of the very opening of consciousness onto the world and things. But it was reinterpreted as part of a conception of the interiority of consciousness (of its "immanence") that opposes a sphere of absolute being and absolute certitude to everything that falls outside it: the world and myself insofar as I am a thing of the world. On the one hand, intentionality is the key to going beyond psychologism; on the other, it is also the means of preserving in hardly modified form the Cartesian doctrine of evidence, the impenetrable boundary between interiority and exteriority, and the crux of the skeptical problem that gave rise to Descartes's innovations, starting with the "cogito."

In setting out to describe the irresolvable tensions that are constitutive of the concept of intentionality, my goal is not to deny that this concept could be relevant within certain limits. I wonder whether intentionality can play the central role many have sought to give it for phenomenology as a whole, and my doubts heighten when it is a matter of understanding experience in its "original" meaning (what one traditionally calls "perceptual" experience) by means of the concept of intentionality. Approaching perception in terms of intentionality will, for Husserl, entail endorsing (in an undoubtedly contradictory fashion) both (1) that perception opens onto things themselves and not onto some hypothetical mental intermediaries and (2) that the content of perception could nevertheless be divided into immanent, absolutely given content (i.e., such that there can be no doubt regarding what they are about) and into content that is transcendent to consciousness, which could, in essence, always turn out to be illusory.

In maintaining that immanent contents, given in absolute evidence (the well-known *Abschattungen*), differ in kind from the objects that appear through them, this second side of intentionality inevitably leads to separating what the first tried to unify, since the contents can remain what they are even if these objects did not exist. But maintaining this entails, in fact, that these *Abschattungen*, these "adumbrations" [*esquisses*], again become—despite all Husserl's denials—mental intermediaries, since they remain what they are *regardless of whether the thing that gives itself in profiles exists or not*. They are no less present "in" consciousness in the case of veritable perception than they are in that of illusion, with the sole difference being that in the case of perception, they follow upon one another in a concordant way, whereas in the case of illusion they enter into conflict with each other and "break up." The world is then nothing more than the correlate of a presumption of existence constantly confirmed, which entails that this presumption of existence can always be revealed to be false and the world dissolved in illusion: this possibility of a generalized illusion can never be entirely eradicated regardless of the care we use to assure ourselves about what we perceive. To the realist side of intentionality, the one that maintains that all perception opens onto the world itself, an idealist (transcendental) side is superimposed, which leads to the declaration that what perception is open to is, in truth, not a necessarily existing world, one that precedes all the ways in which I intend and relate to it, but only a world as pure horizon of my constituting operations, a transcendental, universal correlate of constitution that could at any moment dissolve into nothing because it is in fact nothing but the "intentional product" of a pure *ego*. These two tendencies are constantly combating one another in Husserl's writing and neither prevails in a decisive manner.

How do you propose to get out of this dilemma?

I propose, for my part, to cut this Gordian knot and radically to change course by abandoning the notion of *Abschattung* as Husserl conceived it without, however, abandoning the distinction between what appears and its modes of appearance. It must then be said that these modes need not be "reified" as *immanent* givens, as real "mental things," and that they are, rather, nothing but the things that appear, but considered *in their relation to ourselves*. Phenomena are the things themselves in their relation to us and not at all the immanent contents of consciousness. To take up Wittgenstein's formula: "The phenomenon is not the symptom of something else, rather it is reality."[11]

In order to make this point more precise one can proceed in two steps. The first step: the idea that one could distinguish in the phenomenon an immanent component (evident and necessary) and a transcendent component (uncertain and contingent) in such a way that when I perceive, for example, the color and form of your pullover, I am certain that I perceive this form and this color but can never be certain that there is really a pullover in front of me at this moment that is as I see it—this is in reality an *untenable* idea, for it rests on a bad phenomenology of perception in its difference from illusion. It is simply not true that illusion is only a flux of *Abschattungen* entering into conflict with one another, or, correlatively, that perception is only a flux of these very *Abschattungen* ceaselessly confirming and corroborating themselves in the unity of experience. Between perception and illusion there is no common element, and that is why the notion of *Abschattung* is to be banished. Here, I make contact with what is referred to in the Anglo-Saxon world as a "disjunctive" concept of perception, but I propose to justify this position by arguments of a strictly phenomenological nature.

Take common illusions: I am startled by an animal passing by, but it was only the wind that shook the branches, or again—what comes closer to a minor hallucination—I hear the sound of footsteps, but no sound was made; I see lightning or a trail of light when nothing, no lightning, was produced. It is not an accident if, in each of these cases, we are dealing with ephemeral, elliptical, elusive phenomena: there is nothing here in our experience that resembles a "sequence of adumbrations," however one understands it. This unstable, floating, or fluctuating character is characteristic of the majority of illusions and hallucinations and has no equivalent in perception. Of course, one could object by referring to the existence of more stable hallucinations, at least in appearance: that of the schizophrenic who always thinks he sees his mother resting under the window, sitting on a bench. Upon closer examination of this example, however, there is no denying that the schizophrenic does not "take his hallucinations for realities" in the sense that he or she would *confuse* the illusion with the perception and would be incapable of noticing the least difference between them. Exactly the opposite is true. In fact, the mentally ill know very well that they're dealing with a hallucination, and despite their knowledge, they cannot help but "believe" it and give it a *kind* of reality. Merleau-Ponty cites the experiment in which a doctor takes the place of the hallucinated mother, putting on her same clothes, assuming an identical posture as that described by the sick person. But the person suffering from the hallucination quickly sees the difference. It would be necessary to pursue these analyses further, but the point that I would like to stress is this: the temptation to in some way put perception and illusion on the same plane, to think of perception as a confirmed illusion and illusion as a contradicted perception, does not issue from a rigorous description of phenomena but is rather the consequence of a prejudice.

And the second step?

The second step of the description consists in going beyond a disjunctive theory of perception in order to adopt what I call a "holism of experience." In fact, the prejudice to which I just referred rests on an implicit inference borrowed from skepticism. From the fact that there is always room, in any perceptual experience, for a *punctual and limited* illusion, one wrongly concludes that there is always room for an illusion affecting all of experience. From the fact that one can always be mistaken about something in perception, one infers that it's possible to be mistaken about everything, which is the skeptical inference *par excellence*. But this inference must be rejected, and, again, this time for phenomenological reasons. In fact, what is an illusion (or a hallucination, distinguishing between them does not matter for my purpose)? What does it mean, phenomenologically speaking: What is the *mode of givenness* of an illusion? The response is the following: an illusion can manifest itself as such only against the background of a stable and coherent world, that is to say a *real* world, beyond any possible illusion, for an illusion is a *simple* appearance that contrasts with all other phenomena and only manifests itself in and by way of this contrast—in sum, an illusion is less a phenomenon that appears than the appearance of a phenomenon, and this appearance needs "truthful" phenomena, *modes of appearance of things against the background of the world*, in order to emerge. It is only against this background of a world (removed from all possible illusion) that an illusion (necessarily punctual) can come about and exempt itself from the world by its very mode of appearance. The idea of an illusory world is therefore a *contradictio in adjecto* not for formal-logical reasons or even for "grammatical" reasons but because this idea violates the conditions of any correct description of the essence of these phenomena.

It would appear very easy to raise an objection here . . .

Yes, one could object that, although an illusion manifests itself *as an illusion* only against the background of the world, this does not mean that an illusion only manifests itself against the background of the world. On the contrary, so the objection continues, before I know that I am suffering from an illusion, I find myself in a situation where I am unable to tell the difference between this simple appearance and a true perception. In this situation, the illusion is *indistinguishable* from the perception. This objection does not appear to me to be decisive. It rests on a questionable premise, according to which, when I am the victim of an illusion, I am in a "mental state" indistinguishable from that of a perception, and—since these states are indistinguishable—I have no choice but to be mistaken. But I think this premise has to be rejected: it is false to say that I can be mistaken (in perception as elsewhere) only when it is positively impossible for me to avoid error. I am frequently mistaken in situations in which the error was avoidable. It is not at all necessary to defend the idea that perception and illusion would be indiscernible at the moment when they are experienced in order to explain the source of my error: it suffices that it possesses a large resemblance. That is why I claim that their mode of phenomenological givenness differs straightaway, which does not exclude that we could take one for the other. For the illusory "phenomenon" is such, from the start, that it fails to enter into the world, that it constitutes a strain in the fundamental cohesion of perception: from which we get its "unstable," fluctuating, and volatile character.

In fact, the very idea of comparing an isolated perception to an illusion is problematic. Nothing can be a perception *in isolation*. Perception has an intrinsically holistic nature. Inversely, one could say that all illusions are *in essence* isolated: the isolation of illusion with respect to perceptual experience in its totality belongs to its mode of manifestation. This point allows me to introduce the notion of the "holism of experience" to which I alluded a moment ago. What is generally misunderstood in all these discussions surrounding a so-called illusory world (a notion that Husserl took to be valid until the end and that led him to his theory of *Abschattungen*) is the holistic constitution of perception and, therefore, the holistic constitution of the perceived world itself. An experience is a perception only if it is integrated without hiatus into all of perception, which is to say if it presents a structural cohesion with all other perception within this whole. And, correlatively, something can be characterized as part of the (perceived) world only if it possesses a cohesion with all its other parts and with the (perceived) world in its totality.

How are you defining "cohesion" here?

An experience presents a cohesion with other experiences when they are all subordinated to a system of structural invariants, for example, to the spatio-temporal invariants that allow us to identify a thing as the same through its successive positions. "Cohesion," as I understand it, here designates a system of structural legalities, what Husserl called material a prioris. This cohesion differs from coherence (in the logical sense). The latter concerns *propositions* whereas the first occurs between *phenomena*. As Husserl suggested with his concept of the material a priori, the world is a phenomenon of structure. But we must go further than Husserl. It is at the very least strange that, after having maintained that there are necessary structures of appearance, he could, following in the footsteps of the skeptical tradition, still defend the view that a chaos of phenomena, by generalized conflict of *Abschattungen*, remained perfectly possible and thinkable . . .

To return to what I just said, cohesion is not an adventitious and accidental property of perceptions, as though perceptions could either be or fail to be "coherent" with one another (and, in those cases where they are not, "illusory"), as Husserl believed when he analyzed perception as a flux of *concordant* adumbrations (therefore also *possibly discordant*); cohesion is what *defines* all perception as perception, what constitutes the essential trait of the (perceived) world as world. A world that would not exhibit structural cohesion would not be an *illusory* world; it would simply not be a *world*—so a perception that would not introduce this character of cohesion with other perceptions and with perception as a whole would not be a *false* perception, it would not be a *perception* at all. I do not want to say that one *could not call* it a "perception," for, to repeat, the considerations I am advancing do not concern the use of this expression, its "grammar." I do not want to say that a perception devoid of structural cohesion with the rest of perception could no longer *be qualified* as "perception" but rather that a perception could not be deprived of structural cohesion with the rest of perception and continue to *be* a perception. This truth is a truth of *essence* relating to perception as such and not a "conceptual" truth relative to the use of the word "perception." The difference is quite obvious: in the case of a conceptual truth, the necessity is *de dicto*: "No bachelor is married" obviously does not mean that a bachelor cannot marry—on the contrary—but that a bachelor cannot marry and continue to be called a "bachelor." In the case of an essential truth, the necessity is *de re*: "No perception can be exempt from cohesion with the rest of perception" expresses an impossibility that has its basis in the thing, that is not limited to the linguistic or "conceptual" order.

If cohesion is an essential trait of all perception (and of its correlate, the world) so that perceptual experience possesses by its essence a holistic constitution, it follows as an essential truth that *there is perception only of the world* (and only in the manner derived from this or that of its aspects or parts). The "relational intention" to the world can no longer be constructed from atomistic experiences and their relations; it is a relation *of totality*, which is to say a relation that must open to the world in its totality in order also to be a relation to this or that of its parts. My point has thus been to show in a *purely argumentative* (and descriptive) manner why, in phenomenology, it is necessary to substitute, in place of the Husserlian concept of intentionality, a concept of being-in-the-world close to that of Heidegger. I'll leave aside the question of how it is also necessary, to my mind, to take some distance from Heidegger in order to think being-in-the-world to the end, starting from its own requirements. But that would take us too far afield . . .

Given your commitment to a pre-linguistic or pre-conceptual understanding of perceptual intelligibility, your work seems to face difficulties that the conceptualist approach does not. The conceptualist can claim to account for how a perceptual judgment has intentional purport by determining the content of perception as itself propositional in form: perceiving means, very roughly, perceiving the contents of a possible "that" clause (that things are so and so). Thus, perceptual judgment and perceptual content are of the same—viz., propositional—kind, distinguished only by the "passivity" of the latter and the "activity" of the former. You, on the other hand, with Husserl and Merleau-Ponty, hold that perceptual judgment and perceptual content are different in kind. How do you establish this difference? How, given this difference, do you understand perceptual content to relate to the content of judgment? And how do you account for the worldly constraint antepredicative perceptual content exerts on perceptual judgment?

Your questions are difficult and technical. They also have a "format," if I may say so, that is precisely that of analytic debates about which we just spoke. Nevertheless, they are important and difficult to avoid.

It is surprising, from my phenomenological point of view, to be asked how to establish the difference between perception and judgment. We don't have to "establish" this difference, it seems to me, since it is the point of departure for all reflection on these problems. On the other hand, we should ask ourselves in the terms and conceptuality according to which an adequate account of this difference can be given. The idea that we have to "establish" this difference already presupposes what, to my mind, arises from a grave confusion: namely, that perception could be called "propositional," which means we could bring together, if not completely identify, perception and judgment. That being said, analyzing the relations between perception and judgment is a complex enterprise that can only be handled *in concreto*. I will thus make do with brief remarks.

How should the *relation* between the content of perception and the content of judgment be understood? This question is impossible to avoid from a perspective like that of McDowell, for whom what matters is understanding how the "logical space of reasons" and justifications embrace perceptual experience itself, according to a perspective that I have characterized as *erkenntnistheoretische*, which underlies his principal formulations. To respond to your question in a word, and in a clearly insufficient manner, I would say this: one of the presuppositions of McDowell's "minimal empiricism" lies in the assertion that for an experience to be able to justify belief, the experience must be structured like belief, which is to say that its content be conceptual (and eventually propositional).

Yes, that seems right.

But why would that be so? Why should what exerts rational constraint be structured in the same way or possess the same characteristics as that on which it exerts constraint, namely belief or judgment?

It seems to be an essential premise in the argument that, in some sense, whatever does the constraining must be like what it constrains, that there is no other way to get the world to constrain belief and judgment.

Why should perception be conceptually *articulated* in order to be able to furnish reasons for believing something, and why would it not be enough for it to be conceptually *articulable*? On this latter hypothesis, perception would have the status of a justification only from the moment it would be formulated in a judgment, so that we would return to a more classic thesis according to which only a judgment can justify another judgment. Note that by denying perception a conceptual status and a "direct" justificatory role, as it were, we do not end up depriving experience of any of its meaningful, motivating character, but rather affirming that its meaning makes unique appeal to a "practical comprehension," a way of orienting ourselves in the world, of evolving with and acting in it, which, as such, remains anterior to judgment. The "practical vectors" that motivate us in our everyday commerce with the world are immanent to experience thus understood, insofar as it is meaningfully structured, and they are themselves of a pre-conceptual and pre-linguistic provenance.

In this regard, the first "constraint" that pre-linguistic experience exerts on us as living beings belongs to a network of motivations and practical meanings (appetitive vehicles, Gibson's "affordances,"[12] etc.) addressed to our corporeal intelligence prior to any judgment. As for judgment properly so called, it is also an act, and as such it can be motivated in different ways. But—to respond to the third part of your question—justification in a proper sense only takes place on the level of reasons, which requires conceptual and propositional thought, and, therefore, only has a place between judgments. In sum, a judgment of perception, to return to your example, is *motivated* by what I see, but it can be *rationally justified* only by a system of judgment and beliefs.

You've just recently published a book on color, and in Au cœur de la raison, *you devote two chapters to the fascinating debates on color and the status of color propositions, debates that took place during the first half of the last century (Vienna Circle, Husserl, and the post-Tractarian Wittgenstein). Your discussion culminates in the strong defense of the material synthetic a priori. Three questions: How does it cement your broader commitment to a "logos immanent to the sensible"? How does such a pre-linguistic logos relate to the phenomenological concept of reason? And how does the phenomenological concept of reason relate to or differ from other concepts of reason?*

In order to understand the originality of Husserl's concept of the material a priori, the originality of his concept of the a priori must first be understood. Husserl's use of this concept is not the same as that of Kant. For Kant, "a priori" means "independent of any experience," but the sense of this independence remains somewhat indeterminate. Should this independence be understood in a genetic sense, in the sense that experience does not play any role *in the acquisition* of concepts and of a priori knowledge, or only in the sense that experience does not play any role *in the justification* of this knowledge and these concepts? However the question is answered, Kant closely links the a priori to the human *Gemüt* [mind] in its finitude, for it does not seem that there could be a priori knowledge for an archetypal understanding in which the two sources of knowledge would not be separated and for which thinking of and intuiting an object would be one and the same. In sum, throughout the *Critique of Pure Reason*, the a priori is referred to the finite mind as such—and notably to the *human* mind—and to its faculties. "We can know a priori of things only what we ourselves put into them."[13] This "we" is decisive; it refers back to transcendental subjectivity as *human* subjectivity. This is what gives the Kantian a priori a double character. First, it is subjective, in the sense that it relates to the subjective sources of knowledge, even though it clearly possesses objective *validity*. Second, it is still tied to the formal, whether of the a priori forms of sensibility or those of the understanding, the categories, insofar as it is what in the human mind precedes all empirical material and every given whatsoever.

And Husserl?

Husserl sees in these characterizations of the a priori only so many unacceptable limitations. The a priori is not bound to subjectivity, even less to *human* subjectivity. "Anthropologism" is the original sin of Kantianism. On the other hand, the a priori is no longer placed exclusively on the formal side of the equation: there is an a priori of content as such, and it is precisely this that Husserl calls the "material a priori." In reality, I would personally hypothesize that, to critique Kant on this point, Husserl paradoxically took his inspiration from Hume. In a letter to Arnold Metzger,[14]

Husserl wrote that he learned incomparably more from Hume than from Kant, in relation to whom he maintained a true antipathy. I think the problem of the a priori provides a good illustration of what he meant. It is well known that Hume distinguishes between two types of science: sciences of fact or experience that are about matters of fact and whose propositions are contingent, in the sense that their opposite does not entail contradiction, and the demonstrative sciences that rest only on the relations between ideas and whose propositions are necessary. Even if Hume doesn't use the word, the latter are a priori. But what does it mean that they are a priori? Hume takes the example of arithmetical and geometric truths: "The square of the hypotenuse is equal to the square of the two sides" is a proposition that, as far as its truth is concerned, is not dependent "on what is anywhere existent in the universe," he writes.[15] A priori truths are therefore truths that as such do not depend on any fact in the world for their validity. The force of Hume's criteria radically frees the a priori from any psychological or anthropological consideration. The a priori has nothing that intrinsically links it to the human mind. Now, that is exactly the criterion of the a priori that Husserl takes up. Not what precedes any given in subjectivity, in the manner of a pure form, but rather what *is independent from any fact in its validity*, what precedes all facts from the point of view of its validity, is a priori according to Husserl. Hume was, therefore, right on this point, but he did not go far enough, since he immediately limited the a priori sciences to algebra, geometry, and logic. But since "a priori" means "of a validity not dependent on any fact of experience," there can also be a priori truths in other domains, beginning with experience itself.

Which is very strange from a Humean perspective . . .

It may, at first glance, seem paradoxical, but there isn't anything paradoxical about it. Take the domain of sounds: we know sounds by experience, of course. But it does not follow that we know everything in the domain of sounds in an empirical manner. There are truths in this domain that are independent, *with respect to their validity*, of what happens in the world, since they define what a sound is, in abstraction from the question of whether something like a sound has ever been made. Take as an example a truth of the following type: "All sounds have a pitch, timbre, and intensity." The same for colors: "All colors have a shade, clarity, and saturation." Why are these propositions a priori? No doubt, in order to understand what they mean, we need to have experienced the clarity or saturation of a color, the pitch or intensity of a sound. But their truth does not depend on these experiences in the sense that it would be justified by them. In this sense, it does not depend on any "fact." Truth be told, Husserl's formulation does not seem entirely satisfying, it seems to me. It should rather be said that these truths do not depend for their validity on any fact (for they are not susceptible to being invalidated by any fact) *with the exception* of the very fact of the existences of colors, therefore of our having a perceptual apparatus of a certain kind that allows us to perceive them. It is this "boundedness" to a fact that distinguishes material a priori from formal a priori (e.g., "There are no wholes without parts," "If A shares with B the relation R, then B shares with A a relation the converse of R"). Thus, it would be preferable to say that these material a priori truths concerning sounds or colors, a priori truths that pertain to experience itself and its content, these "a priori truths of content," so to speak, are such that they depend only on a general fact: the physiological constitution of living beings of a certain kind in a world of a certain sort, which is to say their possession of a visual apparatus in the world where there is light and an auditory apparatus in a world where there are elements through which sound waves can propagate. Apart from this dependence on a very general fact, these a priori truths depend on nothing that happens or could happen in the world. And what makes this clear is that *we cannot even conceive of a state of affairs where these truths would not obtain*. No fact can render them false, since no such fact is even *conceivable*: for something that would not have clarity, shade, or saturation would simply not be a color at all (I leave the problem of "achromatic" colors aside here). There is no possible world in which this truth would be not be valid, for even in a world where, for contingent reasons, no animal would be capable of seeing the least bit of color, one can still maintain that this truth, even so, would not become false. This is why it is a priori and necessary in an absolute sense. The same goes for another classic example of the material a priori: "A spatial object can be perceived only by adumbrations." This truth certainly depends on a fact, the fact that whoever perceives is situated in space by his body, and that all perception requires a point of view. And yet, *it is not the result of an empirical generalization*.

Before responding to your other questions, I would just like to indicate in what sense Husserl's response to Hume is a lot stronger than that advanced by Kant. Kant essentially responds to Hume's skepticism: the truths of physics (among others) must have objective validity, objectivity entails strict necessity and unconditioned universality, therefore empirical truths must in themselves harbor an a priori element, since strict necessity and rigorous universality are characteristics of the a priori; and this a priori element emerges on one side from the a priori forms of sensibility (space and time) and on the other side from the categories of the understanding.

But, to a large extent, this response to Hume neglects the question that he formulated. In effect, this response presupposes what has to be established, namely that the truth of the empirical sciences, for example the truth of Newton's propositions, possesses strict necessity and unconditioned universality. Now that is what Hume vigorously denied: in fact, he responded, we do not have to demand more certainty from the empirical sciences than they can give us, and the validity of the sciences of fact (which Hume clearly never doubted) rests only on generalization from experience. These sciences are objective in the sense that they permit us to predict, to a certain extent, what will happen, but they are not objective in the sense that Kant gives to this word by defining objectivity in terms of necessity and universality *in a strict sense*, for they always leave open the possibility of a phenomenon that will come to contradict this generalization. Insofar as Kant did not establish that all objectivity must be as he defined it, he did not establish anything at all. In this sense, the dialogue between Hume and Kant is really a dialogue of the deaf, and Kant's response is question-begging.

Now, Husserl's response is completely different; it turns Hume's own assertion against him. Hume says that every truth is either factual and contingent or is necessary and rests on a "relation of ideas." And he defines the necessary and the contingent in logical terms: "contingent" means that its contrary does not entail a contradiction and "necessary" means that its contrary does entail a contradiction. If, in following a predominant Humean exegetical tradition (which extends to the Vienna Circle and even beyond), the first type of truth is called "synthetic" and the second type "analytic," one can conclude then there are only two kinds of sciences and two kinds of truths: synthetic contingent truths and analytic necessary truths. But is this the case? This is precisely the question that Husserl raises. Take the previous proposition: "All sounds have a pitch, timbre, and intensity." This proposition is clearly necessary: we cannot conceive something that is a sound and that doesn't have pitch, timbre, or intensity. Inversely, whatever has pitch, timbre, and intensity is *ipso facto* a sound. It is, therefore, a necessary proposition, since its contrary does not express any thinkable state of affairs. And, for all that, its negation *is not a logical contradiction*, is not of the form "A and not A." Hume did not establish the impossibility of truths that are both necessary and non-analytic (not resting only on the principle of non-contradiction or, better, on the principle of non-contradiction and an ensemble of logical truths). And it should be added that the Vienna Circle didn't do any better.

In fact, in his discussion of causality, Hume says something that turns against him and challenges his own distinction between two types of sciences. Hume claims that the causal laws of nature do not rest on a priori reasoning but only on generalizations from experience, on empirical conjectures that can always turn out to be false. They only have a *limited* generality, *so long as* they are not challenged by a new experience: on this point, Hume is right, against Kant. But does the fact that truths of the causal variety are not known a priori lead to their *all* being known a posteriori? Yes, if there are only two types of sciences. However, Hume himself puts forward a truth about causality that goes as follows: in any causal relation, he says, the cause must be distinct from the effect: "Every event is an event distinct from its cause . . . . " Now, isn't *that* an a priori truth? It cannot be an empirical truth. But it is no more a truth the contrary of which would be purely and simply *contradictory*. Logic tells us nothing about the nature of causality. But then Hume opens the door for the existence of truths that he elsewhere says are impossible: for example, a priori truths on the nature of causality, which are not, however, analytic (deduced from the ensemble of logical truths and them alone). They are synthetic a priori, which is to say they are essential truths that belong to the sphere of the "material a priori," as Husserl calls it. And, of course, if it is necessary to allow for the existence of material necessities (in the sense I've been discussing) when it comes to causality, others must be admitted, many others. Contrary to what we find in Kant, Hume finds himself refuted *on the basis of his own premises*. It would be necessary to explain how the dialogue continues with the neo-empiricists of the Vienna Circle, but that would take too long. I simply wanted to indicate where to situate the force of Husserl's response and, from there, the idea of the material a priori.

Given your acknowledgment of the role you assign to certain general facts of nature in the constitution of material a priori truths, such as our possession of a certain audio and visual apparatus, it seems that you are not denying anthropology unconditionally or without reservation . . .

Of course, the idea of a material a priori poses numerous problems that I try to address throughout my book. Let me make clear that I am far from endorsing everything Husserl said on this subject. I just indicated that the a priori ultimately hangs on a very general fact: *our own anthropological constitution in a world of a certain kind*. Thus, I believe that the general objection of "anthropologism" that Husserl formulated at least needs to be nuanced. The anthropological horizon seems to me *impassable* when it comes to describing the structures of experience. Phenomenology can only describe the structures of *human* experience and not those of a transcendental subject supposedly freed from its factual anchoring in humanity. Even Heideggerian *Dasein* conserves irreducible links with factual humanity, so it is too quick to say with the existential analytic that "the entire anthropological problematic" had been "overcome," as Heidegger himself says in the letter to Richardson.[16] It nevertheless remains the case that by describing the structures of *human* experience, phenomenology does not describe anything "empirical" in the sense of the empirical sciences; in no case does it limit itself to making generalizations on the basis of contingent experiences. What it strives to bring to light are rather the possibilities, impossibilities, and necessities (in the strong sense) that relate to human experience as such and that structure *all* experience of this kind in such a way that a phenomenon that departs from these necessities and impossibilities is positively *inconceivable*. At the same time, these necessities and impossibilities are not in any sense purely "logical" (they are not "analytic," contrary to what the Vienna Circle believed) or purely grammatical, contrary to what Wittgenstein thought.

These truths, the opposite of which is inconceivable (without being contradictory in the strict sense) are therefore what one could, following Husserl, call "truths of essence." To talk about truths of essence and of grounding phenomenology in such truths does not at all—not in my case—imply subscribing to the Husserlian idea of *intuiting* essences, a *Wesensschau*, or even the idea that these essences should be thought of as Platonic objects. On the contrary, I defend a conception of essence that I call "adverbial" and that could be summed up by the following: there are no essences (in the sense of *sui generis* objects that would be essences), but things are *essentially* such and such. Finally, although phenomenology takes descriptions of essences as its point of departure, it is hardly exhausted by this task. Phenomenology, like philosophy generally, is a historical activity; its descriptions are always necessarily conditioned by prejudices, by particular interests, by an inherited conceptuality it must try to clarify by critiquing its sources, legitimacy, and limits, in order to be able to carry out successfully its descriptive enterprise. In this sense, the description of essence is only the first word of phenomenology; the last word has its place in a historically learned and careful hermeneutic that questions the origin and limits of its own conceptuality, as well as the presuppositions within which it moves. The concession made to a certain understanding of essence need not lead to a dogmatism regarding the "vision of essence" or to the idea that there has to be only one correct way of describing phenomena, something like a pure description, absolutely adequate to phenomena, free of all prejudices and any historical conditioning.

These remarks allow me to outline (I could hardly do more) a response to your second question, on the phenomenological concept of reason. The idea of phenomenological essential truths, which is to say of material a priori truths, effectively leads to a remarkable extension of the notion of reason beyond discursive and inferential thought, toward the pre-linguistic structures of experience themselves. There are two concepts of reason, Husserl tells us in a decisive passage from the *Crisis*: there is an essentially narrow rationality [*une rationalité au cœur étroit*], an *enghertzige Rationalität*, which implies—Husserl leaves more to be understood than he positively asserts—that there is also a rationality in the broad sense [*une rationalité "au grand cœur"*], a rationality [*raison*] that is capable of accommodating its other (i.e., sensibility and experience) within itself, a "reason" that begins from the level of our sensible, corporeal, pre-intellectual, and pre-linguistic openness to the world, of which reason in the narrow sense, the reason of intellect, discursive and inferential reason, is the continuation. This idea, which gives sensibility and *praxis* a rank equal to that of discursive thought for comprehending and determining human intelligence, appears to me to have an import that contemporary philosophy is far from having taken the full measure of. It seems by its nature to open perspectives that we only glimpse for the moment.

Simplifying things a great deal, one could say that the Kantian distinction between *Verstand* (understanding) and *Vernunft* (reason)—which, for Kant himself, went hand in hand with a rethinking of practical rationality and the advent of an aesthetic rationality obedient to its own requirements—opened a breach in classical rationalism and bequeathed the task of "expanding" reason to all post-Kantian philosophy, the different historical figures of which can be listed: Hegelian logic, *qua* dialectical sublation (*Aufhebung*) of the logic of the understanding; Nietzschean "grand reason," a reason of the body opposed to the little reason of the intellect. And yet one could say that these two attempts, grandiose as they were, took the Kantian problem seriously only up to a certain point and ended up failing in their conditions of possibility [*et finissent par échouer au lieu même où se situaient leurs conditions de possibilité*]: they manage to say that there is a more profound, ample, original reason that overwhelms and includes reason in the sense of discursive and inferential thought, but they fail to say how this more ample or profound reason still remains, despite everything, *reason*. Hegelian discourse is the dialectical auto-deployment of the Concept, absolute reason thinking and speaking itself, but this auto-deployment does not tell us what norm of validity it obeys or what the proper criteria are in light of which to measure its success or failure, its truth or falsity. By becoming the subject of discourse and the very place of truth's auto-manifestation, reason conquered its absoluteness, but did it not abdicate, in the very same stroke, any criterion that would render its verdicts justified or justifiable? In other words, in refusing to separate truth and method and by claiming that method is only "the form of automovement interior to its content," therefore truth, doesn't Hegel, having refused the very principle of justification that underlies truth and method, abolish the possibility of both? Of course, one could point out that Hegel's purpose isn't where I've placed it and that his originality consisted in overturning the very coordinates of philosophical discourse to such a degree that the idea of a discourse that should advance theses and issue "truths" in the traditional sense of the term must be abandoned. This is how Gérard Lebrun reads Hegel in his major book, *La patience du concept*. Whatever the case may be, the sense of the word "reason" is so transformed with Hegel that his pan-rationalism could just as well appear, in another respect, as an irrationalism, this distinction itself becoming uncertain and maybe even, under his pen, *undecidable*.

As for Nietzsche's "grand reason" of the body, which goes to the point of *positively challenging* all the traditional attributes of reason (truth, universality, objectivity, etc.), it can only raise itself to the rank of "reason" by a kind of forceful takeover whereby it relieves the latter of its prerogatives but in order to become its inversion and parodic subversion. Nothing really allows us to understand what justifies, *from the point of view of reason itself*, this destitution and substitution.

And Husserl?

One could say *cum grano salis*, but not without a certain truth, I believe, that Husserl succeeded where his predecessors had failed. He succeeded as one "succeeds" in philosophy, of course, which is to say that he only failed more magisterially in his very success, if it is true as Heidegger said—and as I believe is true—that "all great philosophy fails." Husserl "succeeded," if you like, because, unlike his predecessors, he managed to give meaning to the idea of an expansion of reason while putting forward rigorous criteria that allow this expansion to be thought of as an expansion *of reason*—the "*logos* of the sensible world." Thus, this expansion sacrifices neither criteria nor justification nor method: it is carried through in a "rationalist" framework. The Husserlian expansion of reason is a *rationalist* expansion that nevertheless leads reason beyond its restricted acceptation and, in extending it to sensibility, preserves in one and the same stroke the autonomy of its relation to discursive thought and to judgment.

Let me add that if these historical indications have some pertinence, it would still be necessary to situate the two other great currents—empiricism and neo-Kantianism—in this picture. The basic characteristic of neo-Kantianism (and this is the reason why it was able to converge at certain points with the *nova methodo* empiricism of the Vienna Circle) is that it basically responded to the Kantian problem of the distinction between *Verstand* and *Vernunft* by proposing what one could call a "Hegelianism of understanding," a Hegelianism that "logicizes" sensibility entirely but refuses the absoluteness of the Hegelian *logos* and, therewith, its dialectical character. In the end, they identified *Verstand* and *Vernunft* (suturing the gap between them while at the same time reabsorbing Kant, who divided the two sources of human knowledge), they entirely subordinated sensibility to understanding/reason while denying to Kant's transcendental aesthetic the least autonomy in relation to logic, and went on to attack all the "myths of the given," including the one they continued to see in Husserl's nascent phenomenology.

The specificity of this position consists precisely in the fact that it renounces any idea of an expansion of reason and any idea of a possible autonomy of sensible and ante-predicative experience vis-à-vis the superior forms of thought and judgment. It renounces any rationality immanent to sensation not conferred on it by the intellect. (I'm of course simplifying a bit, since Cassirer's position is surely not that of Hermann Cohen or of Paul Natorp.) A position of this kind could easily converge with that of a neo-empiricism that strongly maintained a separation between formal sciences and empirical sciences, opposing form and content, analytic and synthetic, a priori and a posteriori. Here too, any idea of an expansion of reason is in principle excluded. Today, it seems to me that a certain convergence between a neo-Kantianism and an empiricism would allow us to circumscribe the space occupied by a good part of "analytic" philosophy—if something of that kind still exists—rather well. On one extreme of the spectrum we find the heirs of logical empiricism. On the other, we find the heirs of neo-Kantianism, who insist on the normative and inferential character of all rationality and exacerbate the gap between nature and culture, animality and humanity (Robert Brandom, for example). Reason is for them reduced to inferential processes of giving and asking for reasons. It is not merely that they say that reason and reasoning are linked (which is obvious) but that reason is *exhausted* by inference. I say "neo-Kantianism" rather than "Hegelianism" here, since, like the neo-Kantians, Hegelian reason has been purged of both the absolute and the dialectic and reduced to what Hegel called "understanding."

Wittgenstein's place seems ambiguous here . . .

It seems to me that Wittgenstein would instead require a reading that situates him on the side of those who have prolonged the inquiry regarding the expansion of reason. With Wittgenstein, we get a contextualized reason, a reason anchored in practices and forms of life that form its background and resource, and as a result a reason that is no longer sovereign but dependent, including on what is inexorably "animal" in us—"I would like to consider man as an animal," to take up the formula of *On Certainty*.[17] He would be better placed on the side of Husserl, Heidegger, Gadamer, and Merleau-Ponty. But it would be necessary to be able to demonstrate that in detail, not an easy task.

Interestingly, in your work on the concept of the event, you've sought to surpass what you see as the limitations of classical phenomenology, whereas in Au cœur de la raison *you seem more interested in reconstructing the normative basis of phenomenology. How do you understand the relation between these projects?*

I try to write *different* books because that is the only way not to bore myself while writing (and of hoping not to bore the reader) and because it is through difference that the continuity or path of a thought is all the more sharply revealed. If there is really something singular and unique in your project, writing different books will only make this come out more clearly!

In the case of *Event and World* and *Event and Time* on one the one hand, and *Au cœur de la raison* on the other, we are effectively dealing with books that are rather distinct in their approach to problems, in their style, and above all in their respective investigations. The first two constitute an attempt to rethink the human being in light of the consideration that man is the only being among living beings to experience events in the strong sense that I give to the term: critical transformations in which his existence is brought into play as such and in its totality. Such upheavals oblige us to pose anew the question "Who am I?" There arises the possibility for the one to whom they happen to come to himself by integrating this radical transformation as a moment of his identity, or be crushed by that which surpasses all power of appropriation and presents itself then in the form of a trauma. Trauma is in a certain way an "anti-event" surpassing our powers of appropriation and experience. I try to show in these works that this dimension of vulnerability to the event, to my mind constitutive of the human as such and central to its comprehension, was eclipsed by Heidegger's existential analytic, himself following in the footsteps of metaphysics as a whole, which thinks the event in the first place as an accident, which is to say as something extrinsic to essence and removed from intelligibility, and thinks its novelty as an "ephemeral part of things," to cite Valéry's expression.[18] Actually, thinking about the event challenges a number of fundamental phenomenological concepts, beginning with the transcendental and constitutive status of the Husserlian *ego* or, in a certain sense, that of Heidegger's "post-transcendental" *Dasein qua* basis of the world's configuration and origin of sense.

In *Au cœur*, the problem that guides me is completely different. The questions that I formulate there are for the most part prior to those I posed in my "*herméneutique événementiale*" in that they bear on the very possibility of something like phenomenology. Nevertheless, this way of presenting things is a bit too summary. The transformation of phenomenology as I try to rethink it in *Au cœur de la raison* conforms to certain requirements that I formulated in my first works, so that the former could constitute in certain aspects the basis of the first, while the first anticipate questions (sometimes left in suspense) that begin to find a response in the latter. For example, the necessity of abandoning the transcendental paradigm, a necessity formulated in my first works within a limited space of questions regarding the event, is justified more "internally" in *Au cœur de la raison* by the aporias that engulf this paradigm. While *Event and World* builds on a concept of "sense" enlarged beyond linguistic signification without searching to justify this concept any further, the adoption of this enlarged concept of "sense" was the object of long and patient argumentation in *Au cœur*. Whereas *Event and World* hardly engaged in a reflection on sensibility as such, *Au cœur de la raison* strives to make up for this insufficiency. These, then, are a few examples of the links that exist between these two parts of my work. But there are, of course, many others.

Taking all the risks the genre of auto-interpretation involves, there is, more deeply, an underlying motif that seems to cut across all of my work and perhaps unify it: the problem of what Husserl brought out under the name "archfacticity" (*Urfaktizität*) with increasing insistence as his reflections progressed. Very early, I wrote works devoted to the question of the a priori in Husserl, in which I tried to show how Husserlian essentialism, first, clashed with this archfacticity as to something unthinkable. Second, I endeavored—not without difficulties—to give archfacticity a status within his discourse on essence. From archfacticity to the event, considered as what both takes place by transcending any horizon of preliminary possibilities and prescribes to human existence one of the dimensions of its intelligibility, the path had been traced. By following the guiding thread of the event, I also took on specific ambiguities of essentialism that are found in *Being and Time* and, in a certain way, through it to the *Seinsfrage* itself. In *Au cœur de la raison*, I try more clearly to formulate what appears to be the acceptable nucleus of a phenomenological essentialism—which is necessary if one wants to be able to respond to contemporary versions of the nominalist paradigm without this essentialism leading to a congealed and "eternal" vision of the phenomenal world (one that would misunderstand the radical novelty of what is possible to be produced there) or yet leading to a dogmatism oblivious to its conditioning by the history of philosophical understanding. These are some of the challenges that I attempt to pick up again in this book.

Claude Romano, thank you for your time.

Thank you for your perspicacious and difficult questions!

Translated by Larry McGrath

Notes

1. The expressions "logical space of reasons" and "myth of the given" are taken from Sellars, *Empiricism and the Philosophy of Mind.*

2. Paul Natorp was a neo-Kantian philosopher and the cofounder of the Marburg school. Hermann Cohen was Natorp's teacher and responsible for the revival of Kant in Germany from the last quarter of the nineteenth century to the end of the first quarter of the twentieth. He is the author of *Kants Theorie der Erfahrung.*

3. See Husserl, *Formal and Transcendental Logic*, 291–92.

4. See Wittgenstein, *Philosophical Investigations*, §497.

5. Ibid., II, xii.

6. See Cassirer, *The Philosophy of Symbolic Forms.*

7. Husserl, *Ideas III*, 30.

8. See Stumpf, *Tonpsychologie*, 1:11.

9. Erwin Straus was a German-American phenomenologist and neurologist and is the author of numerous books, including *Phenomenology of Memory* and *Phenomenological Psychology*. Viktor von Weizsäcker was a German physician and physiologist and is the author of *Der Gestaltkreis*. Frederik Jacobus Johannes Buytendijk was a Dutch anthropologist, biologist, and psychologist and is the author of *Allgemeine Theorie der menschlichen Haltung und Bewegung*. Kurt Goldstein was a German-Jewish neurologist and psychiatrist and is the author of *The Organism* and *Human Nature in the Light of Psychopathology*.

10. See Aristotle, *The Complete Works of Aristotle*, 1:686: "Let us now summarize our results about the soul, and repeat that the soul is in a way all existing things; for existing things are either sensible or thinkable, and knowledge is in a way what is knowable, and sensation is in a way what is sensible: in what way we must inquire."

11. See Wittgenstein, *Philosophical Remarks*, 283: "A phenomenon isn't a symptom of something else: it is the reality."

12. See Gibson, "The Theory of Affordances."

13. Kant, *Critique of Pure Reason*, Bxviii.

14. Arnold Metzger was Husserl's assistant from 1920 to 1924. For Husserl's letter of September 4, 1919, to Metzger, see Husserl, *Husserliana Dokumente*, vols. 3 and 4, 411–14, esp. 412.

15. Hume, *An Enquiry Concerning Human Understanding*, 28.

16. See Richardson, *Heidegger*, xx: "Man here is not the object of any anthropology whatever."

17. See Wittgenstein, *On Certainty*, 62: "I want to regard man here as an animal; as a primitive being to which one grants instinct but not ratiocination. As a creature in a primitive state. Any logic good enough for a primitive means of communication needs no apology from us. Language did not emerge from some kind of ratiocination."

18. Valéry, "Choses tues," 478–79: "Il est étrange de s'attacher ainsi à la partie périssable des choses, qui est exactement d'être neuves." See also Valéry, "Tel quel," 560: "Le nouveau est, par définition, la partie périssable des choses."

Context, Realism, and the Limits of Intentionality

JOCELYN BENOIST

Who were your teachers? What was the intellectual milieu of the École normale supérieure (ENS) like during your student days, and how did you find your way in and around that milieu? How would you mark the decisive moments in your intellectual development?

Didier Franck was my first philosophy mentor [*maître en philosophie*]. When I entered the École normale supérieure in 1986, his intellectual persona dominated the philosophy department. The context was rather morose. The great teachers of the 1960s or 1970s were dead or at least no longer involved. In a certain sense, what might be said to define my generation (I was born in 1968) is that it lacked teachers, unlike the generation that came before, which perhaps had too many. We had instructors [*enseignants*] but very few mentors [*maîtres*] with the magnitude of intellectual brilliance and authority involved in the notion of a mentor. This lack was, to my mind, a catastrophe; it adversely affected our formation. A discipline like philosophy cannot be dissociated from a personal relationship of the Socratic type. Only in the footsteps of a mentor, and probably (inevitably) in the revolt against him, does one become a philosopher. For that to be possible there must be mentors, individuals who take their philosophical vocation sufficiently seriously and yet possess the distance and humor necessary to play a mentoring role. Without a doubt, for me and a number of others the presence of Didier Franck at the ENS partially filled that void.

His philosophical rigor and the radicality of his thought exerted an intense fascination on us.

Then came Jean-François Courtine, from whom I learned to discipline my enthusiasm and do the history of philosophy in the grand style, an important step in my formation. He imparted to me a sense for the historicity of concepts and an enduring taste for erudition. Even when I distance myself from him today, I still have history, and a lot of history, in my mind.

Finally, toward the end of my studies at the ENS, I was strongly influenced by the thought of Jean-Luc Marion, even though I was never directly his student. I was still very young: I left the ENS at age twenty-three. Didier Franck once told me that I'd "make for an atheist Marion." That wasn't untrue. The influence can be felt in my first texts on Husserl, which date from my years as a *normalien* and were later included in *Autour de Husserl: l'ego et la raison*. This apparently contradictory situation captures rather well the aporia in which I found myself then. In fact, the paradox is that it was the properly theological part of Marion's work that influenced me, despite the fact that I was and fundamentally remain an atheist. I have always had more trouble taking the historical part of his work seriously, which seems to me to suffer from the French defect (to which I myself, like everyone else, paid heed in my thesis) of projecting things onto the author studied. By contrast, his way of posing the question of God "after the end of metaphysics" had a lasting effect on me. In a sense, a big part of the work I did at the very beginning, a part that extends further than you might think in the work I did until a considerably later date, could be identified with the question of atheism after the end of metaphysics: What is it to be atheist and how might one be an atheist in such a historical [*historiale*] situation? From this point of view, I have always admired *L'idole et la distance*—to my mind, Marion's most radical work—and I still have a soft spot for that book. For me to distance myself from this field of inquiry, it was necessary that the (post-) Heideggerian theme of the "end of metaphysics" progressively lose its sense for me, and that was a very slow and laborious process in the displacement of my interests and projects.

You also did some work on Kant . . .

Yes, in my thesis on Kant, which I defended in 1994 and published in 1996, I had already taken some distance from these themes, even though I was in a sense still involved with them. My reinterpretation of Kant in light of contemporary French phenomenology—taking a formula of Merleau-Ponty's as its guiding thread—pointed in the direction of Lévinas and Michel Henry. Not because, like my mentors, I found in them the promise of a "post-Heideggerian" phenomenology but rather because I found in them the reality of a non-Heideggerian path to that same phenomenology, a path that deliberately ignored the destitution of the subject orchestrated by so-called fundamental ontology and positively devoted itself to the exploration of such a subjectivity in its concretion. At that time, the question that interested me was the question regarding the link between subjectivity and sensibility, and if I expected anything from phenomenology it was from this aspect of it.

My education, then, was essentially phenomenological. But beyond my personal tastes, there was, no doubt, something characteristic of the times: the 1980s were marked by a kind of *revival* of phenomenology in France. Phenomenology occupied the philosophical scene yet again. The return was made possible by the ebbing of structuralism, and we cannot fool ourselves about the fact that this gave rise to a "conservative revolution." Philosophy once again became the queen of disciplines, sure of itself, often against a background, if not of outright resentment, then of ignorance and disdain for the human sciences. More generally, what dominated the phenomenological current (or what took itself to be such) was a certain form of anti-scientism that quite often—as the result of a poorly digested Heideggerianism with a properly reactionary dimension to which we were no longer sensitive—amounted to hostility pure and simple toward "science" or, in any case, toward what one placed under that heading. There was something there that made me deeply uncomfortable. I did not like what I saw: diffuse spiritualism, badly made-up as a philosophy of immanence, a certain philosophy with a phenomenological inspiration, nothing more than the irrationalist pose of a certain aestheticism nourished by what was, at bottom, most conventional in Heidegger.

I realized that what a certain philosophy (nostalgic for its prerogatives) called "science" was no less a myth than the "rationality" it denounced as metaphysics and that what needed to be sought out and questioned were reasons *at work*, there where we actively try to give ourselves reasons in the effective reality of discursive practices. I also was not too comfortable with my fellow philosophers. For me the real philosophical friendships came later. At the ENS, I spent five years in close contact with scientists and, more particularly, with mathematicians.

You were among the first, if not the first, French phenomenologist to engage seriously with the analytical tradition. In your work, you make ample reference to figures such as Austin, Wittgenstein, Putnam, James. And as you've just made clear, a certain uneasiness, even suspicion, about the status of phenomenology as a philosophical idiom seems to have affected you much more than any other phenomenologist working in France today, virtually all of whom continue to explore what they see as the "internal possibilities" of the idiom, as it were. And yet, despite everything, your philosophical concerns remain, in a certain sense, deeply phenomenological. What sense of phenomenology and its history does your current work reflect?

On this point, I have evolved a lot, and I will no doubt answer you differently now than I would have a few years ago.

My critical relation to phenomenology has gone through different phases. First, very soon after the thesis—this began in the fall of 1993 when I had submitted but not yet defended the thesis—a certain kind of critique of phenomenology imposed itself on me, one that came from the philosophy of language, essentially thanks to Jacques Bouveresse.[1] I had the feeling that phenomenology—as, etymologically, a "discourse of phenomena"—lacked sufficient understanding of itself as a discourse. Simply put, it lacked a philosophy of language. Of course, I could not ignore a certain tradition of the phenomenological sort: namely, the Heideggerian tradition of assigning a majestic place to language. But this very hypostasis of language, far from responding to my expectations (to understand what it is to talk about phenomena and what it means that we have to talk about them), seemed to me to constitute an obstacle to accounting concretely for language as language, that is, language in its effectivity and in its difference from what is not language. If everything is language, or is "always already" language, it isn't easy to see what "language" is supposed to mean and, at the end of the day, it could very well be that nothing can seriously be called "language" anymore. In any case, at a minimum this means that language has not been thought in its concrete determination: we have not thought enough about what speaking, as a regime of specific action, is. An entire phase of my inquiry, from 1995 to at least 2001, was devoted, then, to trying to give phenomenology the philosophy of language it did not have, or in any case did not really have: in a way, to give phenomena speech [*rendre aux phénomènes la parole*], to use a formula I have come to use to characterize my research at that time in a synthetic way.

Following this route, I was quickly confronted by the fact that phenomenology, in its beginnings, developed a very rich theory of signification and even, in Husserl, defined itself in part as such a theory. This fact, which I thought had been underestimated by continental phenomenologists (including the most serious interpreters of Husserl), and which had been brought to my attention by the highly original reading that had been proposed in France by Jacques English, nourished the hope in me that it would be possible to restore to phenomenology the philosophy of language that, in a way, it lacked by reviving the Husserlian theory of signification in its richness, which seemed to me to anticipate many of the discoveries and current debates in so-called analytical philosophy.

Thus, I developed a kind of "analytical phenomenology" (heterodox within the field of contemporary phenomenology) characterized by the primacy of signification and the critical function played by taking into account forms of discursivity in relation to all hypostases, be they mental or metaphysical. I was thus fighting on two fronts at the same time: against the mentalism of traditional phenomenology and that of today's analytically inspired philosophy of mind (which often agrees with the former without knowing it) and against the phenomenologically inspired metaphysics (which multiplies and hypostasizes entities) and today's neo-analytical metaphysics, which, here too, oftentimes agrees with the former.

It was in 2002–2003 that I became aware of the defective character of such a synthesis, for a number of reasons that came together then. First, I evolved even further in my reading of Husserl and was led to re-evaluate an extremely important aspect of his thought, whatever aspects of his discourse there might be that go in the opposite direction: namely, the very firm thesis of the irreducibility of the perceptual, the fundamental distinction between signification and intuition, which is not necessarily a gap, because there is no reason at all to think that one needs the other or is necessarily drawn toward the other, but which is rather a distinction that is, from the start, purely and simply a conceptual distinction. From that moment on, my investigations partially, but permanently, reoriented themselves in the direction of a philosophy of perception.

Consistently, a dramatic reversal also took place in my search for a "philosophy of language of a phenomenological kind" (that is, a philosophy of language that incorporated certain constraints of phenomenology, beginning with descriptivity and a certain kind of attachment to the sensible as horizon of the manifestation of what is described) that made a dramatic return. In fact, what became clearer and clearer to me is that a "theory of signification" as I found it ready-made in Husserl, far from constituting the philosophy of language in action [*en acte*] I was looking for (taking into account *what speaking is*), was on the contrary a major obstacle on the path of such an elucidation. To understand what it is to speak, one needs first of all to be interested in the efficacy of speech (which is what, in the footsteps of Merleau-Ponty, I had done for a while) and, above all, to place speech back in context, to apprehend it in its constitutive relation (condition of the very possibility of a language) to what is not linguistic. What I needed was a non-hermeneutic (thus non-Heideggerian) theory of context, for which meaning is not "always already given" but rather always constructs itself with its limitations in an effective relation to what is not linguistic—beginning with what is given in perception.

Such a theory of "meaning under constraint" is what I expressed in my first really personal book, *Les limites de l'intentionalité: Recherches phénoménologiques et analytiques*. Clearly, meeting the American philosopher Charles Travis in 2002–2003, a philosopher whose radical contextualism in the tradition of ordinary language philosophy contributed to opening my eyes to the conditions of what giving an effective account of language would be, played a decisive role in this turn.[2] From then on, motifs borrowed from this tradition (which I had gotten used to thanks to ongoing contact, since 1994, with the work of my wife, Sandra Laugier)[3] have constantly played for me the role of a corrective to and a critical principle of phenomenology.

However, what I was aiming for at that time and until 2008 (the year I finished *Sens et sensibilité: l'intentionalité en context*) was a form of critical phenomenology, more precisely: a phenomenology that would have passed through the crucible of analytic criticism (retaining only those authors from the analytical tradition who have espoused a critical style in philosophy: Frege, the Vienna Circle, Wittgenstein above all of course, Austin and ordinary language philosophy) and that was characterized both by its attention to ways of speaking and to the various linguistic formats of phenomena as well as a robust perceptual realism. By returning phenomenology to its effective conditions of enunciation (to what it is to "say the phenomena," according to a title I had previously given the theme of my inquiry), I also intended to purge it of the idealism of its principle *qua* idealism of meaning whose conditions of effectuation had not been thought (Husserl) or had been poorly thought (Heidegger). Such a program, however, still presupposed that the principle of the phenomenological approach was right.

In what sense?

It was still a matter of the structures of manifestation, of the appearing of anything whatsoever, be it on the linguistic or perceptual level, even though I sought to bring a reality constraint to bear upon these structures. This presupposed that the notion of "appearing" was pertinent on both levels. Phenomenology was thus corrected but not annulled, and its fundamental, methodological and, *therefore*, metaphysical presupposition was maintained.

What is the presupposition?

In a way, I've never had occasion to state this explicitly, but the idea I had arrived at was that one needs to accept that any investigation of a phenomenological kind (therefore, into the conditions of appearing) includes something that exceeds it. Any such investigation supposes that, in a certain sense, one already *has* the thing in question—this thing that has to appear—or, in any case, something related to it. In other words, there is no phenomenology without its own metaphysical charge, however cumbersome or unpleasant that term might be. One cannot speculate about that which appears or "is given" in the world without accepting a certain number of theses about what there is in the world, and any phenomenological investigation carries with it, in its inevitably local and contextual character (which is to circumscribe the form of this or that appearing), its own presuppositions. What I call "metaphysics" is nothing but the name of such "presuppositions"—that which, in relation to a definite appearing, is not "given," cannot be given, since it is that which must be there anyway for it to make any sense to reason in terms of this or that appearance [*apparaître*] (i.e., in this instance, also to treat anything whatsoever as something that appears [*apparaissant*]).

Now, recent developments in my work (since 2008) have led me to believe that such a "phenomenological realism" (or a phenomenology corrected by realism) is a dead end. I now think that it is not only a certain, abstract way of asking the question "How can things (or this or that kind of thing) be given to us?" that has been vitiated, but the question itself. In a way, one could say that my latest research has been devoted to the deconstruction of this question, as, for example, in *Concepts: introduction à l'analyse* and *Éléments de Philosophie réaliste: réflexions sur ce que l'on a.*

How do you mark that difference, and what, if anything, remains of phenomenology in your more recent thinking, if only as a function of the transformations you have just described?

I now favor asking about the forms according to which we put into play, in one way or another, what we have, instead of acting as if we could think independently of this having and as if it made sense to ask ourselves how we could have what we (in fact) do have. My research on the concept of perception, that is, on what we understand by perception, has played a major role here, leading me to renounce any problematic of presence (which has the misfortune of carrying its opposite with it: in order to be said, it supposes that one can place oneself ahead of it). But once the knots associated with a certain concept of perception (which phenomenology inherits from modern epistemology with the goal of criticizing it) are undone, the perspective on language also changes radically: language is henceforth understood as a form of orientation in the having of things instead of constituting something like the inverse of their phenomenalization.

Here, I think, one can say that I have left phenomenology behind on this point. My thinking is fundamentally no longer a thinking of phenomenalization. Concepts like the "given" no longer play a central role and, at least in a certain "absolute" usage, appear as nonsensical. Nevertheless, it is clear, first, that I was educated in the phenomenological tradition and that I remain and probably will remain enduringly marked by it. A large part of what I do remains unintelligible without reference to phenomenology. Second, when I first took the path of a "critical phenomenology" only to end up in all likelihood abandoning the very concept of phenomenology (because, at bottom, I abandoned the concept of the "phenomenon"), it certainly was a disappointed love: the result of the conviction I had reached that phenomenology did not live up to its own initial demands and did not reach the kind of result it aspired to in terms of descriptivity and the capacity to assume the concrete, those "things themselves" it had promised us. I was then led to go and look for such results elsewhere (in Wittgenstein and Austin) and ended up becoming aware that in reality it was the question that, from the beginning, had been poorly posed (in terms of "phenomenalization"). Third, finally, in my current philosophical style, there remains much phenomenological content (in the sense that it comes from phenomenology in the instituted sense of the term) and, more globally, what one could call a "phenomenological concern" in the sense of what I just said regarding my phenomenological education. From this point of view, one may think of the theory of "experiential concepts" that I largely take over from Husserl and that plays a central role in my *Éléments de philosophie réaliste*. There is something like a trace of phenomenology at the center of the edifice: there are "phenomenological concepts," and they are a fundamental lever of our orientation within the real. On the other hand, this point is conceptual and does not refer back to an a priori of phenomenalization. It simply takes note of the fact that the qualitative dimension of what we call "experience" constitutes an essential aspect of our world—that is, of what we call "world."

Once again, it's not so much that I want to erect a "linguistic phenomenology." It's more that, when it comes to taking into account the way in which we inhabit this world, orient ourselves in it, and, especially, speak in it, the experiential dimension (the "effect" things have on us), which one may always call "phenomenological," remains essential. It is here, in my view, that today, against all odds, we must retain something of phenomenology. From my perspective, then, phenomenology is no longer possible as universal grammar, according to which the philosophical approach to anything whatever would be subordinated to the examination of the conditions of its experience, as if one were, in a way, to find the thing only in experiencing it and to constitute it absolutely starting from this experience. I no longer believe in this primacy of appearing over being that characterizes phenomenology properly understood. Or, if you like, I do not believe in "givenness" as the ultimate figure of the absoluteness of the phenomenological. Or, to put it in yet another way, I do not believe in the priority of the "possible" over the "effective."

You do not approach experience from a transcendental point of view.

Right, which is not to say that the notion of "experience" has no meaning or that we need to conceive things as if we did not experience them, or independently of such an experience. As a matter of fact, this experience, with all its qualities, is a very important part of all kinds of concepts we ourselves make of things. A certain philosophy, against what it perceived as its half-real, half-invented adversary's scientism and objectivism, has got it into its head to restore to the world its colors. In doing so, it has forgotten, first of all, that nothing (and certainly not a philosophy) could deprive the world of these colors, since they are *its* colors, and there is no place for "restoring" them. There is nothing here that one could "give" to the world. This is where the fundamental vanity of the concept of "appearing," which constitutes the heart of the idea of phenomenology, lies. From another angle, this philosophy has equally forgotten that, if there is nothing here one could give to the world, it is because what one would give it is what one has always already placed in its *concept*: What do we call "world" if not that which has colors? There is no point here from which it would be necessary to reconquer color and thus no space for a phenomenology, because it is the concept of world itself, or in any case a certain concept of world, that is "phenomenological." In this sense, the exhaustion of phenomenology, the fact that in the end it becomes purely "conceptual"—and, therefore, transparent—is also its truth or, rather, its *reality*.

In L'idée de phénoménologie *you criticize the predominance of the Heideggerian narrative of "the" (one) "history of metaphysics" (and its "end") in contemporary French phenomenology as a return to a certain form of historicism. You also criticize what, to your mind, has become something of an obsession in contemporary French phenomenology: the "transgression" of the so-called onto-theo-logical constitution of metaphysics, the "frenzied" search for phenomena irreducible to the conditions of the possibility of experience (however defined: Kantian, Husserlian, or Heideggerian). With respect to the so-called "theological turn" in French phenomenology, for example, you say, among other things, the following: " . . . in God, phenomenology was in a way confronted with its Other, the great Other par excellence, in the sense of 'that which in principle exceeds and goes beyond the level of phenomena.'" What possibilities of phenomenology, if any, do you understand a certain current of contemporary French phenomenology to occlude?*

I think that diagnosing French phenomenology or post-phenomenology with historicism is a little less exact today than it was ten years ago. What is certain, in my eyes, is that the historical predominance of the Heideggerian track in French phenomenology, starting from the 1960s, had a considerable perverse effect: that of an excessive form of historicization. As if the thing itself could be reduced to a narrative of the successive ways of saying it. Phenomenology in France has largely functioned as a life raft for a certain history of philosophy—as it has also, often convergently, for a certain metaphysics.

Whatever the importance, which one should not underestimate, of the historical determination of concepts (a determination, however, that requires a different treatment than phenomenology's epochal approach, a treatment that interrogates practices of thought in their reality and that turns to effective transmissions) there was something there that was extremely harmful. We nearly lost the sense for the thing itself that the founder of phenomenology had so ingeniously put forward. French phenomenology (or, as it would no doubt be more exact to say, post-phenomenology of the 1980s) was incredibly poor in descriptions and no longer had a sense for the concrete at all. It was entirely locked in a debate with its own tradition. This historicist bent, to my mind, was such that it prevented what constitutes the true philosophical requirement: the interrogation of all concepts in their relation to reality (and not to doctrines alone). There is a moment when, as Nietzsche says, one has to "smash the windows [. . .] and leap into the open!"[4]

As to the second aspect of your question, I do in fact believe that one of the notable characteristics of the revival of phenomenology in the eighties was a kind of exacerbation of the motif of phenomenality. Once more, there is no phenomenology in the authentic sense of the term if there is no doctrine of appearance. In a sense, 1980s phenomenology was no exception: it made this idea its very theme. By thematizing it, it made it into a problem. One could witness at the time a characteristic one-upmanship around the notion of appearance: as if this notion only became interesting, or showed its full extent, where it found itself confronted by the challenge of accommodating that which does not appear, or in any case by whatever puts the most stress possible on it. The phenomenology of the eighties is systematically and deliberately excessive. It believes itself to be inscribed in the Lévinasian practice of hyperbole, not seeing that this practice, in Lévinas, confirms a pure and simple exit from phenomenology: the transition to a dramatics that, as such, cannot be a dramatics of "phenomena" but of *discourse*.

There is something very striking about the thematic choices of a phenomenology that privileges, against the supposed standard of a classical (Husserlian?) phenomenology, phenomena that it constructs as "extremes" or "limits." It is as if Husserlian harmony, the ideal of "adequation" according to which the appearing lives up to its intentional aim, had been broken: either the appearance goes toward exhaustion and only the aim remains (Derrida), or, on the contrary, its profusion no longer manages to return within the framework of the aim, or in any case the framework of a *single* aim (Marion). However, this presupposes that we are still within the perspective that reasons in terms of an "aim": the aim and only the aim is the measure of the lack or excess of the appearance. The alleged excess [*dé-mesure*] is nothing but a perverse effect of measure, ignored in its purely grammatical sense and made substantial, the very norm of the appearance.

This, however, is only the first step of the analysis. In truth, going further, one becomes aware that this is what the very concept of appearance carries within itself. The concepts of appearance and of the aim are not really two different concepts but two aspects of one and the same concept. Reasoning in terms of "appearance," as phenomenology does (it cannot do otherwise, for that is what defines it), is always already to have placed it under an "aim" and thus to expose oneself to questions such as: "Is this appearance adequate to, lacking, or in excess of such an 'aim'?" This is inscribed in the very concept of appearance. The rollercoaster of excess and lack into which 1980s post-phenomenology wanted to drag appearance does not, therefore, constitute a simple deviation, as I thought for a long time, but an intrinsic pathology of phenomenological reason. It is essential for appearance to be able to be qualified as "lacking" or "excessive." It was made for that. The whole question hinges on knowing that in relation to which it is to be measured. There is no *intrinsically* "lacking," "excessive," or "adequate" appearance. But that is because there is no longer intrinsic appearance—independently of such measure—either. That is what this entire phenomenology of the extreme has forgotten insofar as it was the culmination of, and wanted to be an overcoming of, phenomenological reason, according to the very terms fixed by that which it had "overcome" and by the logical space it assigned for such an overcoming. Not for a second did one wonder whether there is any sense in saying that what we *have*, that with which we are always confronted, "appears."

This may be a good time to raise some questions regarding your own, positive project. In Sens et sensibilité: l'intentionalité en contexte, *following a certain reading of Austin and Wittgenstein, you develop a "contextualist" approach to intentionality and signification according to which the normative conventions of a determinate "form of life" fix "contexts" of possible speech acts and, in so doing, determine (to a considerable, but by no means absolute, degree) the various possibilities of signification (and, importantly, non-signification) vis-à-vis the context in question. How do you define "context" and to what problem(s) does a "contextual" approach to intentionality respond?*

The notion of context is not without ambiguity. I tried to clarify it a bit in *Sens et sensibilité* by introducing a distinction between "context" and "circumstances." But I'm not sure that that suffices. In a few words: it is possible to distinguish between a normative and a non-normative concept of context. On the one hand we find the idea that a speech act, but also a mental attitude, defines a certain normed framework according to which things can be evaluated as conforming or not conforming to the speech act or the mental attitude, respectively. This minimally supposes that a situation is of this or that kind, and it is only in this kind of situation that a speech act or mental attitude has normative efficacy and that things can be judged to be in conformity with them. On the other hand, there are the things such as they are, such as they do or do not satisfy the norm, or even such as they annul the sense there is in applying such a norm. What is important here is reality's capacity for exercising pressure on norms, to lend itself to their application, and to fall under their jurisdiction, but also sometimes to undo them and to put them in question once more, to lead to their transformation.

For me, this was a very good interpretive principle of the dynamics of mental life: a constant process of adjusting meaning, within the real. At the time, I called this a "pragmatic conception of intentionality."

The contextualist theory of intentionality has a double import: from the semantic and epistemological point of view (if it makes sense to speak of a mental semantics, which I am less and less sure about), on the one hand, it provides an answer to the fundamental question of the determination of *intentional content*. It is in the adjustment of the act or attitude to the context, in the kind of normative connection they weave with the context, that its principle can be found. On the other hand, from the "metaphysical" point of view—in the (positive) sense outlined above—such a theory very much anchors the "mental," or, at the very least, the terms by which we describe it, back in the real. It opens the perspective of an intentional history of the mind, which is always a *real history* with its objective circumstances and encounters.

Looked at through the prism of contextualism, intentionality stops being an empire within an empire. It is restored to its ground in reality and is no longer anything but the very format of the way we have of orienting ourselves in reality. Such an approach raises considerable problems not addressed in *Sens et sensibilité*, which, like *Les limites de l'intentionalité*, builds on a certain direct transferability of the results obtained in the analysis of linguistic acts to the philosophy of mind. In effect, it is not at all certain that a mental attitude has a context in the same sense in which a linguistic act has one. I do not say a "mental act" because that would suppose the problem to be resolved: it is likely that the very notion of a mental act is held in place by a seductive parallelism with the notion of a linguistic act, and it is not at all certain that there are such things as "mental acts" at all.

Intuitively, we would like to say that linguistic acts need contexts (in order to be effective), while mental attitudes, in a certain sense, have already integrated a context: there is no mental attitude the content of which is not already fixed, and this content is only fixed by having absorbed contextual traits. The context, here, has been (logically) interiorized, and that is what produces "the mental."

And yet, it is also true, of course, that what we call "mind" is characterized by a certain transferability of forms of identification or of normation that we call its contents. Thus, on this level as well, the problem of a certain contextuality arises: What are the conditions of transferability of mental content? What exactly does it mean? That is the question I tried to advance in *Concepts*. The difficulty of conventionality is one aspect of this problem . . .

Despite your frequent use of the concept of the "conventional" throughout Sens et sensibilité, *you've made known your discomfort with a thoroughgoing "conventionalist" account of intentionality. What, to your mind, are the sources of such discomfort? Being uncomfortable with a thoroughgoing conventionalism would seem to require, at the very least, some kind of philosophical anxiety about the allegedly unwelcome consequences such a commitment might entail . . .*

Where linguistic acts are at issue, they obviously put conventions into play, and conventions support the normative wiring of these acts with the world. But where mental attitudes are at issue, will we find anything whatsoever that is analogous to such conventions? It is doubtful that there is any sense in representing thought as anything conventional at all. Thought does not escape convention, as those who subscribe to a substantial conception of intentionality seem to think (as if it were logically possible that it succumb to convention), simply because it doesn't make sense to submit it to such a question: the very grammar of the notion of intentionality excludes its having anything to do with the division between the conventional and the non-conventional.

It is instead a matter of seeing the conventions that regulate uses of language, as well as the problems of adjusting such conventions to reality, as revealing the "contextual" tenor of the very contents of thought, of their own contextuality insofar as, from one occurrence to another, the very conventions of language will lead to expressing them in a differentiated manner. A (conventional) contextuality functions here as the prism of another (non-conventional). But that is a project that largely remains to be constructed . . .

In Concepts, *you emphasize the flexibility and/or plasticity of our concepts vis-à-vis the world not as an accident that merely happens to befall certain of our concepts but rather as a condition of our having concepts at all, or at any rate as an intrinsic feature of our life with concepts. You mention, in this connection, the possibility of a "contextualist philosophy of mind."[5] What do you understand this to mean and what relation does it bear to contextualism in the philosophy of language? How, moreover, might this "contextualist philosophy of mind" relate to your ongoing interest in the "limits" of intentionality?*

The question concerning the delimitation of concepts has several aspects.

First of all, it is essential for concepts to have a delimitation. A concept that would apply to anything whatsoever, that would not make any difference, would not be a concept. And when I say, "that would apply to anything whatsoever," I mean to say, "that would give a value (including the false) for any object whatsoever." In exact opposition to what Frege thought, it is absolutely essential that, for all concepts, it be possible to find objects that the concept determines neither positively nor negatively, objects in relation to which the judgments elaborated by means of that concept are neither true nor false. Such indetermination has no positive meaning, it is not a third type of determination—as though "neither true nor false" were positively a third type of truth value. It refers simply to this fundamental logical fact: the scope of any concept is limited. This is also what gives a concept its strength and its pertinence as a concept insofar as it is referred to certain matters.

In turn, this delimitation cannot be dissociated from the concept being effectively put to work—that is to say from the possibility of effectively putting it to work. In a very essential sense, it cannot be anticipated.

What I mean by this, following others (here, I owe much of my inspiration to Charles Travis), is that the question of knowing whether a concept can effectively apply to an unexpected situation for which it was not a priori made cannot be posed in the abstract. To settle this question, there is no other solution but to try to apply the concept to the situation such as it is in its richness and complexity. Sometimes that which at first sight (abstractly, independently of an effective confrontation with reality) appears perfectly pertinent to a situation is not pertinent at all. At other times, the contrary is the case and that which seemed a bit too coarse or out of place finally functions in the situation in question. That is to say, precisely, that *we find the means to make it work.*

From this point of view, it seems to me that a certain misunderstanding prevails about the point of the contextualist position, namely the idea of the sensitivity of terms' signification (or, at the very least, of what some would call "cognitive meaning") to their future use. It seems as though there is something magical there, and it rightly worries rationalist epistemologists: How could that which is not given (future uses in their diversity and unforeseeability) influence what is supposed to be given (present meaning)? Obviously, those who ask themselves the question ought to begin by asking themselves what it might mean that "present signification" be "given" and that is exactly where the problem lies. It is likely that such formulations conceal gross errors concerning the notion of meaning. Simultaneously, the balloon of so-called future uses must be deflated. To say that the signification of a term is, in a sense, sensitive to future use draws attention to the nature of what is called "usage" when one says that it is where meaning is decided. We are in no more a position to imagine all future uses as potentially contained in present use (a potentiality that would be filled with all these virtual meanings, independent of new uses that would eventually put in play the meaning of the term once again) than we can conceive present use as *dependent* on uses that have not yet taken place, about which questions cannot perhaps even be asked at this stage. In fact, the thesis on sensitivity to future uses is essentially only a thesis about present use: it is a matter of bringing out its character *as* a use, that is, as something that we *do*, something about which it would be wrong to think that it could maintain itself independently of this doing [*faire*]. As for the future, the question is: In determinate circumstances, do we or do we not do the same? It could be tempting to say that for us to do the same, the minimal conditions for it to make sense for us to do the same must be met. Yet such a verdict is rather imprudent: very often, in a given situation, we end up doing what a particular aspect of this kind of situation, an aspect now lacking, would lead us to do. It is thus the fact that we *do* so, definitively, that gives the situation its meaning, and not the inverse. Thus, in the present, there isn't really an answer to the question about the future. But it is fundamental that the present be itself thought as a species of a future, as that for which there *is* a response to the question for which there isn't one for the future, and for the same reason: because, in the present, *this is what we do*. That is what the sensitivity and the openness to future uses means.

As for the difference in perspective between a "contextualist philosophy of mind" and a contextualist philosophy of language, once again I think it is important to keep in mind the asymmetry between the respective logical functions of thought and expression. To take seriously the "linguistic turn" and become aware of the extent to which it is by means of an examination of the effective employment of our forms of language that we are to outline the very physiognomy of what we call "thought" is certainly not to identify thought and language and, above all, even less to reduce it to a sort of language beyond language that would come to redouble it in its effective use. It is fundamental that the given linguistic means, used in a certain way in a context with its own thickness and characteristics, express a thought content. They can only produce this result if they are used in a certain way and in a certain context. This is the principle of linguistic contextualism. The content that is expressed is not of the order of the means of expression or even, truth be told, of the order of a means in general. Of course, in a certain sense, it is possible to say that thoughts, insofar as they are ready-made, available thoughts, can themselves become means of thinking: one relies on a thought in circulation as a motive from which to produce thought. Yet, first, it is likely that this becoming instrumental of thoughts is entirely indissociable from their formulaic expression, which fixes them as, precisely, "means." On this point, I refer you to the remarkable work done by my student Thibaut Sallenave on the fecundity of "clichés." Second, such an instrumentalization of thoughts themselves does not, for all that, identify them with signs. Thoughts do not express anything and above all not themselves. Therefore, they certainly cannot be contextual in the sense in which statements [*énoncés*] are. It is contextually and only contextually that statements can express the thoughts they express.

If we forget that this is a grammatical point, a simple clarification of the functional value we assign to the terms "thought" and "expression," we risk concluding from all this that if the expression is contextual (in the sense that it expresses only within a context), thought is not contextual. We contextually express thought contents that are what they are and, by construction, acontextual. And in a sense, that's true: thought contents are certainly not contextual in the sense in which expressions are.

Nevertheless, and this is the difficult point, it is not true that they are acontextual, and contextualism is also a thesis of the philosophy of mind, even a thesis of the philosophy of mind above all. The contextuality of linguistic use, in a certain sense, only reflects the contextuality of thoughts. This in the sense that thoughts are not cut off from the world, they entertain complex and subtle connections with reality. And it is this contextual inscription of what we call "thoughts" that manifests itself in the fact that a certain sequence of signs, to express this or that, requires being used in a certain way in a certain context, or, inversely, requires that, in another context, it is another sequence of signs, taking into account its typical uses, that will become pertinent for expressing it. Once more, here, one contextuality indicates the other, but they are not of the same nature. A thought's contextuality is, so to speak, indirect: it becomes apparent from the fact that this thought is "what would be said in this way in these circumstances" but "in this other way in other circumstances" and perhaps "could not be said in yet other circumstances" (there would be no means of saying it because there would be no logical place for such a content in such circumstances). The idea, if you like, is that our thoughts are exactly what, contextually, our statements express. But it is difficult to draw all the consequences from this idea.

Erecting a contextualist philosophy of mind in a non-hermeneutic sense, a philosophy that does not place the mind in a relation of exteriority to itself (as though it were intrinsically and not just, as it sometimes is, accidentally its own interpreter) and that does not confuse thought and its expression (a distinction that is the very condition of linguistic contextualism, properly understood) is, in my view, the great philosophical issue of our time.

As for the relation between the point of view I defended in *Concepts*, which effectively is the very first sketch of such a "contextualist philosophy of mind," and the preceding idea of "the limits of intentionality," there, the problem is a little more complicated. In fact the existence of boundaries for any mental attitude, and in general any normative grasp that we exercise on the world, could pass as a form of this very idea. Yet that is not entirely the case. The notion of a "limit of intentionality" still refers to a phenomenological apparatus, intentional in a substantial sense, where everything happens as though intentionality, to do what it does (provide the access it provides, according to the terms of this apparatus), needed an outside contribution. Such was the intentional externalism I was tempted to defend. Yet such an externalism, like all externalism, presupposes as *terminus a quo* a relatively robust sense of interiority: as though intentionality were something substantial to which something comes from the outside. That is what is evacuated once you start reasoning in terms of "concepts," that is, formats of a typical grasp of the world. The notion of "concept" is logical: it does not refer to a mental content in the real sense of the term. You'll notice that the notion of intentionality, with the trap it involves (the amphiboly of the logical and the real), is pretty much absent in *Concepts*. That is a major difference from *Les limites de l'intentionalité*. It comes back again in *Éléments de philosophie réaliste* but entirely slimmed down, grammaticalized, precisely insofar as it is a pure format of description.

In your historical work, you've worked out, in considerable detail, the late nineteenth–century philosophical debates that led to the formation of both phenomenology and analytical philosophy. What, broadly speaking, was the substance of these debates and how do you understand them to have affected the development of philosophy in the twentieth century?

In a certain sense, I returned to using the history of philosophy with an "agenda" in mind. By definition, it is only now that we will find the solutions to our problems, not in the past. I now think there was something naïve in looking, as I did, for an analytical truth of phenomenology, or a *via media* between phenomenology and analytic philosophy, in the protohistory, partly shared (in any case overlapping), of these two movements. Yet it is obvious that these historical studies have taught me a lot. The close contact, especially with an author like Bolzano,[6] has for me been a school of rigor, and I am filled with admiration when I look at the degree of analytic sophistication of his treatment of the relation between semantic and metaphysical questions. This entire but little-known phase of German thought opposed to German idealism has an incredible richness to it.

In the rediscovery of this forgotten continent something major is at stake in terms of understanding what happened in the twentieth century, and especially the genesis of the break between "Continentals" and "Analytics."

One thing often strikes me. At the end of the nineteenth century, in the authors who laid the foundations for the phenomenological and analytic traditions, first among them Husserl and Frege, we find a relatively common way of writing philosophy taken to its highest point of artistry, a way of writing that consists in analyzing concepts, in taking and reworking examples, in formulating hypotheses and in logically reasoning from them. One could call it the scientific style in philosophy. It had its limits, of course. No doubt the presuppositions of science must be interrogated. All the more so when a discourse like philosophy is at issue, where it is not certain that it can or should lay claim to the name of "science." Yet, even taking all of these criticisms into account, I don't see what philosophy could be if it isn't the illustrated and argued analysis of concepts questioned in their application. I think that the tragedy of what is called "continental philosophy" at the beginning of the twenty-first century (first so-called from the outside, polemically, and has since identified itself with that norm) is that, while it freely takes pride in itself in its role as guardian of the supposedly eternal essence of philosophy threatened by "analytic philosophy," it has, on the one hand, largely renounced substantial philosophical questions, privileging their narrative over their treatment (when the great founders at the end of the nineteenth century, on the contrary, believed in a new departure for these problems and consecrated all their energy to it), while on the other it has also largely repudiated the definitional and conceptual norms of that great tradition, abandoning these norms, without even knowing it, to an adversary who, for its part, often caricatures and impoverishes these norms. In my opinion, this is a true intellectual catastrophe because in many ways the current scene seems to place us before the alternative between a philosophy that has lost the ability to instantiate its concepts and a philosophy that has renounced its task of analysis and conceptual elaboration and, for that reason, is no longer a philosophy.

Against all this, I believe that, in learning from these great founders, including from their failures (which constitute the very path of the twentieth century's intellectual history), and in trying to understand their reasons, our current task is to maintain and bring to life the demand of conceptual analysis, of the ever necessary clarification of our ways of saying and of understanding, insofar as these ways face the things themselves. In this, the sense of instantiation that constituted the best of phenomenology and, ultimately, its essential methodological content, remains, to my mind, on the agenda more than ever.

Translated by Nils F. Schott

Notes

1. Jacques Bouveresse is a French analytic philosopher and professor emeritus at the Collège de France since 2010.

2. Charles Travis is a professor of philosophy at King's College and the author of numerous books, including *Perception, Objectivity and the Parochial, Occasion Sensitivity*, and *Thought's Footing*.

3. Sandra Laugier is a professor of philosophy at the University of Paris 1 Panthéon–Sorbonne and the author of *Why We Need Ordinary Language Philosophy, Wittgenstein*, and *L'Anthropologie logique de Quine*.

4. Nietzsche, *Thus Spoke Zarathustra*, 26.

5. Benoist, *Concepts*, 149.

6. Bernard Bolzano was widely recognized as one of the most important logicians of the nineteenth century.

Material Phenomenology

MICHEL HENRY

The following "interview" was compiled specifically for this volume by Jean Leclercq and Grégori Jean of the Fonds Michel Henry (which opened in 2010 at Université catholique de Louvain à Louvain-la-Neuve, Belgium) from the body of available interviews conducted over the course of Henry's life. Below, a preface to the "interview," written by Leclercq and Jean, offers a brief picture of the basic motivations behind Henry's work. We translate it here:

Although Michel Henry (1922–2002) attributed more importance to his published books than to other kinds of contributions, the various interviews that he gave, which themselves trace the significant moments of his work, provide remarkable summaries and offer further insights and valuable clarifications. The extracts that we present here, collected with the approval of Anne Henry, thus offer an overall look at a path of thought that surely stands out in an original and decisive way within contemporary phenomenology.

While trained in the tradition of French post-Kantianism, Henry's starting point lies in his dissatisfaction with its idealist posture and, more generally, with what he interpreted very early on as a "philosophy of representation." But if it is for this reason that in the historical context of philosophy after the war he turned rapidly to the works of Husserl and Heidegger, the reading of these early masters immediately takes the form of a very personalized interpretation animated by a challenge to the equation of the phenomenal and the visible, which was, to his mind, the characteristic paradigm of the phenomenology of intentionality.

Far from wanting to "substitute" his phenomenology of life for those of Husserl and Heidegger, which he acknowledges even here to offer "extraordinary descriptions," he nevertheless accuses them of a unilateralism that he would later name "historical phenomenology," the positive side of which will lie in the development of the phenomenology of the "invisible"—this being understood as a primary, radical, secret, and absolutely indubitable "mode" of phenomenalization.

He explicitly noted: "The ultimate problem of phenomenology is that of how the phenomena are given to me; it is the problem of givenness, of the appearing or, better, of the phenomenality of the phenomena considered as such."[1] Therefore it is in contrast to "exteriority," "representation," "Being-in-the-world," and even the "horizon" that a more original phenomenality is reached, of which the "how" itself and the specific mode of revelation will be situated early on in an original affectivity, in a pathetic and instinctual life, of which the structures, foreign to the world and its proper "visibility," are nothing other than a "feeling oneself feeling."

This powerful project of the exhibition of the actual conditions of a transcendental affectivity will then be expressed in the two inseparable dimensions of a philosophy of subjectivity and corporeality. It will first be expressed in corporeality because the "flesh" is simply nothing more than this "pure affective substance," where, in its affects and impulses, it is given to itself by life. It is not noted often enough that this occurs even in this world from which it is not separated, for the specificity of its phenomenological material allows it never to be lost. In fact, life for Henry is no more anonymous than it is "objective," and the phenomenology of the flesh is coupled with a phenomenology of incarnation inseparable from a fundamental egological intention founded on a strong theory of ipseity. And here we locate the dimension of subjectivity, which is thus the opposite of every narrative or hermeneutic paradigm through the intrinsic link of the singular ego with an original ipseity itself engendered in and through Life—such are the different ways through which each individual is found affectively given to himself. In other words, he is found apprehended by this absolute Life that engenders him and that becomes manifest through such affective givenness. A new conception of human finitude emerges from within this thesis that will gradually impose on Henry the notion of a "transcendental birth," opened to the event of Life, but singular each time in its modes of revelation.

In opposition, therefore, to every form of naturalism and psychologism, avoiding every reduction and objectification in leading back to an impressional and pure, pathetic matter, it is in the name of life—no longer biological or moral but rather transcendental—that Michel Henry breaks with "historical phenomenology" in reviving the great intention of Nietzsche, which can be already found in Schopenhauer: to question every metaphysics of representation and pave the way for a phenomenology of the most radical affective lived experiences and of our singular experience of existence, as it is expressed through work, economics, politics, aesthetic experience, psychopathology, as well as religious and even erotic experience.

In this respect, the importance of this selection consists not only in providing an overview of a philosophy falsely conceived as monolithic but also in bearing witness to the views that Michel Henry himself had on the various movements of his oeuvre and his "phenomenology of the unapparent," from its beginning in *L'essence de la manifestation* to the final books devoted to Christianity. It is precisely because life is and remains for Henry the original site of all subjectivity and all knowledge that the phenomenology that responds to it is open to a plurality—a plurality of phenomenological material as well as to the modes of exposition required. In this way, the interviews in which Michel Henry talks about his own literary writing as a way of expressing life marked by the imaginary rather than the concept become all the more significant. If for Henry life is felt and, above all, experienced even more than it is thought, the lifework of this philosopher will have been simply a concerted attempt to say it.

Jean Leclercq & Grégori Jean
Fonds Michel Henry
Université catholique de Louvain
Translated by W. Chris Hackett

[Intellectual History][2]

My education resulted from the philosophy that was taught in high schools and preparatory classes in Paris after World War I. It concerned the French reception, between 1870 and 1940, of Kantian thought through a series of philosophers like Lachelier, Lagneau, Boutroux, Alain, Nabert, Lachièze-Rey, etc.[3] In spite of the remarkable character of their analyses, I felt a sense of disagreement with them from the outset. For me, this Idealist thought let something concrete escape: what I am at the basis of myself, my real life.

The World War II era was marked by the emergence in Paris—notably, through Jean Hyppolite, Alexandre Kojève, and Jean-Paul Sartre—of Hegelian philosophy and especially German phenomenology. I had a strong attraction to phenomenology, and I can say that it was at that time that I became a phenomenologist. And yet, while studying it with passion, I felt a dissatisfaction similar to the one I had experienced with traditional philosophy; the essential was missing. But I was now able to grasp the essential in a rigorous way, phenomenologically, and to understand why both traditional thought and contemporary phenomenology missed it. From that time on, I realized that philosophy had always presupposed a certain conception of phenomenality since the Greeks, one that refers the phenomenon to a horizon of visibility in which it appears outside of us. This exteriority defines how it is shown to us in its "phenomenality." In modern thought, one can find this concept of phenomenality in the interpretation of "consciousness" or the "subject" as representation—that is to say as the act of placing in front; this philosophy of representation reaches its culmination in Kant. And traditional phenomenology presupposes the very same concept of the phenomenon. Husserl's intentionality as well as Heidegger's Being-in-the-world at the time of *Sein und Zeit*, later the "ek-static truth of Being," are only various ways of interpreting how things can be shown to us as their arrival in a primal "outside." This is the "world" taken as the horizon of visibility about which I was just speaking. This arrival "from the outside" founds the "objectivity" of the object and ultimately all knowledge, including scientific knowledge. However, what I am at the basis of myself, my life, is foreign to the world's horizon of visibility. My life as I originally experience it in myself is never an object; it can never be seen in a "world." Its essence consists precisely of the fact of experiencing oneself immediately, without distance, in an "auto-affection" in the original sense. This means that life is not affected first by something else, by objects or by the horizon of a world. It is affected by oneself. The content of its affection is itself, and it is only in this way that it can be "living." To live is to experience oneself and nothing else. The phenomenality of this pure experience of oneself is an original affectivity, a pure "pathos" that no distance separates from oneself.

My philosophical journey can thus be summed up as a route that led through phenomenology and resulted in the rejection of the assumptions of traditional phenomenology, both Husserlian and Heideggerian. Those presuppositions consist of an intentional conception of phenomenality as "worldly." Rejecting them leads to the discovery of a more original phenomenality, the phenomenality of life in the invisible embrace of its drives and pathos.

[The relation between Henry's phenomenology and the history of phenomenology][4]

My phenomenology of life is not intended to be a substitute for the phenomenologies of the world. The phenomenology of the world has its own proper role. There are extraordinary descriptions of this world in Husserl and Heidegger, but their phenomenology is unilateral. If we cannot see life, it is because we feel it. I worked upstream, in another region. My progress was to discover a phenomenality that does not belong to the order of exteriority but that resides within us even though we cannot see it, an invisible phenomenality. This phenomenality of the non-apparent entails a modification of the Greek concept of *phainomenon*, whose Indo-European root *pha* means "light"—this is a light of the world, of exteriority, and of what we see. Descartes had the hunch that we do not see our profound being. Indeed, who has ever seen his or her own suffering? Who has ever seen his or her own despair, which is only perceived in its external manifestations or symptoms? What we are cannot be seen, and it would be absurd to say that it is like a table that feels nothing or a pebble on the road. This is where the efforts of my research are focused: on understanding that affectivity is a primary form of revelation and of the appearing of reality.

[Genesis and context of the doctorat d'état, defended in the early 1960s: L'essence de la manifestation*]*

L'essence de la manifestation is not a starting point. It is the result of a long life of research. The ten or eleven years devoted to writing it followed four previous years at the Centre national de la recherche scientifique (CNRS) and the writing of *Philosophie et phénoménologie du corps*, which was initially a chapter of it. The length of the book is explained by the dissatisfaction I mentioned above. Husserl had helped me to define the phenomenological framework for my work. I was looking in vain for what I had not found in him—the recognition of the originary phenomenological dimension of transcendental life—throughout the Western philosophical tradition. By identifying some analyses in the tradition that seemed crucial to me, each time I showed that they were subordinated to the same phenomenological assumption that hid the essential (at that time, I called it ontological monism, but it should instead be called a phenomenological monism). Hence the excessive length (but it could have grown endlessly) of a large antithesis that takes up more than half of the work [. . .].[5]

In *L'essence de la manifestation* I did nothing but make a phenomenological distinction, if I may, between two ways in which things show themselves: in the world and in life. In the space of light that is the world and also intelligible space, I see circles and triangles in a kind of mathematical space, by a seeing of thought. This first way that things have of showing themselves presupposes a gap, a horizon of visibility. It is because there is a screen behind things that they are able to appear on this screen. This screen is a transcendental screen, and Heidegger's philosophy is ultimately a description of this horizon as time. This is what he calls an "ek-stasis," that is to say the fundamental "outside" in which the phenomenality of things emerges. And, according to phenomenology, consciousness is fundamentally outside. That is why I enter into relation with things. All this is quite true but unilateral. And the effort of *L'essence de la manifestation* was to take up these descriptions by showing not only their validity but also their limits, since they completely obscured a much more original mode of revelation, which is life. My aim was to establish that this mode of revelation is itself completely different from the showing of things in exteriority. This revelation is an affectivity, an original feeling of oneself that is literally the flesh of our being. Every feeling of something thus presupposes this feeling of oneself. That is where our life is situated. And in short, even the world is only possible if we are first in life. Our opening to the world is a fact of life, and it must reach a point where it experiences itself in this immediacy where there is no light. This invisibility is also the most certain. The word "invisible" should not be taken as negative from a phenomenological standpoint. In reality, the invisible refers to the first and most radical form of revelation. It is secret because one cannot see it. But it is undeniable because one cannot say that one does not experience what is experienced. The revelation of life occurs at that level, and I have treated it as the original revelation.[6]

[Relation of L'essence de la manifestation *to Henry's other work]*

I consider my work as a whole to be dominated by a unifying principle that consists of this conception of the specific and fundamental phenomenality of life [. . .]. By applying this phenomenology to Marx, I was able to propose a completely new interpretation of this great thinker and extract him from the Marxist ideology that disfigures him. I refer you to my two volumes—*Marx: une philosophie de la realité* and *Marx: Une philosophie de l'économie*—originally published by Gallimard in 1976. Similarly, by applying this phenomenology of life to the problem of the unconscious, I was able to present a new understanding of Freud and psychoanalysis in *Généalogie de la psychanalyse*, originally published by Presses universitaires de France in 1985. I did the same for the problem of art, especially that of painting. I was able to show the decisive significance of Kandinsky's theses about abstract painting in *Voir l'invisible* originally published by François Bourin in 1988. [. . .] In each of the domains I explored, I was able to evaluate the fecundity of the phenomenological presupposition that I had grasped in life. Over-specialization is no longer opposed to the unity of a comprehensive philosophy, if such a philosophy has an overarching principle of intelligibility that is discernible within any essential human activity. Today, I would even say that only a phenomenology that can go back to this essence of life, and thus make use of a "radical" principle of explanation, can overcome the crisis of a culture that has shattered into multiple specializations unaware of one another and that no longer allows human beings to give life a unified meaning. Life is the only thing that is capable of conferring such a meaning onto its multiple manifestations. In the end, it is only life that can understand itself and, more deeply, act toward its total fulfillment or its destruction, as seen in the nihilism that characterizes modernity. Nihilism has not just a theoretical side but also a practical one. It is recognizable in behaviors of flight as well as self-destruction. This is expressed in all of the ideologies, especially scientific ideology, that deny the specificity of a human essence by reducing one's subjective life to an objective series that is said to determine it.[7]

[Relation between Henry's literary activity and philosophical research]

My whole life has been divided between philosophical research and this literary activity that I opened by writing my first novel, *Le Jeune Officier*. What these two attitudes share is the intention to tell the truth, to detect something essential through events or forms of existence. This truth can be expressed in two ways. The first is the path of conceptual analysis, which is a path of rigor and abstraction—I have followed this track for very many years. But I have met up with its limits. This is because analysis is performed through the mediation of a technical language reserved, if not for experts, at least for initiates. A reversal of perspectives occurs then. Philosophical language sought a universal truth that is communicable to all, but instead it becomes a very particular language that is addressed to a limited public and cut apart from this universality. The drama of twentieth-century culture is to be a culture shattered into specialties and techniques that no longer understand one another. Philosophy had sought to become the *sapientia universalis* that would dominate specific forms of knowledge. In fact, it has become one of these forms of knowledge that is juxtaposed with the other ones. It no longer plays the role of reunification and synthesis. [. . .] Because the novel does not use conceptual indices but the imagination [. . .], it is addressed to a wider audience and, especially, to those who are different from me. When I publish a book of philosophy, I talk to philosophers. But the world is not populated only by philosophers—so much the better, indeed! Besides, I love telling stories. My philosophical research had repressed this taste, pleasure, and need. My philosophical development itself helped me to appreciate that human existence is not thinking but sensibility, affectivity, bodily activity. These are singular events where the imagination also matters. Imagination expresses this incredible faculty of life to always go beyond what is given. To imagine is to posit something other than what exists. Becoming a novelist, for me, was not an escape; it was the possibility to give a place in reality to what is essential.[8]

[The concept of "life" and the thesis of a "phenomenological dualism"]

Actually, the word "life" should not be understood in the traditional sense. When the Greeks speak of *bios*, of life, for example, they are speaking *in the world* about a certain category of *beings* (being-there), to use Heidegger's term. Some beings are inert and others are alive, like bees, and then there is the life I am and that is *Dasein* (Being-in-the-world). In the traditional sense of the word, life is seen as a kind of being in the world, and biology studies living beings. The inert thing has no world, the animal is poor-in-world, and me, the human being, I am in the world. That is to say that I am enlightened by the light of exteriority. For my part, I give an absolutely new and different meaning to life, since it is no longer a being in the world but refers to appearing itself [. . .].[9]

The question of life has indeed guided my thinking and, today more than ever, does not result from a "choice," strictly speaking. It is imposed on me by issues raised in phenomenology that, it seems to me, needed to be completely rethought. The ultimate problem of phenomenology is to know *how* phenomena are given to me. It is the problem of givenness, of appearing, or better, of the phenomenality of phenomena as such. As soon as one identifies this decisive question, one can see that the same concept of phenomenality dominates almost the entire development of Western philosophy. Instead of questioning this phenomenological presupposition, phenomenology leads it to its goal. It produces a more rigorous and more adequate formulation of this phenomenality rather than any reversal of it. This is why phenomenology, instead of opposing it, carries on traditional philosophy. This is also why, if another concept of phenomenality arose, it would run up against disbelief on the part of phenomenologists as well as the proponents of classical thought—be it philosophy of knowledge, epistemology, political philosophy, aesthetics, or the social sciences.

So why is there another concept of phenomenality? Once again, this was not the result of my decision. Phenomenality phenomenalizes on its own, and in its own way, prior to and independently of any effort of thought to grasp it. The "way" in which phenomenality originally phenomenalizes is precisely life, and this mode of phenomenalization has nothing to do with what dominates Western thought. Traditionally, it understands phenomenality on the basis of the phenomenon "world" and, indeed, as being identical to it. Naturally, throughout the development of this tradition and in spite of its revolutionary character, most of the current issues and major changes are situated with this spontaneous or explicit interpretation of the "phenomenon" that delineates the horizon of all questioning. But, apart from a few marginal but very important thinkers, these changes have never called into question the traditional concept of phenomenality. From the Greeks to Heidegger, the phenomenon continues to be understood as the opening of a first "outside" where everything that can be shown to us is shown in the horizon of visibility that is hollowed out by this externalization or ek-stasis—consequently, as external, other, "facing" or "object."

The nature of life is that it is never given as other or external to itself; instead, it feels *itself* in an *auto-affection* in the strict sense, such that the content of this condition suffered by life is nothing other than itself. It is only *in* and *as* this immediate experience, impassable and invincible, that something "living" is possible. To put this otherwise, in its original phenomenalization, appearing is not carried out of itself and does not turn away from itself. It is not transcendence or intentionality but rather an auto-appearing in which what appears is appearing itself. The concept of life is auto-appearing as something exclusive of any otherness. Life is only possible as auto-appearing and the non-appearing of anything else. Now the ultimate question of phenomenology becomes to know what concrete phenomenality, what phenomenologically pure matter, makes appearing possible as an auto-appearing and, in this way, as life. I have shown that it is the non-ekstatic *pathos* of a transcendental affectivity that constitutes a pure affective substance, the "flesh" of this embrace of oneself that is found in any feeling, no matter how simple it is.

I turn to [a difficult] question: How is it the case that phenomenology, and more broadly traditional philosophy, knows nothing about that which phenomenalizes as the oldest phenomenality and about that which is given before any other thing? How can one explain this misunderstanding of a phenomenology of life among philosophers in general and, in particular, among those who are concerned with the phenomenon in the phenomenological sense, that is to say, the phenomenon thematized in its manner of givenness? I see at least three reasons for this paradoxical situation.

The first resides in the very nature of the phenomenalization of life, in short its non-ekstatic, "invisible" life. Based on the naiveté of the natural attitude, the "phenomenon" has always been taken in the sense of something that is shown by becoming visible, in a space of light. Moreover, it is in this space that the regard of thought moves; it seeks and discovers everything that it finds there, in this "outside" where life is never shown. As its own phenomenological essence, there is something in life that is irreducible to thought, and so it is not surprising that philosophy, which is a mode of thinking and knowing, misses life in principle. To know life in thought presupposes an extraordinary method that I have explained in a recent text on the phenomenological method. Knowing life in *an indirect way*—only life "knows" itself directly—is not just the task of a phenomenological method that is constructed on the basis of its own impossibility. It is also a practical knowledge that humanity has used from the beginning and to which we will return in a moment. In spite of these modes of knowledge that all depend on a phenomenological and ontological substitution that is defining and decisive, it is nonetheless the case that—and this is precisely the cause of this substitution—the way of revealing life withdraws from the Greek phenomenon as well as the conceptual systems based on it. Foreign to every ek-static horizon of visibility and not relating to oneself through the mediation of this horizon, life is a night without division. It is an immemorial and absolute forgetting where, however, nothing is lost from the pathetic embrace of life. But while this pathos cannot be completely misunderstood because it always proceeds from the very stuff out of which it is made, thought interprets it as an opaque content that can only be illuminated through thought itself. It is thus the immemorial character of life that explains not only the constitutive forgetting of its own essence but also thought's forgetting of it, whether it is thought and knowledge in general or philosophical thought in particular.

The second reason is thus the inability of phenomenology to break with tradition. In spite of its criticisms, it repeats the essential occultation. Concerning this tradition, we can also add this: because life tirelessly continues its work within us, it is hardly possible to reject it entirely. One thus sees in this tradition, at the moment where its objectivism culminates in a metaphysics of representation, that it is broken by the emergence of Schopenhauer's will-to-live. His opposition to representation signifies nothing less than the irreducibility of life to the conditions of phenomenality defined by the Kantian transcendental aesthetic. From that moment forward, and despite philosophers' contempt for Schopenhauer, the clandestine return of life reflects both its irreducible character and the ruinous phenomenological deficiency of Western philosophy.

Adding to the first reason and transforming it into an almost invincible prejudice, the third reason is what I call the Galilean arch-fact (i.e., the methodological elimination of subjectivity by the rational project of a scientific knowledge of the material world). We are indebted to Husserl for having seen the decisive consequences of that project for the constitution of modernity. But Husserl understands this putting out of play of subjectivity as a putting out of play of intentional subjectivity and not of life in the radical sense that I understand it. It is thus a matter of referring every "objectivity" back to a constituting consciousness and of grasping the world as a life-world and not as this life itself that is prior to any world, which is a non-ekstatic pathos where our timeless essence is carried out. The fact that philosophy and phenomenology itself, let alone Galilean science, can forget our true essence forces us to go back to this arch-revelation that Western phenomenality does not promote or contain. Thus the weight of tradition, the Galilean opening of modernity, and most radically the essence of original phenomenality are the three factors that explain the isolation on the theoretical level of research centered on life.[10]

[Relation between the phenomenology of life and the concept of the body]

My reading of Maine de Biran allowed me to anticipate what I then called ontological dualism, that is to say the fact that appearing is double. It sometimes appears outside oneself in the world and sometimes appears in the impressional and pathetic immediacy of life. These are two heterogeneous ways of appearing. [. . .] By studying the phenomenon of the body in Maine de Biran, I discovered—which was really the philosophical revelation of my journey—that he had deepened Descartes's *cogito* by stating that this *cogito* is an "I can" and that this "I can" is my subjective body—the body-subject that is at the origin of all experience [. . .].[11]

Maine de Biran understood for the first time that the "I can" is not the external body but that it makes use of an "organic body" that is lived internally as what gives way to the effort of this "I can" and is nothing other than what resists it. It arises the moment that this resistance, lived internally through this effort, no longer gives way. The "I can" then experiences, in the invisibility of its obscurity, the real body of the world, which is itself invisible. Because of the duality of appearing, it so happens that this entire process is not simply experienced in the invisibility of our flesh in which effort is carried out but also is given externally in the world. This is the case not only for the real body of the world that shows itself to us as a sensible body that one can see and touch. The subjective bodily "I can" thus appears to itself from the outside as an external body among others, as an "empirical individual" identified with this body that is distinguished by its objective ability to touch other things and to touch itself, to move itself, etc. In this way, the subjective and pathetic movement of the originary

"I can" is conjured away to the benefit of purely objective phenomena in which our life is lost. This is how the reign of the visible is extended everywhere and draws everything into itself.[12]

[The "reign of the visible" opposed to the "knowledge of life"]

The knowledge of life is extraordinary because this knowledge is the source of everything we do. It makes life possible, coincides with it, and is its essence. For example, to study a treatise on biology you read a book with printed characters, and this means that you use sense knowledge allowing you to see the letters and read them. This is followed by another kind of knowledge because the letters have a meaning. This requires the knowledge of a consciousness that forms meanings. The ability to form meaning is not merely an ability to perceive, because mysteriously our mind can form the meaning of a thing in its absence and even without representing it. So a meaning is formed in a different way from an image. That is the knowledge of consciousness—consciousness creates meanings and also creates images. The reader of the treatise on biology is one in whom both sensible vision and intellectual knowledge are functioning. The knowledge that allows for an intellectual grasp of the meanings contained in the words is the knowledge of consciousness. When this reader gets worn out from effort and leaves the library to have some rest, he or she must stand up and use the most simple, primordial knowledge—this knowledge is already involved in sensible knowledge and intelligible knowledge. How can one stand, walk, leave, etc.?

Well, it should be noted that the great philosophers stumbled into this difficulty. What does Descartes say? "I am a thing that thinks," a *res cogitans*. A *cogitatio* is an invisible thing that one cannot see or touch, even though this invisible thing is the most certain. This *cogitatio* is already in the knowledge of life. In *The Passions of the Soul*, Descartes says that, if I dream, everything I see in my dream is false. And Descartes's dream argument summed up an entire tradition—though he radicalized it—in asserting that with respect to sensible vision what I see is false, as is the case with respect to intellectual vision, the seeing that sees that 2 + 2 = 4. Suppose that the evidence of the rational truths is challenged. If an Evil Genius deceives me when I see that 2 + 2 = 4, if everything is a dream, what is left as certain? Whatever remains cannot be dependent on seeing. But Descartes said that if I feel fear in my dream, this fear is real, and it is even the only thing about which I can be certain. Moreover, fear is true exactly how I had it, that is, exactly as it is. There is thus a revelation of fear that owes nothing to seeing. This self-revelation of fear is a pathos, a transcendental affectivity that is totally independent from seeing. That is life. Life reveals itself to itself, without distance, immediately, without anything seen. This immediacy is not a concept; this feeling that life has of itself never ceases. All the modalities of life, including those of knowledge, are of that order. That is what I call a radical phenomenology.[13]

[Phenomenology of life and the phenomenology of the "unconscious"]

The problems posed by Descartes, which were not well understood, inaugurate the modern age, whether it takes them to be true or false. [. . .] Western thought only believes in representations, whereas Descartes is basically the first to question them. This means that the Heideggerian interpretation of Descartes is completely wrong: "I think" means anything but "I represent myself." And from the time that Descartes questions representation, phenomenality, falsely identified with representation, becomes the unconscious. In his 1915 article "Das Unbewußte," and in other texts of this period, Freud is able to introduce the concept of the unconscious precisely because representation disappears. One of his major arguments is based on the analysis of memory. I think that anyone who examines the world of representations and its structure can clearly see that, before my eyes, there is only room for one thing at a time. The horizon of light in which I see is limited, such that the thing that I see quickly leaves this area of clarity in order to make way for another—this allows me to see another object. But there is a price to pay. In the world of representation, when I see one thing, then I do not see all the others and they will then be called "unconscious representations." At this moment, Freud begins by demonstrating the reality of the unconscious by saying: there are some representations on which I can exercise my thought, but as soon as I cease to do so, they leave the circle of the light of representation that identifies them with the conscious mind. They then become unconscious representations, or memories, and they will fill the container that is my unconscious. Thus is born the aporetic, untenable concept of an "unconscious representation," of something in front of me, that I both see and do not see: this is the case for each one of the representations that I can observe only for a moment and the next moment disappear. This is the first phase of psychoanalysis, the phase where the unconscious stands in opposition to representation. Representation as a finite mode of appearing gives rise to the idea that the authentic reality is unconscious. But what is authentic reality? It is important to recognize precisely that it is another kind of reality than representation, which is deep within myself and that Freud will call the "unconscious." It is invisible but not in the sense of something that is temporarily visible before slipping into a temporary invisibility, in a field of unconscious representations, from which it can return again to visibility, as when I carry out a recollection or an analysis that allows me to recover repressed memories. Here we are in the domain of the passage from the represented to the non-represented, such that this non-represented can always recover its condition as represented. It is the world of representation, the world as such. But our authentic reality is a reality of another kind. It is a very particular reality, which has always been in me and remains there invisibly—Freud would call it the unconscious—without ever becoming visible, or disappearing in the sense of descending into nothingness like representations do. So, should it be called the "unconscious" or should one adopt another term? Its real name is "life." It is life, if life is what I feel, what Descartes discovered in dreams, and what Freud finds at the depths of the unconscious. It is life as it is lived, only invisible, something that I can feel without it ever appearing before my eyes. All my experiences are of this kind. I feel anxiety, but I do not see it. Perhaps it will change my vision, and no doubt it will completely change the world of representation—this is one of Freud's major themes, and it was already brought up by Schopenhauer and Nietzsche. But anxiety in itself has a different nature from that of representation, without being other than myself. It is my own life.[14]

[Henry's reading of Nietzsche in Généalogie de la psychanalyse*]*

The value of Nietzsche is immense, insofar as he did not give a phenomenological description of life in terms of representation—in this putting at a distance through which a horizon of observation becomes possible—but even more important, he defined phenomenality as feeling or pathos. A figure like Dionysus, suffering and enjoying at the same time, is essentially the figure of a living being, because pleasure and pain are, in my view, the primary modalities of life and define it above all else. Life is need, and need implies suffering. It only exists on the affective plane. If need were not felt, it would be nothing. In Nietzsche, there is thus the deep desire to turn life into something splendid and to understand that this beauty comes from the fact that it is a revelation. Or rather an auto-manifestation, since each affect only reveals itself and feels itself. In sharp contrast with this abandonment of the unconscious to obscurity and anonymity, evidence of the phenomenological character of life can be found in Schopenhauer but also, in part, in Freud. This evidence resides in the fact that Nietzsche makes it the *originating principle* of all values, whereas in Schopenhauer it is the source of the absurdity of existence and in Freud the source of delirium, madness, and all kinds of fantasies. It is life that creates values;

values are not in nature or in objects, instead it is life that assigns value to them. From this, it follows that life is also the main route of evaluation. That is why the fundamental question to ask should be the following: Why is this source of any evaluation—life—itself also a value? And why is it a value in Nietzsche's eyes? Because it is good to be alive, because feeling oneself, which is characteristic of living beings and will be taken away from us when we die, is an extraordinary thing. For him, life is analyzed through different figures. One of the most important of them is the figure of the nobles, which is expressed as follows: "We the noble, the good, the happy . . . ." What justifies life is happiness. This is why we need to defend life against everything that violates it and, in particular, according to Nietzsche, against the process that leads it to turn against itself, which is the most terrible of all. One of Nietzsche's most inspired discoveries is to have recognized this movement of self-destruction in human experience. And when he discovers this process, of which suicide is only an external manifestation, he recoils in horror by saying: What a strange animal is the human being, which destroys itself! Then this self-destructive trend is in the service of the bad conscience, the feeling of guilt, and gives rise to self-disgust, fatigue, and malaise. For him, there is indeed a sickness of life, but the most terrible thing is that this sickness is also the consciousness of suffering, except that it is no longer a suffering that leads toward life but a will to destroy oneself. Suffering thus has a dual role for Nietzsche: it brings us into life, in the condition of feeling oneself and, at the same time, it unleashes the process of self-destruction, which we can still see before our eyes in the modern world.[15]

[Returning to this process of self-destruction, Henry explains how the contrast between the knowledge of life and objective knowledge leads to a critique of civilization that, after La barbarie *in 1987 and directly from his study of Marx in 1976, he exposes in 1990 with* Du communisme au capitalisme*]*

In this work, I develop a dual critique. The first is directed against Marxism and shows how ideological Marxism is responsible not only for the totalitarian political deviance of communist regimes but also, more deeply, for their economic failure. And it is precisely with the help of Marx's theories that I strive to make this collapse transparent. Their collapse is due to the fact that Marxism replaced life, "living people," "living work," "subjective work force" (which plays an instrumental and creative role in the economic manuscripts gathered under the heading of Book III of the *Capital*) with a series of abstract, ideal objective entities—like "Society" and its analysis in terms of "classes," "history," its "movement," "contradictions," etc.—that Marx had, in fact, severely criticized. Marx's key insight is that only life and, therefore, individuals (because life for him only exists in an individual form) have strength, power, and effectiveness. The replacement of these acting individuals by abstract entities can only mean, with the elimination of all effective power, immobility, inertia, and eventual ruin. No one has ever seen society or a class doing anything whatsoever, such as digging a trench or building a house. To do this, as Marx said, "there must be human beings." It is this progressive invasion of inertia, the fact that individuals no longer did anything and no longer wanted to do anything, which explains why nothing was done and why it ultimately failed. But, since individuals continue to live, to be hungry, etc., and since the satisfaction of these needs no longer follows the age-old path of labor and effort, it can only be gained by a series of uses of force—the underground market, trafficking, and looting—that ultimately result in poverty. Today, everyone is opposed to Marxism, which has lost, and so the only option now available to humanity are the benefits of "free enterprise" and the "market economy"—that is, in reality, capitalism. Indeed, as equivocal as they may be, the successes of capitalism are based solely on the fact that it has exploited the force of individual work to the greatest degree, and, within a few decades, this is what allowed for the transformation of the face of the planet and for the constitution, according to Marx, of the only true revolution that humanity has ever known. It is needless to recall the number of sufferings and calamities that were caused by this upheaval.

But, and this is the second part, the second criticism of my *Du communisme au capitalisme*, in the past, capitalism has experienced many "crises," and today it has come to the point that its existence, and the existence of the human beings involved in this regime, is becoming increasingly impossible. Marx rigorously examined the various contradictions of capitalism, but through a phenomenology of life it is possible to go back to their ultimate principle. This principle is precisely the same as the one that explains the fall of Marxist regimes. Here again, it is the replacement of life with a set of abstractions that will take its place and gradually take away its right to exist. The ultimate contradiction of capitalism, in effect, is not strictly economic; it is a contradiction between capitalism and technology, which is more noticeable in industrialized countries where technology turns against capitalism in order to erode it from the inside and lead inexorably to its ruin. Let's not forget Marx's central thesis, which takes on a decisive significance in light of a phenomenology of life: only living work—the activity of subjective life—can produce exchange value and money. The unbridled development of modern technology, under the sway of what I call "Galilean science," eliminates in a gradual but inevitable way the living work of the real process of production and, at the same time, the money that is only an objective representative of this actual subjective work. With the trend to eliminate money, the functioning of the economic process of capitalism is compromised; the crisis becomes permanent and widespread. On the one hand, products are exchanged and sold more and more difficultly, and on the other hand, individuals (living work) are excluded from social activity, placed out of economic circuit, and thus reduced to unemployment. The world of technology is invasive objectivity. Productive activity is transferred to more sophisticated material mechanisms, to advanced machines and computers whose functions, which tend toward self-control and self-regulation, replace everywhere the subjective and real work that has defined human existence up to now. The human being thus becomes unnecessary in a world whose surface comes to resemble more and more the microphysics of the material world's substructure. This terrifying situation, where life fades away and gives way to inertia and death, characterizes the techno-capitalist world. Its striking advance appears right before our eyes. If we were to compare this techno-scientific and techno-capitalist world, which triumphs in the West, with the Marxist regimes that just collapsed in the East, we can see that, though they follow different temporalities, the same peril resides within them. By substituting abstractions and dead objectivities for the real life of human beings—abstractions of Marxist theory, on the one hand, and abstractions constitutive of the economy and technology, on the other—they put this life out of play and, along with it, the human beings who are defined by this life.[16]

[The constitutive forgetting of the essence of life]

Life is constantly misguided but never in such a way as to lose itself, because that would be death. Life is such that it also necessarily has life. The only danger that could occur, and this is one of the great insights of Nietzsche, is that it would turn against itself. This is what is happening today with nihilism: because suffering belongs to life and because it is inscribed in the essence of life as one of its possibilities, life refuses suffering and negates itself. Anything becomes possible afterward. It is death. Death in all its forms, collective or personal death, is absolute evil. Our own times seem worrisome due to the nihilism of life that says no to life. Why? The solution proposed in *La barbarie* is that life can no longer bear itself. Life is constantly backed up against itself; it is in a situation of anxiety. Kierkegaard saw clearly that being a self, that is to say someone who affects oneself, is to carry a native anxiety within oneself. There is no other solution than to find, at the bottom of this anxiety, in this crashing into oneself [*écrasement contre soi*], the surpassing of life—because it comes to me and because I am always, by absolutely being myself, surpassed by something beyond me. I do not create myself. This is why Stirner's thesis is absurd.[17] The self does not affect itself in the sense that it would create itself but in the sense that it exists in auto-affection. In crashing into oneself and being thrown by life, there is a possibility in anxiety—a permanent possibility—of a kind of intoxication [. . .]. For enjoyment has the same structure as suffering. This type of enjoyment of oneself is also more than oneself, as is the case in love with the joy of the other. Life is that way. It is the work of God, the absolute. That is a limit to my phenomenology. This is the key to my life as well as to the world. My phenomenology is a dangerous thought, not a watered down spiritualism. It contains in itself the tragic, the possibility of the greatest joys and great adventures, like those of Kandinsky and many others before.[18]

[Kandinsky, art, life, and "the invisible"]

I believe that Kandinsky's example is striking, because he did it with regard to painting. Obviously, painting is a visual art. It is made out of visible elements and its fundamentals are forms and colors. That is why painting has always been considered an art of the visible, whose flesh is the visible. Let's start with colors. Kandinsky shows how a canvas is organized around a color. In a glade near Munich, for example, he sees a color and paints what is around it. He paints a picture that is composed on the basis of red, a red note, etc. But when he reflects on his topic, he says that this color appears to be a part of exteriority. There is a kind of red spot, even though he no longer thinks of this red as the red of a blotting or the red of a woman's lips or her scarf: it is always something that unfolds in a first world, even if this is not a utilitarian world. In truth, he added, the reality of this color is an impression, *a radically subjective impression*. He does not make any philosophical references, but I can say that it is the position of Descartes as well as that of Husserl as a phenomenologist. For Husserl, before color is an aspect or quality of the object, a "noematic color," it *is* a pure sensing. It *is* a *cogitatio* of the same order as fear in Descartes's dream. This is how color is double. First of all, it is a red that I see on the palette, but at the same time I am fooled by an illusion if I believe that red is limited to this spot I see on the palette. In truth, the reality of red is the impression that this red spread across the palette creates in me. This impression is the true essence of color. [. . .] Red is a sensation, and this sensation is absolutely subjective and originally invisible. Originally colors are invisible, but they are extended onto things through a process of projection. [. . .] If one looks, for example, at an adoration of the Magi painted in the Quattrocento, one can admire the scene where the Magi arrive covered with wonderful clothes and bring their presents to the most humble being. This theme gives rise to wonderful compositions. It has been chosen because it allowed for the aesthetic use of sensation. No painter ever saw the adoration of the Magi. The painters had no reason to give Gaspar or Balthasar a yellow rather than red garment. They had no reason to represent them in one way or another. The choice, which seems to correspond to the rich clothing of the time, could only be one that is situated in a place other than objective representation. What is this place? *It is the emotional power of color*. This has been an object of classical reflection since Goethe, but it becomes fundamental for Kandinsky who takes on the task of studying the emotional power of each color. He sees that yellow is an aggressive color coming toward the spectator, while blue is a soothing color that moves away. Therefore blue will be put here and yellow there, depending on whether one wants to give the impression of a thing coming toward you and attacking you or soothing you. Every color will be the subject of an emotional and dynamic analysis, and this analysis will deliver the real reason why a color was used. This reason no longer resides outside, in the visible, but in the emotional, impressional power of the color. The whole law of construction of the canvas is torn away from the world to be situated in a radical subjectivity. One will not try to paint the world but the soul of people, their emotions. But one can also show that if the painter chose to represent this or that thing, it is because this thing, because of its colors, has this impressional effect on him. Even so-called figurative painting confirms this point.

If we consider forms, the proof is even more striking. A form is not a kind of external entity; it is the expression of a force. The point, the straight line, the zigzag line, etc., are the expression of specific forces that are deployed in different ways, either continuously or intermittently, either in the same direction or in a different one. And the theory of forms refers to forces, but it also refers to subjectivity, because forces reside within our bodies, our lived body, and our subjective body, which is our real body. As a result, the world of forms is in some way an encoded world whose true meaning refers back to the play of forces within us and thus to life, because the living body is a body that is made up of forces. That is the origin of the painting. Here again, an invisible element, the *invisible force* with which the living body is identified, is the principle of the composition of painting.

Painting offers an explicit theme for expressing life, and in this regard it is connected with music. Music never sought, apart from representational music that everyone recognizes to be superficial, to imitate the sound of the wind or that of water on stones. It has always sought to express life, thus giving reason in advance for a phenomenology of life. It expresses nothing. It does not express the horizon of the world or any of its objects. [. . .] One can even conceive that all art, even the more external, expresses affectivity and refers back to the living body. [. . .][19]

The image of art is the *resurrection of life in us*. One can try to understand this relationship between the living being and life—how life generates the living being within itself—in the way that Meister Eckhart does. Then, one must be placed squarely in God, which we are not, in order to understand how life necessarily generates—in order to be alive—a first living being. Life can only exist as a self. This is fundamentally what Christianity says. It is the only deep and intelligent thought about the human being.[20]

[Phenomenology and religion]

I did not begin from Christianity but phenomenology. It is later, by rereading the texts of the New Testament, that I discovered, with some emotion, that the theories implied by these texts were those to which the internal development of my philosophy had led—namely, (1) the definition of the absolute (God) as Life; (2) the affirmation that the process of life as coming into oneself and as an experience of oneself necessarily generates an ipseity in which it feels itself and thus is revealed to itself—which is its Word. As such, this does not happen at the end of this process but belongs constitutively to its performance and is thus contemporaneous with it: "In the beginning was the Word"; (3) What we call the human being, that is to say the transcendental living self that each of us is, can only be understood on the basis of this immanent process of life and never on the basis of the world. For me, the "theological turn" of contemporary phenomenology is not a "deviation" or denigration of phenomenology but its fulfillment [. . .].[21]

One can easily see that what philosophers call the absolute, religion calls God. But if the philosopher says that the absolute is life and if John says that God is life, they are speaking about the same thing in different languages. The phenomenology of life is thus not an artificial veneer of philosophy placed over the doctrinal body of Christianity. It simply recognizes that the object of philosophy and religion are the same. And as if by chance, John says not only that God is life but also that God is love; he thus gives God an affective definition [. . .]. Of course, I do not claim to reduce Christianity to a philosophy of life. It is a religion, which is to say that it concerns the mode of life of beings. It does not require them to think this, but to act. I was in my own element when, after my encounter with Maine de Biran in 1946, I came to regard action as more essential than thought. In the New Testament, it is never said that the "truth" is a universal truth in the sense of a rational truth, and being is not reduced to this truth. This corresponds with what I think. For me, the truth, to the extent that it is "life," contains an ipseity, since living is feeling oneself and there is no experience of oneself that does not have a self within it. The truth is thus linked, for essential reasons, to individuality. In the famous prologue to the Gospel of John, one finds that God generates a self that feels itself and is revealed to itself, and this is God's Word.[22]

[Whether this reading of Christianity reintroduces a certain transcendence into the phenomenological immanence of life]

It is a question that I am often asked. I've always avoided it. One must distinguish, in my view, between two radically different senses of transcendence. First, there is the transcendence of the phenomenologists, which simply means the fact that my consciousness is directed toward something. Transcendence in the Husserlian sense means that intentional consciousness goes out toward an object, even the most modest one, which it grasps immediately without passing through a representation. It grasps "the thing itself." And this object is said to be transcendent. Here transcendence has the most trivial sense. It is the transcendent object in relation to my regard. This causes a huge ambiguity because the traditional sense of the word "transcendence" is a religious one that refers to God; it means something that is outside of the world, something that is a-cosmic, like the life that I am talking about. It is invisible because it does not show itself in the world: I cannot see or touch it. This is a huge equivocation. There are two totally different senses of transcendence! However, both the stroke of genius and the ambiguity of Heidegger is that he collapses one sense into the other. This way of reaching the thing in the world and of being in the world, which was the "transcendent" for Husserl, was the transcendence of Being itself [for Heidegger]. "Transcendent Being" for Heidegger is the horizon of exteriority, which is itself already ungraspable, in which I can grasp something. "Being is the *transcendens* pure and simple," he said.[23] There is an evasion and a source of confusion here because people cannot recognize these gods, especially when God has traditionally been defined as the absolute in all of the scholastic or theological conceptions. Then, since Heideggerian being is not the same as the being that is traditionally identified with God, Being appears to have several different meanings. For me, God is life, and for Christianity and Christ also. To say that the human being is the Son of God is to define the human being by life. This is not the case for a rock, which is not the son of another rock. The problem of being, of the Being of beings, and of their difference, appears secondary and foreign to the fundamental and original relationship of the living being to Life [. . .].

I believe that there is a fundamental alterity in life. Egology is surpassed to the extent that there is a transcendental birth of the ego. I no longer begin with the *ego cogito*, like Descartes, but I maintain that the ego was brought into itself. This is the theory of ipseity: ipseity is not at all an egology. One cannot confuse ipseity with the ego, because the ego is only an ego on the basis of an ipseity that gives it to itself and without which it is pointless. Put otherwise, there can only be an ego and an I through the fundamental ipseity of the self, and it is the self of life. Life—the absolute life, the life that is self-generated, the life that Meister Eckhart talks about, the life that auto-affects itself in a radical sense—generates an ipseity within itself through a feeling of oneself. In and through this ipseity, multiple I's and multiple egos become possible. I have shown in my book on Christianity [*C'est moi la verité*] how the ego is engendered by a fundamental ipseity, which is itself engendered by an absolute life. There is a process of transcendental birth of the ego and the only thinker who perceived this without theorizing it was Kierkegaard. He affirmed that we are a transcendental Self, a Self with an upper case S, that there is no human being independent from a transcendental Self, since there is no biological definition of the human being. If one says that the human being is a "rational" animal, one runs up against the fact that reason is impersonal. Moreover, this is also subject to caution since one can conceive of [forms of] reason other than our own, as Descartes did, since, according to him, the rational truths are created. There are thus other possible worlds. There are other structures for apprehending things. But this is not the case for the Self, because the Self is something that one relates to absolutely, according to an unbreakable relation that cannot be other than what it is. To relate to oneself is not an ek-static relation but a relation of pathos. There is indeed a transcendence in the traditional sense, but this transcendence is not at all ek-static. It is the relation, unthought up to the present day, of the living being to life. At bottom, this is the experience that mystics have and that all people experience unwittingly. They live through this experience because they are nothing other than it. But they live through it without knowing it, because they live in a stupor, in a sort of fascination toward the world of radical alienation. The modern world increases this state at breathtaking speed through the media, whose images are anti-art.[24]

[On ethics]

I am convinced that philosophy must have this dimension for the simple reason that ethics has always been what allows us to live. The activities of devotion and creation are the means for life to fulfill itself. This presupposes that life is not something simple. It is a mistake to believe that biology on its own can pave the way for an investigation of ethics. It provides the means, not the ends; it is up to the human being to decide; it is always life that decides. Who can say "Thou shall not kill" except for life? This prohibition is a positive word, because life says that it is infinite. But it is a transcendental life, not an inert life. Has anyone ever seen an electron become world champion? Ethical issues can only be raised on the human level. The legitimacy of this level must therefore be recognized—not to forget the fact that it is by defining this level by something prior to the human that one is situated in the domain of ethics *ipso facto*. [. . .] The etymology of the word "religion"—*re-ligare*—offers a path: this is the link, the link between my life and the absolute. This link itself opens ethics because the way of living this link determines human life, and ethics is nothing more than that. I can live by denigrating this link or by giving it its full meaning. It is not by chance that religions have always had an ethics, and it is not a matter of chance that now that religion is undergoing a crisis, so too is ethics. In *Incarnation*, I reflected on the deep human condition in order to understand that our life is a finite life and, to that extent, that it is an infinite life. Our Self does not bring itself into the self that it is: I am not created by myself. I have come into life, and I did not bring about this arrival. It would be a mistake to believe that I would owe this to my parents who are exactly in the same situation as me. The coming of a Self into oneself presupposes a reality that could be called metaphysical or absolute. It puts me into my privileged condition, namely, of being a living being. If life is becoming, it is because it is located at this junction that we are. We are not only living and finite beings, but we are living beings who live an infinite life that makes us alive at every moment. The purpose of our life is to welcome this life into ourselves and to live from it. This can be done in multiple ways: in the work of creating, in the solitude of cloisters, or the simplicity of devotion.[25]

[The place a phenomenology of life, of these "living beings who live an infinite life," makes for an experience of death]

Death? I do not know what it is. To the degree that the I is carried by life, it *is* at each moment. Here I will also give credit to Descartes and to his profound theory of continual creation: it means that it is in the continual fold of life that my ego is continually formed. So, if this fold were to cease, then it would not be up to me to determine whether I would no longer be formed or whether I would continue to form myself. And I have come to think that we are in the hands of being or God, as is commonly said. Then, without a direct experience, death is an idea that has its foundation in life. Inasmuch as I feel myself at each moment as not being the basis of my being, I have the experience that I can die and that I am under the discretion of that power. The idea of death is the projection into the future of the condition of a being that is not the basis of itself. That does not have to be taken in a negative way. Quite the contrary, this condition signifies the experience of life as an experience that comes to me, from this flow that occurs within me and of which I am not the source. Just like this experience, or connected to it, this gives rise to the idea that this occurrence could no longer happen. This is a very strange connection between the idea of death and the experience of the profusion of life, of the life that abounds in me, without me, and through this phenomenon makes me completely myself. It is a question that today I am defining better and better, but in its mysterious and enigmatic nature. One should not forget that it all comes from pathos, from the non-objective, and that it can never be defined as one would define a square or triangle. One can only refer to something invisible in its own presence, to a pathos.[26]

[Primacy of life over thought]

I think that the most profound project of Husserlian phenomenology was to think life—the transcendental life of the ego that Husserl tended to confuse with the absolute. The phenomenological reduction is always the method for realizing this project, and it always ends up in failure or *aporia*. This is because it is absurd to try to attain life through thought, through an intentional regard—a *sehen und fassen*—that is cast onto the world, where life is never held. Only life can give us access to life. Life is revealed through a pathetic immediacy that is a concrete auto-impression, a "flesh." Instead of thought allowing us to reach life in itself and to "give" us life, it is life that allows each thought to feel oneself originally in this immediacy that was seen by Descartes. Life gives thought itself as a living thought. [This] implies a new concept of the Word that would be able to [call into question] these theories of language that have proliferated without at all suspecting the archaic language of life. Without it, ordinary language would have nothing to say and ideology itself, as Marx admirably saw, is only its "language" [. . .]. [27]

Language is not what was repeated on the basis of Kojève's seminar.[28] Kojève himself, in the 1930s, was repeating the ideas of the young Hegel who believed that language is the murder of reality. From the moment I pronounce the word "dog," I kill the real dog, since the word "dog" is not a real dog. Clearly, the conception of language implied at work in my books is the opposite of this. My language is a happy language. There is no problem of language in my opinion. When I received the Renaudot Prize for *L'Amour les yeux fermés*, I was asked, "What is language for you?" I replied that language does not exist. If I am talking about, for example, how a dog's barking bothers me, language, the words that I use, and the sentences that I form, have no reality in the sense that they are not objects of consciousness. This language is not language itself. It is still the language of something else, and it fades away in front of this extremely powerful reference. If you are in a train and you look at the landscape, you don't look at the glass. Language is this transparent glass. When I say that language does not exist, I mean the discursive language that we use without paying attention to it. In fact, I was concerned about language but otherwise and on another level. When I write, I rewrite every sentence until it gives me satisfaction and coincides with my breathing, and more profoundly, when it is animated by the pathos that I am seeking. Language is perhaps a window but what it lets us see, in the end, is not the barking dog that I don't care about: it is *pathos*. I recently had to rework the question of *Logos*. I noticed that the language spoken by the Greeks and after them by Heidegger is a *Logos* of the world, that is to say, a language that discloses things. As for myself, what I naturally looked for is a language that discloses affects. And to do this, language itself must ultimately affect. That is to say that revelation is not seeing what the word refers to, or what the word lets us see; it is pathos. In short, it is not a *logos* of knowledge [. . .].[29]

In the arch-revelation of pathos, life is a Word and [. . .] every human word ultimately has meaning only in reference to that Word [. . .]. The way that life comes into oneself—its auto-donation as an auto-appearing—consists of the pathos we are talking about [. . .]. Suffering, anxiety, drives, enjoyment: these are the "reference points" that make life into a philosophical question. These reference points have two essential features: they are precisely not the objects that a regard would take into view in order to analyze their properties—they overwhelm us and hold us in an indistinctness that no distance will ever break. From this, a second feature follows—the non-ecstatic crushing and immersion of drives and affects within themselves never ceases. The reference points for a philosophical questioning of life are always there, not in the contingent "there" of the theoretical regard but in the silent arrival of life into oneself that is always auto-impressing in an endless embrace. Thus the transcendental motifs that continually question life philosophically are inherent to the deployment of its essence and are identical to it. Suffering is a reference point that is older than every living being and delivers each one into life and its essential determinations, but in order for there to be philosophy, apart from the suffering that motivates it, this must also be taken into the aim of a regard that can provide a thematic clarification of it. Philosophy as phenomenology is a clarification of this kind and can only be carried out in this way. How could that happen if life withdrew from the seeing of any intentionality whatsoever, including a theoretical one? In the first place, life makes use of the ability to re-present itself, that is to say, to make images of itself. Through a variation of these images, it can construct the *eidos* of its own essence as well as the plurality of its essential features. These noematic essences produced by fiction in eidetic seeing together constitute a rational phenomenology of our transcendental life. Two conditions are required for that: first, the contribution in and through life of what thought will then seek to know, that is, suffering, drives, and their immanent destiny; second, the duplicity of appearing, *the phenomenological arch-fact*, that is, the phenomenality that phenomenalizes in pathos while life also opens onto a world, is such that it is never shown in the world but only reveals itself in the flesh of its pathos. It is represented there, however, and can be represented there, as an image or essence in a noematic irreality. But this representation of life would not be possible if life were not held first and forever in itself—and if this opening onto a world did not auto-affect itself as such. Intentionality only exists as intentional *life* and in this form alone.[30]

Translated by Scott Davidson

Notes

1. "Le statut phénoménologique de la vie," interview with Thibault Dhermy, appeared in *Lettres philosophiques* 6 (1992), and was reprinted in Henry, *Autodonation*, 67.

2. From an interview with Bogdan Mihai Mandache, in *Cronica*, October 1992, reprinted in Henry, *Entretiens*, 87–89.

3. Jules Lachelier was an influential French Kantian, to whom Henri Bergson dedicated his *Essai sur les données immédiates de la conscience*, and is the author of *Du Fondement de l'induction suivi de psychologie et métaphysique*. Jules Lagneau was a student of Lachelier. Émile Boutroux was a French philosopher and historian of philosophy and is the author of *The Contingency of the Laws of Nature*. Alain, pseudonym of Émile-Auguste Chartier, was an essayist and philosopher and is the author of over forty books. Jean Nabert was an influential proponent of "re-

flexive" philosophy and is the author of *L'Expérience intérieure de la Liberté*. Pierre Lachièze-Rey is the author of *Le Moi, le Monde et Dieu*.

4. From an interview with Thierry Galibert, in *Autre Sud* 2 (December 2000), reprinted in Henry, *Entretiens*, 130.

5. From an interview with Roland Vaschalde, "Un philosophe parle de sa vie," in *Michel Henry, l'épreuve de la vie*, ed. Alain David and Jean Greisch, 16–17.

6. From an interview with Sébastien Labrusse, "L'invisible et la révélation," *Autrement* 12 (1993): 79–97, reprinted in Henry, *Entretiens*, 109–10.

7. Interview with Bogdan Mihai Mandache, 89–91.

8. From an interview with Jérôme Thor, "Une politique du vivant," in Henry, *L'amour les yeux fermés*, reprinted in Henry, *Auto-donation*, 224–25.

9. From an interview with Isabelle Gaudé, "Un parcours philosophique," *Le Journal des Grandes Ecoles* (June-July-August 2001), reprinted in Henry, *Auto-donation*, 166–67.

10. From an interview with Thibault Dhermy, "Le statut phénoménologique de la vie," *Lettres philosophiques* 6, (1992), reprinted in Henry, *Auto-donation*, 66–70.

11. Interview with Isabelle Gaudé, 161.

12. Interview with Isabelle Gaudé, 165–66.

13. Interview with Sébastien Labrusse, 107–8.

14. From an interview with Sergio Benvenuto, "L'émergence de l'inconscient dans la pensée occidentale," published in English as "Emergence of the Unconscious in Western Thought."

15. Interview with Sergio Benvenuto, 85–86.

16. Interview with Bogdan Mihai Mandache, 94–96.

17. Max Stirner is the author of *Der Einzige und sein Eigentum* (1845), reprinted in *The Ego and Its Own*.

18. Henry, *Entretien avec O. Salazar-Ferrer*, 48–49.

19. From an interview with Magali Uhl and Jean-Marie Brohm, "Art et phénoménologie de la vie," in Henry, *Auto-donation*, 203–6.

20. Interview with Magali Uhl and Jean-Marie Brohm, 214–15.

21. From "Entretien avec Sabrina Cusano," in Henry, *Entretiens*, 153–54.

22. Interview with Thierry Galibert, 131.

23. See Heidegger, *Being and Time*, 38: "Being and the structure of Being lie beyond every entity and every possible character which an entity may possess. *Being is the* transcendens *pure and simple*."

24. Interview with Magali Uhl and Jean-Marie Brohm, 212–14.

25. Interview Thierry Galibert, 140–41.

26. From an interview with Roland Vaschalde, "La subjectivité originaire. Critique de l'objectivisme," in Henry, *Auto-donation*, 82–83.

27. Interview with Sabrina Cusano, 154.

28. A French philosopher of Russian origin, Alexandre Kojève is best known for his 1933–1939 course on Hegel at the Ecole Pratique des Hautes Etudes in

Paris, which was edited by Raymond Queneau and published as *Introduction à la lecture de Hegel.*

29. From an interview with Mireille Calle-Gruber, "Narrer le pathos," in Henry, *Phénoménologie de la Vie*, vol. 3, 322.

30. Interview with Thibault Dhermy, 70–72.

The Phenomenology of Life

RENAUD BARBARAS

When and with whom did your interest in phenomenology begin?

My interest in phenomenology was sparked very early on, in secondary school, when a professor had me read Heidegger and Merleau-Ponty. I didn't understand it all, but I felt that this manner of thinking corresponded to what I was looking for in doing philosophy. Very early, I saw myself working on Merleau-Ponty, but while I was doing my studies at the École normale supérieure de Saint-Cloud (as well as at university), I found myself thrown into a very different atmosphere, one that was essentially hostile toward phenomenology. It was the end of the 1970s and the philosophical scene was dominated by two kinds of approaches that were opposed in all respects, even if certain individuals lay claim to both simultaneously. On the one hand, there was a Marxist-inspired perspective according to which philosophy was, as it were, in the service of political action. There was thus no philosophy outside of political philosophy, philosophy of science, or epistemology. Everything else was "bourgeois." At the École normale supérieure de Saint-Cloud, this particular current was very strongly represented, and someone like Desanti, whom I had as a professor, was a major reference. On the other hand, another current of thought, which has subsequently become known as the "thought of '68" [*pensée '68*], blossomed primarily at Vincennes and was dominated by Deleuze, Lyotard, and Foucault.[1] And yet—this is quite striking—there was no real place for phenomenology, in any case not for the kind of phenomenology to which I subsequently dedicated myself. That's how I remember it, at least. In truth, one would have to be a bit more nuanced, since Husserl clearly enjoyed a certain prestige on account of the "scientific" character of his project, and Heideggerianism, moreover, was already very active even if it was not represented much in academia, as it later would be in the 1980s. In any case, this period was characterized by the fact that phenomenology was not taught at universities and was often the object of violent critiques, both by Marxist-inspired thinkers and by those whom we called the "desirers" [*les désirants*] at the time (Deleuze, Lyotard). On the other hand, the only phenomenology that was officially recognized was German (Husserl, Heidegger). During this period—which, by the way, lasted a very long time—a strange theoretical Germanophilia was prominent, one that supposed that rigor and seriousness were to be found only in German philosophy and that French authors, however well they wrote, produced merely epigonic philosophy allergic to methodological reflection and without real theoretical consistency.

No "French" phenomenology, then?

It is no exaggeration to say that at the time there was no place for French phenomenology. Sartre was still alive but it had been forgotten that he had written *L'être et le néant*. Lévinas was still unknown. It was precisely these authors, Merleau-Ponty above all, who interested me practically from the outset, and it was starting with them that I worked my way back, as it were, to Husserl and Heidegger. I remember having discovered and read Lévinas's *Le temps et l'autre* toward the end of the 1970s with the feeling that it was the book of a secret writer whom my fellow students had never heard of. And as for Merleau-Ponty, we were lost in the wilderness. Nobody spoke of him, and when he was mentioned, it was either to criticize his political positions of the late 1950s or to stigmatize his lack of rigor and originality and the literary, "metaphorical" (as they put it) character of his work. All these qualifications were clearly signs of scorn. I remember the reactions of consternation, notably at the École normale supérieure, when I suggested the possibility of working on him. I should add that a thinker such as Bergson, whom I have also worked on, was the object of comparable scorn and that we had to wait until the 1990s for him to be recognized as the great philosopher that he is and to be rehabilitated, so to speak. In any case, the consequence of this situation was that my interest in phenomenology was neither excited nor encouraged by anyone; on the contrary, it was forged against the circumstances. Although I've offered courses on phenomenology every year since I began university teaching, I did not attend a single course on phenomenology during all my years of study. I worked alone. I certainly lost a lot of time, particularly in assimilating Husserl's thought, and I still harbor the feeling that I'm something of an amateur. In a sense, I also gave into the pressure in the air, a demand that one work on the history of philosophy, or a classic author or, at the very least, an established figure. After writing a master's thesis on Leibnizian dynamics and metaphysics and obtaining the *agrégation*, I began a doctoral thesis on Leibniz. What interested me in him was precisely that which escaped the sphere of logic and the principle of non-contradiction, that which seemed to go beyond his powerful rationalism, namely, everything that touched on the question of the world and its creation: compossibility, the point of view and finitude of the monad, etc.

How did you get back to phenomenology?

I quickly became aware that the questions underlying my research found much more fertile ground in phenomenology, and so after several years of conceding to the academic norm, I returned to phenomenology with enthusiasm. I discovered Merleau-Ponty's *Le visible et l'invisible* (from the start and for a long time thereafter, Merleau-Ponty's "working notes" for the book fascinated me) and I quickly decided (in the beginning of the 1980s) to devote my doctoral thesis to Merleau-Ponty's ontology. This starting point was clearly quite decisive for my own work. It is significant that there was at the time no specialist on Merleau-Ponty or even a phenomenologist who could have supervised my thesis; so I wrote it under a notable Hegelian, Bernard Bourgeois.[2] Needless to say, for the reasons I've just listed, I found myself completely isolated in my generation. Nobody shared my interest in Merleau-Ponty's phenomenology. It was only upon finishing my thesis that I approached the phenomenologists who had worked on Merleau-Ponty and who were—all of them—appreciably older than me. I'm thinking here of Jacques Garelli and Marc Richir[3]—both of whom lay claim, albeit in different ways, to the thought of Merleau-Ponty—and Françoise Dastur, who distinguished herself in the Heideggerian circles she was a part of by the fact that she bore great interest in the work of Merleau-Ponty.

Nevertheless, your investment in Husserl—you'd be the first to admit—is not at all negligible, and it is significant that, as you say, you "worked your way back" to him via Merleau-Ponty. In your work, you have insisted on the constitutive value of what Husserl referred to as the "correlational a priori" for the entire post-Husserlian tradition (Heidegger, Merleau-Ponty, Michel Henry, Jan Patočka). How would you define the "correlational a priori" and what problem(s) in phenomenology and the history of philosophy did it respond/give rise to?

I became interested in the universal correlational a priori because, following the path opened up by Merleau-Ponty, my own work takes questions about perception as its starting point. Basically, I could say that my initial approach was to take note of a gap in Husserl between the crucial discovery of the theory of adumbration (*Abschattungslehre*) and the conceptuality within which it is formulated. This conceptuality remains tributary to a phenomenology of reason dominated by an ideal of adequation and is, for this reason, removed from, if not in contradiction with, the essence of perception as givenness by adumbration [*donation par esquisses*]. So I had to take measure, as it were, of the theory of adumbration, which meant thinking *according to it* and forging a conceptuality starting from it alone instead of submitting it to one that had already been constituted. Now, perception is a privileged form of the correlation; indeed, correlation is, in the *Crisis of the European Sciences*, specifically elaborated with the example of perception. If I have insisted on the importance of this correlational a priori, it is first of all simply because Husserl himself writes, in a quite remarkable note, that "The first breakthrough of this universal a priori of correlation between experienced object and manners of givenness (which occurred during work on my *Logical Investigations* around 1898) affected me so deeply that my whole subsequent life-work has been dominated by the task of systematically elaborating on this a priori of correlation."[4] In a certain sense, the constitution of phenomenology in Husserl merges with the elaboration of this a priori, which, in turn, represents, to my mind, the necessary framework within which, or beginning with which, phenomenology has developed since Husserl, even when the goal was to criticize or, at the very least, inflect it differently. Husserl formulates the correlational priori in the title of §48: "Anything that is—whatever its meaning and to whatever region it belongs—is an index of a subjective system of correlations."[5] The key point here is to understand that we are no longer on the level of empirical factuality but on that of a universal a priori. Husserl's formulation does not mean that being [*l'étant*] is *in fact* given only in subjective appearances but rather that the essence of being *is* its relation to such appearances, which Husserl calls a subjective system of correlation. Man can only relate to being via subjective appearances.

Husserl means something quite specific by "subjective" here . . .

The a priori rediscovers the obvious fact that everyone sees things and the world only as they appear to them, a fact that, accepted as such, leads to skepticism. But Husserl's stroke of genius is to give a radical philosophical sense to this fact by raising it to the level of essence, that is, by giving it an ontological signification. He goes beyond the correlation with an eidetic variation, the only possible mode of access to essence: "No conceivable human being, no matter how different we imagine him to be, could ever experience a world in manners of givenness which differ from the incessantly mobile relativity we have delineated in general terms, i.e., as a world pregiven to him in his conscious life and in community with fellow human beings."[6] If we see things as they appear to us—that is, only via their appearances [*apparitions*]—this is not because we are prisoners of our singular mode of perceiving or that we are separated from being as such by these appearances (which would then be nothing but appearances [*apparences*]). In other words, it isn't a question of regarding our finitude as obstructing access to being [*l'être*], an access that would in principle remain possible. If we see things as they appear to us it is because the essence of a thing, as opposed to that of lived experience, obliges it to reveal itself only via a series of adumbrations, since its being cannot be distinguished from its appearance. So the subjectivity of perception does not obstruct access to, but is rather the condition of access to the thing as such.

What does this say about the relation between being and appearance?

If the being of the thing entails its appearances, then its appearance to a subject delivers the very being of the thing: its appearance [*apparition*] is no longer a mere appearance [*apparence*] but a presentation, an ostension of the very thing. A knowledge that would proceed directly to things, passing over their appearances, so to speak (as classical rationalism would have it), is unthinkable: as Husserl said, God himself would perceive via adumbration. This ultimately entails returning the ground of our finitude to being itself: it is not—no longer—because we are finite and, in particular, subjugated to a sensible body that being dissimulates itself behind appearances. On the contrary, it is because the essence of being entails that it subtracts itself [*s'absente*] from its adumbrations (since they are only adumbrations of it) that we are sensible and finite beings. Husserl manages to situate himself beyond the alternatives of skepticism and dogmatic rationalism: being reveals itself only via subjective appearances, which are, however, the only possible mode of access to being itself, in person. It of course follows that, as Patočka says, "*as itself* and *in itself* are not the same thing"[7]: if, in perception, a thing is present in person, rather than only in a representation or an image, it is nonetheless not present as it is *in itself*, that is, exhaustively. On the contrary, it always retreats behind its adumbrations and subtracts itself from that which presents it.

The correlation is precisely that, a correlation, a reciprocal relation of the subject of perception to the object perceived . . .

Each of the terms in use here—transcendent being and subject (which is the condition, if not the site, of appearances)—determines its relation to the other term; neither of these two poles can be postulated outside of this correlation. A transcendent being that would remain entirely within itself cut off from all appearance—in short, that would exist only in itself—would not *be* at all. Likewise, a subject that would not relate to a being, that remained closed within itself instead of aiming at something other than itself, would destroy itself as subject. Here—one can see it—the choice between a certain realism and a certain idealism has been surpassed. We are beyond realism because being is always appearing being, relating as it does to subjectivity rather. It doesn't stand on its own. That it is being *for* a subject, however, does not entail that it is *in* the subject or that its being merges with that of the subject (as is the case, for example, in Berkeley). On the contrary, being's relation to subjectivity does not compromise its transcendence, since the being of subjectivity consists in transcending itself toward being: it is in its very transcendence that being is the correlate of a subjective system. There is no alternative between being given in appearances, on the one hand, and remaining transcendent, on the other: the transcendence of being corresponds to the inexhaustible character of the series of appearances—to nothing but that. This is the true sense of the theory of adumbration. If being is entirely relative to the subject, we are talking about a subject that remains thoroughly open to something other than itself. Thus we remain on this side of idealism, at least of dogmatic idealism. One can see, moreover, that the major themes of phenomenology follow from this correlation. To say that transcendent being is by its essence relative to appearances—that is, to a subject—is to open a path to the *épochè* as a neutralization of the thesis of existence. Indeed, the meaning of the *épochè* is that the thesis of existence is nothing to the world and that the world remains the world when it is suspended, which means that the being of the world is nothing other than its being for a consciousness. Likewise, to recognize that consciousness is by its essence relative to a transcendent being comes down to saying that its essence is characterized by *intentionality.*

To my mind, this correlation defines the minimal framework and, so to speak, the criterion of a phenomenological approach. The phenomenologist is one who knows that we can only arrive at the sense of being via its modes of appearance, the one who makes of our finitude the very measure, as it were, of being (and not only of phenomena, as in Kant), and who, for this reason, interrogates appearance as such and tries to make appearance appear. The phenomenologist is one who understands that consciousness is not a substance (as Descartes thought), one who is aware of the pitfalls of transcendental realism made evident by Husserl. The phenomenologist knows that the mode of being proper to consciousness cannot be identical to that of the objects of the world and must therefore be investigated for itself. In this sense, phenomenology places itself beyond the alternative between dualism and monism. It refuses the real or substantial duality of consciousness and the world since it places their correlation in the foreground. This amounts to a refusal of dualism. At the same time, phenomenology does not go beyond this correlation in order to posit a common element or fabric to which both subject and world would relate, which would abolish the distance that constitutes the correlation. In such a case the very dimension of appearance *to*—insofar as it entails a recipient distinct from that which appears—would be definitively compromised.

You say that both that the correlational a priori defines the minimal framework of phenomenology and that, in Husserl, it remains subordinated to a phenomenology of reason, defined by an ideal of adequation. How does one preserve the correlation without a phenomenology determined by this ideal?

Well, the ontological meaning of the correlated terms has to be investigated in the light of the correlation. Instead of reconstructing this correlation from a world and a subject whose ontological meaning has already been determined, we need to reconceive their ontological meaning starting from the correlation itself. Now, it isn't certain that Husserl fully succeeded in thinking the subject and the world from the standpoint of the correlation—I mean without any metaphysical prejudices. On the transcendent side, the difficulty is to respect the coordinates of appearance, I mean to think of a being that is relative to its appearances without letting this relativity compromise its transcendence. This implies recognizing an excess of that which appears [*l'apparaissant*] vis-à-vis its appearances [*apparitions*]—an excess that is nothing but its transcendence—without founding this excess on a positivity: the being that appears differs from its appearances without, for all that, being *other* than them. We are dealing here, in Merleau-Ponty's terms, with a pure transcendence "without ontic mask,"[8] a transcendence that can only have the meaning of an "identity within difference," identity within the difference between that which appears and its appearance. This means, this time in Husserlian terms, that we must separate originarity (*Leibhaftigkeit*) from adequation: that a thing presents itself does not mean that it presents itself *itself*—that is, that it is present as such in that which presents it (the appearances). As Merleau-Ponty clearly saw, to perceive is, in principle, not to know that which we perceive. Now, it's not certain that Husserl succeeded in preserving this disjunction between originarity (perception) and adequation (knowledge). Indeed, the phenomenology of reason imposes an equivalence between the rational thesis and being: to say of a thing that it is, is to say that I can in principle know it adequately. This affirmation runs into a head-on conflict with the theory of adumbration. Husserl resolves the problem by recourse to the Idea in the Kantian sense: there is an Idea of the adequate givenness of a thing as the pole of an infinity of adumbrations, an Idea that, as such, is finite and allows perception to progress. Suffice it to say that there is a tension between the point of view of reason and that of perception, and that, in the end, the ideal of an adequate givenness of the thing—that is, of a transparence of the real to knowledge—teleologically commands perception itself.

How does the matter stand with post-Husserlian phenomenology?

Post-Husserlian phenomenology will be particularly attentive to phenomena that prohibit this convergence and impose a disjunction between originarity and the horizon of adequation—all phenomena whose originarity excludes fulfillment and whose carnal presence implies a constitutive dimension of non-presence. Three orders of phenomena can, according to Husserl himself, be characterized in precisely this way and will, therefore, go on to constitute the privileged themes of the research undertaken by all of his successors. First, the *world*, which, as the prior frame or scene that guarantees perceptual fulfillment—that is, the continuability of experience [*continuabilité de l'expérience*]—can in no way be adequately or exhaustively given. The world is an originary presence with an irreducible dimension of absence: the world as such can never be fulfilled, or only "indirectly," by means of the perception of worldly beings. This theme will be dominant particularly in Merleau-Ponty and Patočka.

Secondly, *temporality*. With retention, we are in fact dealing with perception in a very particular sense, since what is presented is none other than an absence. Retention is an intentionality totally foreign to the intentionality that gives the object: it opens onto a pure transcendence and only possesses the past in being dispossessed by it. One could even claim—without risk—that all post-Husserlian phenomenologists have this in common: they brought into the foreground, no doubt according to very different modalities, this intentionality that constitutes originary temporality and, in a sense, saw in it the very model for all intentional performances [*prestation intentionnelle*].

Finally, the experience of *others* [*autrui*] highlights the disjunction between givenness in person and the possibility of fulfillment (and, a fortiori, of adequation). If others are present in person, they are present only in an apresentation, never a presentation (which would abolish their constitutive alterity): their presence contains a definitive absence, a presence I can only apprehend and confirm indirectly, by means of their bodies. Merleau-Ponty confessed very early on that the phenomenon of *others* turned him away from idealism and toward phenomenology. It goes without saying that Lévinas's approach could be described as a radicalization of this situation: others are not an object and they exceed the very order of the object, which is the order of the Same.

What about the other side, the side of the subject?

Well, on the side of the subject, the correlational a priori gives rise to problems that are possibly even more difficult. My own research is primarily rooted in tackling these problems. The subject of the correlation is submitted to a double constraint. On the one hand, insofar as it is the one to whom a thing appears—the operator or, at the very least, the recipient of appearance [*l'apparaître*]—it clearly cannot exist in the same mode as worldly beings [*étants mondains*]. When Husserl criticized Descartes for being a transcendental realist, this is what he meant. I believe that Husserl was profoundly aware of the necessity of radically desubstantializing the being of consciousness and of the difficulty involved in doing so. In an unedited manuscript, he writes that he who delivers us from the reification of consciousness will be the savior, if not the founder, of philosophy.[9] Husserl, I think, always tried to struggle against the reification of consciousness, and dereification is, to my mind, a watchword, a fundamental priority for the phenomenological enterprise. But, as Heidegger saw, Husserl doesn't go far enough: he doesn't interrogate the meaning of the *sum* (that is, the existence of the subject). This prevents him from thinking the *cogitare* and the *cogitatio* (that is, phenomenality itself) in a satisfying way. In any case, because Husserl remains prisoner to the presupposition according to which the meaning of worldly beings can only be univocal, he thinks that the *difference* in meaning between the world and the subject can only be one in which the latter is exterior to the world: the transcendental subject can only be different by being elsewhere, from which follows the affirmation that an "abyss of meaning" separates this absolute (consciousness) from reality. Of course, this position is correlated to the principle according to which objective reason has no limits: Husserlian subjectivism is the other side of an objectivism. The world can only adequately or transparently give itself to a consciousness that surveys it without being in it. Now, as Heidegger has emphasized, the fact that the world cannot be illuminated in its appearing by returning to a being with the same mode of being as the world "does not mean that what makes up the place of the transcendental is not an entity at all; rather, precisely at this juncture there arises the problem: What is the mode of being of the entity in which 'world' is constituted?"[10] Thus, if the mode of being of the subject and of the "transcendental" is other than that of worldly beings, it nevertheless remains the case that consciousness is still a being of the world. So the ontological meaning of the subject finds itself submitted to a second constraint: it can only constitute the world as such if it belongs to it like other beings, even if, of course, the meaning of this belonging cannot be the same.

And this follows from what you refer to as the "originary" meaning of the correlation?

Indeed, givenness by adumbration means that the subject of perception relates to the thing according to a perspective, such that it is necessarily situated in the world. The partial givenness of the thing is correlated to the intra-worldliness of the subject—an intra-worldliness of which its own body is the manifestation, if not the cause. Merleau-Ponty's merit consists in having drawn all the consequences from the fact that this relation between a situated subject and a world that only gives itself partially is not a simple state of affairs, one that doesn't call the claim to adequate knowledge [*le droit de la connaissance adéquate*] into question, the claim to the transparent coincidence of subject and world. This relation is the originary and irreducible situation from which the ontological meaning of both the subject and the world must be defined. The correlation is a correlation between a world that remains at a distance from a subject who belongs to it by his body.

However, in recognizing this correlation, one does not so much solve the problem as reformulate it. The question to which the correlation leads us, and that I have attempted for my part to confront, is the following: What is the ontological meaning of the subject insofar as it is at once the condition of the appearance [*apparition*] of the world and inscribed through and through within it? How does one reconcile—in one being—both the phenomenalization of the world and belonging to the world? Note that the formulation of the problem already points the way to its solution. It is a matter of thinking the ontological meaning of a subject that both escapes all forms of reification (and is, therefore, foreign to the mode of being of worldly things) and yet belongs fully to the world. Such a subject can clearly be situated in terms of movement: movement is in no way a thing (since it is the active negation of substantiality and identity), but it can nonetheless only unfold within the world, its space of play [*espace de jeu*]. In a sense, the subject needs the world in order not to be a thing. Thus, to escape from the reification of consciousness is to think of consciousness itself *as an effective escape from reification*, that is, as self-negation, movement. Only a dynamic phenomenology allows us to reconcile "transcendentality" with belonging . . .

How does this "dynamic phenomenology," grounded on the concept of corporeal movement, reconcile transcendentality and belonging?

One further step will, I believe, allow me to explain my own perspective: if substance is indeed that which needs only itself in order to exist, then to say that the being of the subject is absolutely non-substantial comes down to recognizing that the subject *needs something other than itself in order to exist*, that its being does not reside within itself—in short, that it is characterized by a *lack* of being.

If substantial being is defined by plenitude, then the being of the subject of the correlation is defined by lack. This means that the kind of movement by which it seems to me necessary to define the subject is not movement in the ordinary sense: its dynamism is governed by a search for the self in the other—it is aspiration. The world is in its being such that the subject actively moves toward it and, by this activity, both distinguishes itself from the things of the world and places itself thoroughly in the world. The major difficulty is thus to gain access to a mode of being where phenomenalization and belonging join together, both a difference vis-à-vis the world and a continuity or ontological kinship with the world.

Is it your considered view that Heidegger and Merleau-Ponty tried but failed to gain access to this mode of being?

Both Heidegger and Merleau-Ponty recognize the necessity of taking into account and articulating the two dimensions I just emphasized, but it seems to me that neither of them managed to think the unity of phenomenalization and belonging—ultimately, a meaning of being from which one or the other could be derived. Heidegger does emphasize the intra-worldliness of *Dasein,* but he does not give himself the means to ground this intra-worldliness in the existentials of *Dasein.* Nothing in his characterization of *Dasein*'s mode of being allows us to account for its belonging to a world. No doubt, the function of *Befindlichkeit* is to reveal *Dasein* and its *Geworfenheit,* to uncover it in its "There." But one could easily demonstrate that such an existential does not sufficiently account for all the dimensions of intra-worldliness—in short, that it supposes a flesh without defining it. In other words, *Dasein*'s potentiality-for-being [*pouvoir-être*] would remain incomprehensible were a more originary possibility not already given to us, a possibility that has us more than we have it and that is none other than the capacity to move ourselves, in which the true meaning of corporeality resides. The limit of the Heideggerian perspective consists in the fact that he never wanted to include the flesh among the existentials of *Dasein,* probably because he remained dependent on a naïve conception of the flesh as relevant to *Körperlichkeit*[11] [corporeality] and, therefore, *Vorhandenheit* [presence-at-hand]. Patočka was well aware of this: "It seems that the analytic makes Heidegger's ontology of existence too formal. Praxis is in fact the original form of clarity, but Heidegger never takes into consideration the fact that original praxis must be the activity of a *corporeal* subject, that corporeality must have an ontological status that cannot be identical with the occurrence of the body as present here and now."[12] Thus, Heidegger affirms an intra-worldliness that he does not truly ground in *Dasein.* He doesn't have access to an existential conception of the flesh. Ultimately, intra-worldliness is sacrificed for existence.

And Merleau-Ponty?

Intra-worldliness is Merleau-Ponty's real starting point, since for him it is a matter of accounting for perception—that is, of the pregnance [*prégnance*] of sense in the sensible—by returning to an incarnate subject as its unique and true condition.

Thus, in Merleau-Ponty's eyes, the dimension of the subject's belonging to the world is straight away thought in terms of corporeality: to say that the subject is of the world is to recognize that it has a body. However, insofar as reference to the subject's own body functions to account for perception (the incarnation of sense in the sensible supposes the incarnation of the subject who apprehends this sense), Merleau-Ponty does not raise the question regarding the ontological meaning of the body. In his work, the body is given more as a solution than as the index of a problem. The consequence is clear: the body is inevitably compromised as a body (*Körper*), that is, as a fragment of matter, which is supposed to found the belonging of the subject to the world. Subjectivity is forced into corporeality rather than corporeality being reintegrated into existence. Another consequence: in order to understand the body as one's own—that is, in its difference from other bodies—Merleau-Ponty has no other solution than to make consciousness intervene, such that the body is now nothing more than its "vehicle" or "mediator." Hence, subjectivity and belonging are merely juxtaposed rather than genuinely articulated. For that to be the case, instead of taking the ontological meaning of the body to be self-evident, it would be necessary to interrogate it and, instead of leading this subject back to its body, to ask how the body could be the body of a subject. In short, if Heidegger thinks existence without incarnation, Merleau-Ponty thinks incarnation without existence. That's why he inevitably falls back to the level of *Körperlichkeit*. Whereas Heidegger never asks how existence can possess a body, Merleau-Ponty never demands how the body can be the body of an existence. Now, if existence is in fact incarnated, its body must have an existential signification: it is precisely a determination of the body as existential that is missing in Merleau-Ponty. For both Heidegger and Merleau-Ponty, the two conditions under which the subject of the correlation falls remain exterior to one another: neither of these two authors turns toward a more originary meaning of being from which this articulation could be thought. In this sense, we have to situate ourselves beyond Merleau-Ponty and Heidegger, at least when it comes to this question.

Where exactly do you see that as being? Since Le désir et la distance *(1999), you have been developing what you call a "phenomenology of life." What are we to understand by "phenomenology of life" and how does it respond to the problems associated with the correlational a priori?*

My hypothesis is precisely that *life* constitutes the only possible response to the problem I just posed. Indeed, beyond existence and corporeality there is a life that articulates the one onto the other, or, rather, constitutes a more profound dimension than their very distinction. Indeed, life is nothing other than existence *qua* incarnated, corporeality *qua* corporeality of an existence, which comes down to recognizing that life is the only possible way to the true ontological meaning of existence and corporeality. It would be particularly easy to show, against or beyond Merleau-Ponty, that moving beyond the body as *Körper* (falling under *Vorhandenheit*) and doing justice to its true meaning, which will prove to be dynamic, only becomes possible by thinking the body as a property of life, rather than life as a property of the body. It must be added from the very beginning that this theoretical proposition only has a sense insofar as it keeps to a *neutral* meaning of life and, in particular, does not confuse it with what biology has to say about life. Indeed, the concept of life in play here refers to its *verbal* sense, "to live," which, in French, possesses both the intransitive sense of being alive [*être-en-vie*] (*leben*) and the transitive sense of experiencing something [*l'épreuve de quelque chose*] (*erleben*). It should also be noted that it is by counting on this indetermination that Husserl is able to speak of "transcendental life" when referring to lived experiences (*Erlebnis*). My hypothesis is that this ambiguity is fruitful and philosophically revelatory: it allows us to make clear a more originary sense of living, one that is more profound than the pair "being alive" and "lived experience" and determines their possibility. One might say that, on the one hand, there is no purely intransitive life and that all life, even the most basic, is already a mode of phenomenalization. On the other hand, there is no experience, however "elevated" and apparently removed from the vicissitudes of life it may be, that does not in reality refer back to a being that lives (*leben*). Living is more profound than the transitive and the intransitive pair. Now, while transitive living (*erleben*) is another name for phenomenalization, intransitive living (*leben*) corresponds to belonging (a living being that would not be a part of the world, involved in exchanges with it, is unthinkable). Indeed, it is in life, or rather as life, that the two dimensions of the subject of the correlation are articulated: insofar as each is a part of life, each dimension goes beyond itself toward the other. Indeed, as living (*leben*), belonging to the world necessarily encompasses phenomenalization, whereas, as merely corporeal, it prohibits phenomenalization, unless a consciousness is added to it. In the same way, as transitive living (*erleben*), phenomenalization entails belonging, whereas, characterized merely as existence, it in no way permits of belonging. Life is indeed that which relates the body to existence and, equally, that which confers upon existence its belonging to the world. Life is the element in which the co-belonging of subjectivity and intra-worldliness is grounded. Now, insofar as the task of phenomenology is to elaborate the correlational a priori and, in particular, the ontological meaning of the subject of the correlation, it is necessary to conclude that phenomenology is only possible as phenomenology of life.

Certainly, access to this originary sense of life, which is none other than the ontological meaning of the subject itself, presupposes that a certain acceptation of life, one that dominates common sense and is historically predominant, has been surpassed. As Hans Jonas definitively showed in *Le phénomène de la vie*, the modern age is characterized by a considerable transformation, which concerns precisely the status of life. Whereas previously, the framework was a universal ontology of life, for which the living being was the ontological norm and death the exception, after the modern age, death and, with it, inert matter became instituted as the norm, such that life now appears as a sort of exception and, consequently, as a problem.

Life is inescapably understood, particularly by biological thought, according to the framework of a "universal ontology of death." This means that life remains an isolated modality of being in a universe ruled by the laws of physics, that it is destined to return to the universal regime of being, that is, to death. One might say that, as an ontological exception, life is perpetually threatened by its return to a state of non-differentiation from the physical universe—in short, by its extinction—and that its life in the active sense (its living) consists in containing this threat. Life is first of all thought in the horizon of this negation, death, and this is why it is necessarily understood as the negation of this negation, namely, as *survival.* Living means nothing but the maintenance of life, that is, the struggle against death. All its activity is at the service of its being: it does nothing if not endure and do what is necessary to continue enduring.

So what does phenomenology have to say about life that biology, given the presuppositions you've just described, doesn't?

Now, this ultimately very restrictive conception of life is totally dependent on the ontological presupposition I just outlined. To access life itself, rather than conceive it starting from its other, it is necessary to neutralize this presupposition and proceed to what I have called an "*époché* of death."[13] It is a matter of thinking life from itself, rather than from the point of view of what threatens it. By proceeding this way, attention is turned toward a dimension of life—namely, that of gratuitousness, profusion, and pure expenditure—which, however incontestable, has hitherto remained obscure, because it had no place within the ontology of death. Certain authors in the German anthropological tradition have stressed this "surplus of impulsions" that leads life beyond—infinitely beyond—the requirements of simple survival, the preservation of life. This profusion traverses everything from play to art to theoretical interrogation and the exploration of the earth. The important point here is that, by approaching life from itself, we discover that it is characterized by a form of activity that isn't subordinated to, but radically exceeds the simple necessity of being. As such, it encompasses a dimension of phenomenalization. Characterized in itself, living necessarily entails an activity of exploration and vision, which is to say, ultimately, of knowledge. In short, in the light of an *epoché* of death, living can no longer be reduced to an intransitive act of maintaining life, but, on the contrary, entails an essentially transitive dimension. Here, the ontology of life converges with phenomenology: the essence of life is situated beyond the distinction between transitivity and intransitivity, of being alive and phenomenalization.

What role does your concept of "desire" play in this convergence, and how does it relate to self-movement as you understand it? In both your work and that of Lévinas, for example, "desire" seems to open the very possibility of transcendence insofar as it constitutes the most basic kind of relation to exteriority . . .

The demand for a desubstantialization of the subject, coupled with its necessary belonging to the world, leads us to conceive it in dynamic terms. The phenomenology of life confirms this. Movement, at least in the Aristotelian sense—that is to say, as change—is indeed a part of the subject's minimal determination: to say that we are living is to recognize that we are able to move ourselves. The phenomenology of life places movement at the heart of the subject and can thus avoid reification, as Husserl called for. Movement constitutes the answer to the question posed toward the end of my critique of Heidegger and Merleau-Ponty. It is as movement that existence can be incarnated: reconceived existentially, the body is the capacity for self-movement. In other words, the power that is originarily given to me and is the condition of my potentiality-for-being [*pouvoir-être*], including the most proper potentiality, is my capacity to move myself.

We have to be careful not to subordinate our idea of movement to uninterrogated presuppositions, for we then run the risk of understanding this movement as a simple displacement and of once more separating corporeality from existence by forcing it into objective space. Movement needs to be rethought in light of the concept of life as I have defined it, namely as an existence within the world that necessarily encompasses a phenomenalization. As something that takes root in life, indeed as the movement of life itself, our movement is an advance that makes its end appear by approaching it, or, if you like, a phenomenalization that is not to be distinguished from an advance. From the point of view of life, there is no distinction to be drawn between moving-toward and seeing, because there is no distinction between living intransitively and living transitively. One could say that, for life, sense is always the pole of an approach, that there is *signification* only as *direction*. In short, the movement of life is situated beyond the distinction between mere displacement and pure vision (phenomenalization): it is more than mere advancement and less than contemplation.

Now, to get back to your question, how can this "movement," which only apprehends its "object" by moving toward it and only discovers it via the inclination that carries it toward it, be described if not, precisely, as desire? I chose the concept of desire to name the being proper to a life more profound than the distinction between self-movement and perception, a life that, as a result, only apprehends its object, whatever its degree of reality or ideality might be, by carrying itself actively toward it. Desire is neither movement nor knowledge but—because initially we have no choice but to use concepts we seek to go beyond—knowledge by movement or movement that yields knowledge. Of course, insofar as it names the very essence of life in its fundamental indistinction between *leben* and *erleben*, desire must first of all be relieved of all the psychological and affective connotations we are inclined to confer on it. The desire I am talking about is not in the first instance a relation to others, since it is fundamentally only another name for intentionality and designates that which underlies relations with all beings. It is certainly not foreign to affectivity, but it is not an affect like others: it corresponds, rather, to the very condition of every affect, to something like an originary affectivity that founds in every affect the co-belonging of e-motion and motion. However, if desire cannot be forced into this erotic relation to the other, which it usually designates, it is clearly and necessarily that which constitutes its source or foundation. Erotic desire has its source in an originary desire that is synonymous with our life, and one of the tasks that my approach calls for, the task in which I am myself engaged, is to understand how empirical erotic desire can be derived from the originary, constitutive desire of the subject.

So my perspective differs radically from that of Lévinas, even if he does employ the term "desire." Of course, for me, desire has the function of opening up transcendence, but it is a matter of the transcendence of the world. This transcendence is given, as it were, only negatively, in the form of the dimension of dissatisfaction characteristic of desire, a dissatisfaction that persists in the very heart of all satisfaction. This means that the world is nothing but the horizon of our quest, which is opened up by all experience insofar as it contains a dimension of dissatisfaction; finite appearances [*apparitions*] are the negations of this totality, which only reveals itself in these negations as that which exceeds them. In short, there is only desire as desire for the world. The gap, at the heart of desire, between plenitude (never attained) and satisfaction, is a function of the difference between the world and its appearances. Now, this definition of the transcendence of the world—immanent to finite beings, since it implies no alterity—Lévinas clearly does not evoke. Lévinas does not think transcendence as this transcendence within the Same, which is the difference or depth of the world; rather, he conceives transcendence as *other to the Same*, that is, the transcendence of the infinitely Other. This means that the desire Lévinas talks about is a "desire without satisfaction," without even the horizon of a satisfaction, even though there is no relation to the infinitely other that is not in the mode of separation. Now, what could a desire without any possible satisfaction mean, if not the very negation of desire? A desire defined by its relation to something totally other, which "*understands* the remoteness, the alterity, and the exteriority of the other" and "does not long to return, for it is desire for a land not of our birth,"[14] which Lévinas terms "metaphysical desire," is in no way a desire. A tension that excludes satisfaction and is itself this renunciation is foreign to desire: it is in truth responsibility or holiness.

If, on your reconstruction of the correlational a priori, desire defines the subjective side of the correlation, how does this affect its relation to the object?

A phenomenalizing advance and a seeing that is indistinctly a self-movement are not yet a desire. Desire means much more: it is a movement that aims to appropriate something that can appease it. It tends toward a satisfaction, which, unlike the satisfaction of a simple need, remains impossible insofar as (1) objects, although sought after, never yield this satisfaction and (2) desire is always stirred on by what satisfies it, intensified by this very satisfaction. It is relieved but never fulfilled. Desire nourishes itself. Its fulfillment is but its rebirth. Furthermore, and even more profoundly, desire is always self-desire, a search for the self in the other: it is always the expression of an ontological lacuna. That being said, I need to justify my characterization of phenomenalizing life in terms of desire. Doing so requires that I return for a moment to the other, transcendent pole of the correlation.

Conforming to the coordinates of the correlation, I said earlier that this pole is not an object that can be intentionally fulfilled but a pure transcendence, as irreducible as it is indiscernible, of that which appears [*l'apparaissant*] vis-à-vis its appearances [*apparitions*]. This pole is nothing but the transcendence of the world itself. Insofar as that which appears is nothing but its appearances, it only gives itself in them as that which always exceeds them. The pure transcendence of the transcendent means that it always retreats when approached and steals away from vision precisely because it is a transcendence "without ontic mask." Now, a world that is pure depth, which is, so to speak, its own excess, can only give itself to a subject who is not vision but is through and through desire. The non-positive excess of the world can only correspond to the insatiability of desire. In other words, if it is characteristic of desire to be the desire of nothing (determinate), since nothing satiates it, then only desire can open this nothing of being, this no-thing [*non-chose*], the world. To rethink the two poles of the correlation in light of its own demands is therefore to characterize them as desire and pure transcendence, respectively. Deeper than consciousness standing face-to-face with the object, there is the correlation of a life that is desire and a world that is pure transcendence.

I have evoked above a second determination of desire, which corresponds to its properly ontological signification: desire is fundamentally self-desire and is determined by a lack of being. Within my framework, we understand that the aspiration that carries the subject toward the world can never be allayed insofar as the world, in its essence, exceeds all finite appearances [*apparitions*]; however, we do not understand *why* the subject is carried toward the world. Now, as I have said before, this aspiration can only take root in an ontological lacuna. If the subject moves toward the world, this is because it is a question of the world in its being: desire for the world is fundamentally self-desire. In other words, the ontological lacuna on which desire nourishes itself refers to a separation. If the subject views the world as a place of possible reconciliation, it is because it comes from it: intentional advance [*l'avancée intentionnelle*] is in reality a return. Now, it is impossible to understand this dimension of desire, the most profound, within a strict phenomenological framework. To think of the subject in the light of the correlation as desire is inevitably to be led beyond the strict phenomenological framework of the desire-world correlation and instead to operate on a more profound level, where the separation that governs desire becomes thinkable.

This seems to be the right time to ask you about your sources in the history of philosophical biology, which are quite numerous (Goldstein, Canguilhem, Pichot, Simondon, Jonas, among others)[15] *and have clearly contributed to, if not made possible, your transformation of the traditional conceptuality of phenomenology. Nevertheless, you have, despite all this, remained committed to a certain number of phenomenological theses. How do you understand the relation between philosophical biology and phenomenology? Must we appeal to philosophical biology in order to resolve the basic problems of phenomenology?*

As I said, the correlational a priori constitutes, to my mind, the minimal framework within which a phenomenological approach can be defined.

By specifying the conditions to which the two poles of the correlation are submitted, I was led to the notion of life, insofar as it best responds to the ontological meaning of the subject in its double dimension of belonging and phenomenalization. But it is clear that what really matters to me is having a phenomenological concept of life. It's true that I have worked on philosophers of life, particularly Bergson, Goldstein, and Jonas, but their work only interests me insofar as it might converge with and nourish my own phenomenology of life. More precisely, my recourse to these authors had an essentially negative and critical function, as what I said earlier about Hans Jonas makes clear. For me it was a matter of finding, within the terrain of the philosophy of life, perspectives that would allow me to get beyond naïve acceptations of life dominated by survival and the negation of death. Now, someone like Goldstein, for example, in no way thinks of life as survival but rather as the realization of a singular essence through dialogue with a milieu, such that a life that limits itself to realizing the conditions of survival is pathological. It was important for me to discover philosophies of life for which the scope of life went well beyond that of a strict satisfaction of needs and incorporated a dimension of phenomenalization, of subjectivity at the heart of vital activity itself. Thus, for Hans Jonas for example, the simplest living thing, insofar as it is defined by what Jonas calls "metabolism," encompasses a constitutive dimension of subjectivity and a form of ipseity. The philosophy of life interests me only insofar as it coincides with phenomenology; the place these philosophies have in my work is comparable to that of the physiology and psychology of behavior in Merleau-Ponty's early work: they allow us to go beyond naive prejudices (which are most often those of science) on the terrain of science itself, or, at the very least, philosophies claiming to be science. Philosophies of life interest me only insofar as they inform the *époché* of death I discussed above. This is why philosophical biology never resolves the fundamental problems of phenomenology, which can in truth only be resolved within its own domain. It only allows us to brush aside the prejudices that obstruct the phenomenological enterprise, to go beyond a kind of natural attitude regarding the phenomenon of life.

In the central section of your Introduction à une phénoménologie de la vie *(2008), you elaborate what you call a "privative anthropology" by way of a reading of the Rilke's eighth* Duino Elegie *(a reading you base largely on that of Roger Munier),*[16] *and you develop the core conceptual framework of a phenomenology of life. What do you mean by "privative anthropology" and how does it respond to the problems we've been discussing?*

I must first of all stress that by referring the ontological meaning of the subject to life, I go far beyond the narrow framework of human existence and include, in principle, the totality of living things. To say that the being of the subject of the correlation must be defined as life is to recognize that the phenomenological correlation—that is, phenomenalization—pertains to every living thing. I thus place myself in a resolutely continuist perspective (I admit that on this point I have been influenced by Hans Jonas) and I hence refuse to make the human subject an ontological exception. But with this approach—starting with life—I was faced with the necessity of accounting for the difference of the human subject, a difference that we name with the help of the notion of consciousness. The coordinates of the problem thus became quite restrictive, since it became a matter of accounting for this difference without compromising the constitutive fact that the human subject belongs to life. This excluded adding a positive attribute, such as soul, consciousness, mind, or reason, as a means to thinking the difference of the human. That would bring us right back to making man an exception to life, a living thing *plus* something else, that is, something altogether other than a living thing. In whatever way we think about life and its additional attribute, to proceed by addition is necessarily to subscribe to the thesis that man is a rational animal, to fall back into metaphysical dualism and its impasses. By approaching the situation in this way, we don't resolve anything; we only pose problems instead of pointing the way to their solution. It remains to be understood how an animal can be rational, that is, how rationality can be premeditated [*se préméditer*] within humanity or, what amounts to the same, how consciousness or reason can belong to a living thing. The only way to avoid these difficulties is to place in the foreground man's radical belonging to life, his fundamental kinship with other living things, which consists exactly in his having nothing *more* than them. The question is thus as follows: How do we think a difference that is phenomenologically incontestable yet that cannot be grounded in an attribute without compromising our status as living beings, our complete belonging to life?

This is where negation and privation come in . . .

Yes, as always, the solution is to be found in the formulation of the problem itself: man is distinguished from other living things not because he possesses something more but, on the contrary, because he is made to *lack something* [*quelque chose lui* fait défaut], because he is the site of a negation, a limitation of life. Human consciousness is but life deprived or separated from a dimension of itself. This is what I mean by *privative anthropology*, and it clearly echoes the privative zoology that has been discussed in relation to Heidegger. My approach is, so to speak, the negative of his, in the photographic sense. Whereas, according to Heidegger, life was only accessible via *Dasein*, such that the ontology of life had to determine what must be the case for something to be mere life [*ce qui doit être pour que puisse être quelque chose qui ne serait plus que vie*], according to me, human consciousness is only accessible from the point of view of life and the goal of the phenomenology of life is to determine *what life must be for something like humanity to be* [*ce que doit être la vie pour que puisse être quelque chose qui ne serait qu'humanité*].[17]

So whereas Heidegger's privative zoology discloses life by negating what is proper to Dasein, *privative anthropology discloses the human subject by negating, or at any rate limiting, what is proper to life . . .*

A solution of this kind isn't only necessary for logical reasons: it corresponds exactly to the phenomenological situation that we have already described. I placed in the foreground a concept of life as profusion rather than conservation, whose scope is equal to the depth of the world. This explains why life names the correlation even when understood from the subjective side. Life is what opens us to the world; through it, we relate to its proper depth. In this sense, life is indeed the very fabric of intentionality. Thus, just as every appearance must be understood as a limitation of the worldly totality given in it, the consciousness correlated to every appearance refers back to a negation of the life that opens up the world. In this sense, the correlation of consciousness and object has its origin in the limitation of the originary correlation of life and world. This comes down to overturning radically the relationship between consciousness and intentionality. Intentionality is no longer a property of consciousness; rather, consciousness is a property of intentionality, in the sense that it originates in the limitation of an intentionality that is fundamentally vital activity.

It was here that recourse to Rilke's poetic works seemed valuable to me, particularly the eighth *Duino Elegy*, where he describes the human mode of being in a privative manner in relation to the animal mode of being. The animal is characterized by the fact that it is completely engaged in what Rilke names the Open: it glides through and is carried away by it. The animal merges with its own progressive movement within the worldly totality, and the world is totally present to it: Rilke characterizes this as *outlook* [*vue*] insofar as nothing is yet delimited within this advance and no object is drawn. Man is, for his part, characterized by the interruption or, at the very least, the suspension or limitation of this pure advance. Something like a distance opens up from which the relation to an object is born: while the animal glides through the world, man stands opposed to it. Now, it is from this face-to-face relation (*Gegenständlichkeit*) that the object and the consciousness that apprehends it are jointly born. In other words, man becomes consciousness and the worldly totality becomes objective reality only by virtue of an interruption of the living engagement within the world, by a sort of contraction and withdrawal or recoiling within pure vital activity. This is what Rilke calls the "gaze" [*regard*]: the gaze fixes, cuts out, and delimits objects. Thus, the limitation of the world in the object originates in the limitation of vital intentionality, which results from the interruption of its full transitivity. The best way to put this is that consciousness is born from intentionality, that is, man from life via privation.

This is how you get around grounding the difference of the human in terms of an attribute whose relation to life remains ambiguous . . .

Yes, we come to account for the difference that marks off the human without introducing any positive attribute, without compromising its full belonging to life. Man is nothing but a living thing, not a superior living thing. Or rather, if he is a superior living thing on account of his ability to apprehend reality *as such*—of which the animal is incapable—it is because he is less living than other living beings, or rather because life in him is held back short of itself, withdraws from itself. The humanity of man is born from what we might call an *originary repression* affecting life itself, not a repression that results from our own initiative. In this sense, it is not so much that repression is a product of man as it is that man is the product of repression. Here, of course, we again find ourselves before the concept of desire. Desire is nothing but the trace, in us, of the vital profusion that everywhere overflows us, the presence of vital excess in that which limits it. To say that we desire is to say that, insofar as we are essentially living beings, we are exceeded by ourselves [*nous sommes comme débordés par nous-même*]. It is precisely this excess [*débordement*] that inserts our objects of consciousness into the depth of the world and confers a presence on them, that is, makes them objects of perception.

But now you have to explain precisely what such a negation might mean and account for how it is possible, no? Doesn't a problem similar to the one generated by the dualist tradition emerge at the heart of your phenomenological, vital via negativa*?*

My analysis is exposed to a major difficulty, one that has determined the essential part of my research since *Introduction à une phénoménologie de la vie*. In the end, have we truly resolved the problems with which I began? Have we truly escaped from metaphysical humanism and the thesis of the rational animal? In order to think the difference of the human, I substituted a negation for a positive attribute (consciousness, mind, etc.), but from the point of view of life, this negation is just as incomprehensible as the positive attribute was, and the opposition between a fully positive life (apparently foreign to humanity) and a humanity that seems to owe nothing to life (indeed, less so, since it is but its pure negation) remains. To found humanity on a negation that suddenly affects life is inevitably to understand this negation as having *added* something to life, something *positive*: from the point of view of life, this negation—humanity—is indistinguishable from something positively posited. If we were to maintain this position, we would end up having furtively reintroduced an inverted metaphysical dualism and would fail to have overcome it. One can see the conclusion that has to be drawn from this, and Rilke saw it himself: the negation that determines humanity would remain incomprehensible were it not *preceded* by itself, self-premeditated [*si elle ne se* précédait, *ne se préméditait*] within life. If man results from a limitation of life, and if life thus limits itself in man, it is above all because life limits *itself* in itself [*se limite* en elle-même], because it is already affected by this repression that culminates in man. In short, a negation of life in man becomes thinkable only if this negation is not the product of man (which would ultimately bring us back to ascribing a positivity to him or attaching to negation a secret positive attribute) but rather the product of *life itself*: there is only negation of life in man as the auto-negation of life.

So negation of life in man and negation of life by itself are one and the same . . .

Yes, against all expectations, I have been led to determine the difference of it to the level of life itself. This is required, as we have just seen, because of the very status of negation, which is only truly negative on condition that it never be added to anything, that it always precede itself: negation is only truly negative on the condition that it is originary, which amounts to saying that it can only be at the origin of man by being at the origin of life itself or, rather, by affecting life originarily. The essence of negation entails a sort of recoil, decentering, or originary gap. Even though it negates something other than itself, it cannot add itself or arise from elsewhere; it must already be co-present with what it negates, spring from it. This amounts to saying that there is no negation that is not auto-negation, no negation that has not already affected what it negates.

But how can this be phenomenologically confirmed?

Even if it imposes itself on us for theoretical and speculative reasons, this conclusion also has a phenomenological sense. In fact, it is difficult to dispute, as I pointed out earlier, that simple living things, even the most simple living things, already possess an ipseity and a world, however rough it may be. In truth, in light of my definition of life, when it comes to the living, one must admit that there are never any simple displacements, that all movement is already an approach and entails a dimension of phenomenalization. Contrary to what a tradition of Heideggerian origin, in particular, wishes to be the case, I do not believe that perception is the prerogative of man on the grounds that it is only through man that negativity can take place, because living things are in truth already capable of breaking their coincidence or fusion with the world. I would be more inclined to say that perception—that is, objectification—begins with life but is never fully accomplished, not even in us. It comes from beyond man but does not terminate in him.

This precession of negation (human difference) within life raises two orders of problem. The first clearly concerns the status of this negation. The question is effectively as follows: How can negation refer to something other than itself while at the same time be co-present with that which it negates, proceed from it? How can negation be originary while remaining a negation? In other words, how can we think a negation, which, insofar as it affects man, must affect life itself, but which, as a negation, nevertheless presupposes a life that escapes it?

Here once more, the answer lies in the very formulation of the problem. The only solution is to look for life somewhere deeper within, or beyond, the place where we currently situate it and, consequently, to recognize a sort of duplication of life. If the life of the living beings that we are can already have the negative status of a limitation, it's because it has already negated *another*, more profound life, a life that is neither our own nor even that of living things but rather that of *manifestation itself*. It is thus by making life recoil into the very depths of the world and in recognizing that life is originarily the "life of things," as Aristotle said, that we can understand how the life of the living is susceptible to having an originarily negative status. The justification for this statement can be found in a dynamic theory of manifestation, which understands manifestation itself as a process of which the world is the subject. This perspective, which can be authorized by Jan Patočka's phenomenology, develops and founds my determination of the essence of the subject as living, that is, as a dynamic reality. Indeed, to say that we are movement and that we belong to the world in the sense that we have an ontological kinship with it is quite simply to recognize that this world itself exists in a fundamentally *dynamic* mode. As Patočka says in an unpublished letter to Robert Campbell dated March 20, 1964: "Becoming and the movement that is at the origin of all our experiences would itself remain impossible without an even more profound and elementary becoming that is not the movement in experience and in the world, but the becoming and movement *of* the world as such; ontological becoming."[18] Of course, such a conclusion can be confirmed by an analysis of the essence of manifestation, which leads to the necessity of understanding it as a dynamic process of individuation and to the characterization of the world itself as *physis*. Thus, we bring to light, beyond the two poles of the correlation, that which articulates the one to the other, constitutes their common fabric and which is nothing but the movement of manifestation, of which the world is the subject and our own movement but one modality. I call this movement *archi-movement*. This archi-movement is synonymous with an originary life, an archi-life, which is initially not the life of any person but which is to be identified with the process of worlding [*mondification*], the joint constitution of the multiplicity of beings (by individuation) and the world (not in the originary and dynamic sense but in the derived sense) as the unity of this multiplicity or as totality. Thus, the phenomenological framework of the correlation leads us back to a cosmological framework where the being of the correlation can again be understood.

We may now return to the question of negation. If the life of the living things that we are can be originarily negative, it's because it refers to an originary life, an archi-life, which is nothing but the worldly process of originary manifestation as individuation. But in what, then, does this negation consist, which is nothing but the origin of living subjects (and no longer that of manifestation)? The difficulty seems to be renewed here. How can we think a negation that adds nothing to what it negates and might not be a surreptitious positivity? There is only one possible response: the negation to which the life of the living corresponds can only refer to a *separation*, a scission that affects archi-life. This split affects it through and through but adds nothing to it. The life of the living is no longer (originary) life but a limitation of originary life, because it is deprived of it—deprived of it because it is separated from it. However, nothing in archi-life announces or prepares this separation. It is matter of a movement that affects the movement of manifestation, of a sort of drifting or detachment in this movement itself—in short, of an *event*, which I call the archi-event. To the extent that this archi-event cannot be justified, within neither the phenomenological nor the cosmological framework that supports it, it is necessary to recognize that it falls within metaphysics. It affects the process of manifestation but does not come from it.

How do you justify this?

We can only justify it by saying that it must be presupposed in order to understand the first negativity that characterizes the subjects that we are, because it characterizes all living things. There is a kind of intrinsic finitude of life, a fundamental exile, that refers to the archi-event of a separation affecting originary life and that is, ultimately, the world in its processual essence.

This conclusion calls for two remarks. We now understand the level at which the characterization of the subject as desire takes root, a characterization that we now know, in a sense, to be equally valid for other living things. I said that desire possesses an ontological signification, since it refers to a lack of being, an ontological lacuna, such that it is always fundamentally self-desire and aspiration to reconciliation. We now understand the deepest origin of this desire: if it exists in the world in the being of the subject, this is because it is originarily separated from the world, because its life issues from a scission vis-à-vis originary life. In this sense, desire has a metaphysical signification: the wound it attempts to heal is none other than the archi-event of the separation, the detachment affecting originary life. On the other hand, it follows from everything I've said that it is in this archi-event that the entire meaning of negativity is concentrated, that only this scission allows us to respect the negativity of the negative.

I am now in a position to sketch a response to your question on negativity. In a sense, since *Le désir et la distance*, my whole approach has consisted in critiquing a certain negativism, more precisely, the presupposition of a primacy of nothingness. In this I fully take into consideration the Bergsonian critique of metaphysics insofar as it is subordinated to the principle of sufficient reason and on this basis thinks being from nothingness as that which overcomes a constitutive threat of annihilation. It seems to me that the condition of access to the phenomenal field is an *épochè* of the negative. This *épochè* means, on the transcendental side, that it is necessary to approach being directly rather than as the negation of nothingness. It is on this condition that we definitively get beyond positivity, that is, beyond the objectivity that is inseparable from positivity as soon as we profile being against the background of nothingness.

On the side of the subject, this *époché* means a suspension of death. It is here once again a matter of approaching life from itself rather than from a non-life (death) that this life would be the negation of, which would reduce the meaning of life to mere survival. To suspend nothingness is to give oneself the means to get beyond logical or objective being for the sake of the phenomenal field, to move beyond mere preservation of self to a phenomenalizing life.

This critique of nothingness does not throw us straight into pure positivism. On the contrary, an awareness of the need to think the difference of the human starting from a negation that, as I have just shown, prepares itself within the life of every living thing, is one of the guiding threads of my most recent books. But contrary to the nothing of metaphysics—Merleau-Ponty showed us the extent to which it remains a figure of positivity—the negation that I have tried to thematize is free of positivity. Indeed, we only overcome metaphysical humanism by thinking difference as a pure negation. This negation is nothing but a limitation that refers, in the final analysis, to a simple scission within the process of manifestation. Nothing more, but also nothing less, than this separation is necessary in order to preserve the purity of the negative.

How do you reconcile what you referred to earlier as your "continuist" position with the need to determine what makes human beings different from other living things?

That brings me to my second remark. Indeed, if human difference is already present in every living thing, is this difference not purely and simply abolished? Does the difference between man and other living things not become incomprehensible? Ultimately, all living things are individuated by separation, all are affected by the archi-event of the scission. That's why they all desire and all possess a world. In what does the difference between the living beings that we are and other living beings consist? They both stem from the power of archi-movement [*puisent dans la puissance de l'archi-mouvement*] and are affected by the archi-event. However, while the animal still gathers up the power of archi-life and thus bears witness to it in a privileged manner, man is closest to the archi-event, affected by its violence, to which he attests more than any other living thing.

In this sense, if the animal is a cosmic creature, man is, for his part, a metaphysical being. In other words, because the archi-event is a singular principle of individuation within the phenomenalizing archi-movement (of archi-life)—that is, the source of the living as such, we must conclude that man is the living thing *par excellence*, whereas the animal is still only traversed by life. Thus, the difference between the animal and man is, if you will, a difference of degree, since the pregnancy of archi-movement and the depth of separation (the archi-event) are not to be found in them, as it were, in the same proportion. Because the power of the process of worlding [*mondification*] continues within the animal, even within separation, its desire is more a *movement* than an ordeal [*épreuve*]: its separation takes the form of an *exodus*. In man, on the contrary, the power of archi-movement is, as it were, dried up by separation, pushed back by the violence of the archi-event, such that man's desire takes place more as something *lived* than as a movement: his singular aptitude for making the world appear for himself is like the power of his powerlessness. In man, separation is *exile*.

A final question about your relation to Michel Henry. What is at stake in the differing conceptions of the tasks phenomenology entailed by your respective concepts of life?

I must first stress that my perspective falls within the scope of Henry's critique to the extent that it resolutely accepts what he called ontological monism. However, it is true that the place I grant life, as well as the determination of life as desire, that is, as a certain affect, justifies the parallel. I would say that I situate myself at once very close to and very far from Michel Henry. Very close, because I defend an essential belonging of consciousness to life, which leads me to think of the being of consciousness as affectivity. Very far, because I think this belonging in a totally different manner and mode. For Michel Henry, consciousness—understood in the pure immanence of auto-affection and its incessant variations—gives itself as a *production* of a life that it reveals. Consciousness is in immediate contact with life, a pure expression of life. In short, it is Life itself in its subjective or phenomenal dimension. There is no trace here of negativity: we are in the fullness of an embrace in which no gap, no limitation, and no negation can ever arise. In truth, this pure immanence and absolute self-intimacy are the product of consciousness, because they are first of all the product of a life that is characterized by a fundamental intransitivity. This is why the fundamental affects that Michel Henry stresses are suffering and joy: in them life supports itself, it is, so to speak, only submitted; in them it experiences the impossibility of doing away with itself. For my part, I have wanted to show that, if consciousness indeed bears witness to life, this is not so much in the mode of a saturating presence but that of a negation. Life has no sense, according to my view, if not as something traversed by a fundamental and, so to say, infinite transitivity. This is why it only gives itself in consciousness as what consciousness has always returned to and what consciousness limits. Life subtracts itself from consciousness more than it gives itself. It follows that only the affect of desire agrees with consciousness insofar as it is the very presence or trace of this absence: life is only in consciousness as that to which it aspires and that is indeed none but its own essence. In short, whereas for Michel Henry, consciousness is auto-affection, suffering or joy (since it is the full presence of life), from my perspective, consciousness ought to be conceived of as desire insofar as it is the auto-negation of life.

Translated by Chris Fenwick

Notes

1. Vincennes, now known as Université de Paris VIII, opened after the academic reforms following the student uprisings of 1968, now located in Saint-Denis.

2. Bernard Bourgeois was a professor of philosophy at the University of Lyon 1 and 2 from 1972 to 1989 and at the University of Paris 1 Panthéon–Sorbonne in 1989. He is the author of numerous books on Fichte, Hegel, and German idealism.

3. Jacques Garelli is a French poet and philosopher and the author of numerous collections of poetry and books on phenomenology. Marc Richir is a Belgian philosopher and phenomenologist. He has written many books on phenomenology.

4. Husserl, *Crisis of the European Sciences and Transcendental Phenomenology*, §48, 166.

5. Ibid., 168.

6. Ibid.

7. Patočka, *Papiers Phénoménologiques*, 123. Jan Patočka was one of the most significant figures in phenomenology in the latter half of the twentieth century and is the author of numerous books, including *Plato and Europe*; *Heretical Essays in the Philosophy of History*; *Body, Community, Language, World*; and *An Introduction to Husserl's Phenomenology*. His influence on French phenomenology can be detected in Dastur, Renaud Barbaras, Paul Ricoeur (who wrote the introduction to the French translation of *Heretical Essays*), and Jacques Derrida, particularly in *The Gift of Death*.

8. Merleau-Ponty, *The Visible and the Invisible*, 229.

9. Edmund Husserl, *Manuscript* A I 36, 193b, Husserl-Archives, Leuven, Belgium.

10. Husserl, *Psychological and Transcendental Phenomenology and the Confrontation with Heidegger*, 186.

11. Heidegger, *Being and Time*, 74; "In their turn, 'body,' 'soul,' and 'spirit' may designate phenomenal domains which can be detached as themes for definite investigations; within certain limits their ontological indefiniteness may not be important. When, however, we come to the question of man's Being, this is not

something we can simply compute by adding together those kinds of Being which body, soul, and spirit respectively possess—kinds of Being whose nature has not yet been determined. And even if we should attempt such an ontological procedure, some idea of the Being of the whole must be presupposed." Heidegger, *Being and Time*, 54, 79; "Being-in, on the other hand, is a state of *Dasein*'s Being; it is an *existentiale*. So one cannot think of it as the Being-present-at-hand of some corporeal Thing (such as the human body) 'in' an entity which is present-at-hand." See also Heidegger, *Being and Time*, 117, 153, 368, 419.

12. Patočka, *Le monde naturel et le mouvement de l'existence humaine*, 93.

13. See Barbaras, *Introduction à une phénoménologie de la vie*, 127.

14. Lévinas, *Totality and Infinity*, 33–34.

15. Kurt Goldstein was a German neuropsychologist and is the author of *Der Aufbau des Organismus*. Georges Canguilhem was Gaston Bachelard's successor as director of the Institut d'histoire des sciences at the Sorbonne and is the author of *Le normal et la pathologique* and *La connaissance de la vie*. André Pichot is a philosopher of science and a student of Canguilhem and is the author of *Petite Phénoménologie de la connaissance*, *Histoire de la notion de vie*, and *Expliquer la vie, de l'âme à la molecule*. Gilbert Simondon was a student of Canguilhem and Merleau-Ponty and is the author of *Du mode d'existence des objets techniques* and *L'individu et sa genese physico-biologique*.

16. Roger Munier was a French translator and writer.

17. Heidegger, *Being and Time*, 75: "In the order which any possible comprehension and interpretation must follow, biology as a 'science of life' is founded upon the ontology of *Dasein*, even if not entirely. Life, in its own right, is a kind of Being; but essentially it is accessible only in *Dasein*. The ontology of life is accomplished by way of a privative interpretation; it determines what must be the case if there can be anything like mere-aliveness [*Nur-noch-leben*]. Life is not a mere Being-present-at-hand, nor is it *Dasein*. In turn, *Dasein* is never to be defined ontologically by regarding it as life (in an ontologically indefinite manner) plus something else."

18. "Le devenir et le mouvement qui est à l'origine de toutes nos expériences est lui-même impossible sans un devenir plus profond et plus élémentaire qui est, non pas mouvement dans l'expérience et dans le monde, mais devenir et mouvement *du* monde comme tel; devenir ontologique." Robert Campbell was a French philosopher and mathematician.

Phenomenology and Finitude

FRANÇOISE DASTUR

How did you come to phenomenology?

In postwar France, secondary studies were still reserved for the children of the bourgeoisie. Coming from the working class, I was initially placed in trade school, but I managed—at the age of sixteen—to catch up with the "classic" stream [*filière classique*] and get into a school where one prepared for the *baccalauréat*.[1] I had the good fortune of being introduced to philosophy by Monique Dixsaut,[2] my high school professor, who is today considered to be the greatest contemporary specialist on Plato in France. It was her first year of teaching, and it was for me an illumination from the very first course: I knew straightaway that philosophy would constitute an essential part of my existence. Initially, I read the philosophers on whom Dixsaut relied as a matter of preference: Bergson, Plato, Nietzsche—Nietzsche above all, the discovery of whom was and remains decisive for me. Naturally, I also read numerous philosophical and literary texts by Sartre and Camus (we were still in the middle of the existentialist era in 1960). It was only a bit later, toward the end of the year, that I read a text of Heidegger's for the first time, "Hölderlin and the Essence of Poetry," and started to get interested in his thought (thanks to Henry Corbin's 1938 translation of *What Is Metaphysics?* and the paragraphs of *Being and Time* dealing with being-toward-death and historicality).[3] I won first prize in philosophy in the Concours Général (a typically French institution),[4] an event that led me to devote myself to studying philosophy at university.

The following year, the death of Merleau-Ponty stirred me to plunge into the *Phenomenology of Perception*, a difficult reading to which I devoted a part of the summer. Unwittingly, I was prepared for two encounters that have decided my philosophical orientation: Paul Ricoeur, who was then a professor at the Sorbonne, and Jacques Derrida, who taught there as an assistant and who, in 1962, put the finishing touches on the great introduction he devoted to a short text by Husserl on "The Origin of Geometry."[5] It was under their respective direction that I began to read the work of Husserl (whose numerous texts remained to be translated) and continued my reading of *Being and Time*, which had not yet been fully translated into French. The difficulties I encountered in comparing the original texts of Husserl and Heidegger quickly convinced me of the need for a stay in Germany, in order to deepen my knowledge of both the language and post-Kantian philosophy, which I'd begun to take an interest in through my reading of Hölderlin. Thanks to a scholarship from the German government, I was able to spend a year studying at the University of Freiburg-im-Breisgau, where Husserl, then Heidegger (who succeeded him) had taught. During the academic year of 1963–1964, I worked under the direction of Werner Marx, the author of *Heidegger and the Tradition*, who had just left the New School in order to take up the vacant chair previously occupied by Husserl and Heidegger.[6] I also followed the seminars of Eugen Fink, who is, alongside Merleau-Ponty and Jan Patočka, for me one of the three great representatives of the phenomenological "movement" founded by Husserl.

I began my studies in Lyon, continued them at the Sorbonne in Paris, and then in Germany at the University of Freiburg, then at the University of Nanterre, created in 1965, where Ricoeur, who directed my master's thesis, had chosen to teach. I finished my studies at the University of Strasbourg, near Germany, where I returned to live starting in 1966 and where I prepared for the *agrégation* in philosophy under the guidance of Philippe Lacoue-Labarthe, who had just been appointed there as an assistant professor. Hegel was one of the two authors on the program, and I was able take full measure of the Hegelian moment in German idealism, which for me represents the summit of Western philosophy.

The necessity of working while being a student (the scholarship granted to me by the French government wasn't enough to meet my needs), in addition to the fact that I had to devote a lot of time to teaching myself Latin and Greek for the *agrégation* and conduct my studies at five different universities, didn't allow me to form many contacts with my fellow students. In any case, having been first in the *agrégation*, I had the good fortune of being appointed assistant professor in the fall of 1969 at the

Sorbonne, where, thanks to the presence of Jean-Toussaint Desanti (who was named professor there in 1970 and for whom I became an assistant), I was able devote the majority of my teaching to Husserl during the years that followed.

You have written extensively on every figure in the history of German and French phenomenology, from Husserl to Heidegger to Gadamer, Merleau-Ponty, Ricoeur, and Patočka, among others. Your philosophical culture has been and remains phenomenological through and through, and your intimacy with the phenomenological idiom and temperament can be seen in everything you have written. What, to your mind, given the diversity of contemporary phenomenological inquiry, defines the singularity of phenomenology at the present time?

I freely affirm the fact that I belong to phenomenology, not as a "school" of thought but rather as a "movement" issued from Husserl that has gathered together figures of thought as diverse as Heidegger, Fink, and Gadamer in Germany; Sartre, Merleau-Ponty, and Ricoeur in France; Jan Patočka in Czechoslovakia;[7] and Roman Ingarden[8] in Poland, to name only the most notable figures. But, for me, phenomenology is not only a movement of thought to which I consider myself to belong; it constitutes the only method that, in my view, is suitable to thought: phenomenology is not a "doctrine" or a philosophical position, it is not a "science of phenomena" that one could oppose, for example, to the "science of being" (ontology), but—and Husserl and Heidegger agree on this point, both of them have underscored it—a concept of method. For me, phenomenology is not a philosophical discipline that one could oppose to others but a style or manner of thought, "the" philosophical manner of thought. In this regard, I am entirely in agreement with Merleau-Ponty's conception of phenomenology. This is why I do not at all feel the need to defend phenomenology against its detractors and am ready to recognize—wherever it may come to light—the phenomenological (that is to say, philosophical) style of thinking. On the other hand, I have no taste for initiatives that lead to positivism or theology. Such initiatives lack that "mystery of the world," which, again according to Merleau-Ponty, phenomenology has as its essential task to reveal.

Given your sense of the task of phenomenology, what, if anything, remains of the Husserlian "breakthrough" into phenomenology?

In a certain sense, the Husserlian "breakthrough" was the event by means of which philosophy was reborn at the end of the nineteenth century, a period marked by non-philosophy (namely, positivism). Husserl's maxim, "Return to the things themselves!" did nothing but clearly formulate that which, so to speak, had been the philosophical manner of proceeding since the birth of philosophy, as opposed to all gratuitous speculative "construction" but also the explanatory method of natural science. Husserl could—and with good reason—see in phenomenology the resumption of the original idea of philosophy, which one finds in Plato and Aristotle. To say that the method of philosophy is phenomenological is simply to say that it is neither speculative nor explanatory but rather simply disclosive [*monstrative*]. This, however, does not mean that it suffices to "describe the given." On the contrary, it means that it is necessary to let phenomena show [*montrer*] themselves by themselves. As Heidegger emphasized in §7 of *Being and Time*, "And just because the phenomena are proximally and for the most part *not* given, there is need for phenomenology." Work in phenomenology consists in "saving the phenomena," snatching them from the dissimulation to which our preconceived ideas and habits of thought relegate them. In saying that phenomenology is the sole possible method for philosophy, I do not in the least have the intention to take up a partisan position in philosophy but simply intend to recall forcefully the purely critical vocation of philosophy, which can never terminate in some integral systematization of the real.

Why, then, given its historical and philosophical pertinence as you describe it, has phenomenology become a primarily French affair?

If phenomenology has effectively become a primarily "French affair," this has, to my mind, become the case for essentially two reasons. In the first half of the twentieth century, the need to take leave of a narrowly rationalist mode of thought—one that gave precedence to the philosophy of science (the French philosophical tradition having been and remaining today of a profoundly epistemological inspiration)—made itself deeply felt. Sartre and Merleau-Ponty, the first French phenomenologists, found in Husserl and Heidegger exactly what they were looking for, a "broadened philosophy, a non-prejudicial analysis of phenomena, the environment in which our concrete life unfolds," as Merleau-Ponty put it in an interview conducted in May of 1946.[9] It was the "deconstruction" (*Abbau*, a word Husserl had already used in *Experience and Judgment*)[10] of Western rationalism that motivated Sartre's and, above all, early Merleau-Ponty's interest in Husserlian phenomenology and Heideggerian thought, and it was this same motive that, in a different manner, was at the heart of those who later situated themselves at the "limits of phenomenology," namely Lévinas and

Derrida. The second reason comes from the fact that the German philosophical tradition, strongly marked until the 1960s by Husserlian phenomenology and Heideggerian thought, later digressed, initially toward Anglo-Saxon analytic philosophy and then, more recently, 1960s French philosophy. The motive here was of an essentially political nature: Germany, having undertaken a critique of Nazism, was led to view the entirety of its philosophical tradition since Hegel with a certain suspicion.

You have written a book as well as numerous essays on the role played by the concept—perhaps one of the most phenomenologically basic—of "finitude" throughout the history of German and French phenomenology, distinguishing its phenomenological acceptation from that of the rest of modern philosophy since Kant, despite what are, no doubt, some very deep affinities. How do you understand the phenomenological concept of finitude in relation to the modern philosophical tradition?

The phenomena of phenomenology are not always given; a procedure is needed to make them appear. To place between brackets the given presence of things in order to reach to their phenomenality itself—that is the program of a phenomenology, which is first and foremost a phenomenology of temporality, since that which it takes into view is not the mere presence of what appears but rather the coming of that which appears, things in their advent, which is not yet an "accomplished fact" ["*chose fait*"], as Merleau-Ponty said, who had so well defined the sensible as the non-positive, the allusive, that which does not have in itself stability and density but that constantly escapes being seized. It appears to me to be evident that the phenomenon of such a phenomenology is time itself. It is in this strict sense that Heidegger used the expression "phenomenology of the inapparent" in his Zähringen seminar of 1973:[11] the inapparent is in play not beyond the visible but, as Merleau-Ponty already said, in the invisibility of the visible itself, the movement that carries it into appearance, the entry into presence of the present. This is why such a phenomenology appears to me to be necessarily a phenomenology of finitude. In the words of Jan Patočka: "Either phenomenology is a phenomenology of finitude or there is no phenomenology."[12] There is here a certain manner in which I distance myself from Husserl and turn more decisively toward Heidegger. As Patočka demonstrates, the relation of the existing being [*l'existant*] to phenomenality cannot be the relation of an impartial transcendental spectator or one of "seeing from on high" [*survol*], as Merleau-Ponty says, but rather a relation of dependence (Heidegger) or flesh (Merleau-Ponty). The reduction must, therefore, accompany the movement of existence, not break with it. It must, as Merleau-Ponty says, be done from within, which entails the double finitude of the existing being himself and that with which he is concerned [*ce à quoi il a affaire*]: being or the flesh. Neither being nor the flesh can receive the status of absolutes but are rather indissociably intertwined with the existent himself in a "chiasm," as Merleau-Ponty says, or in a co-belonging, in what Heidegger calls *Ereignis*.[13] A finitude such as this—which I call "originary" in order to make clear that it is not to be thought of as a lack or a deficiency vis-à-vis a prior infinite—is this place of places [*ce lieu des lieux*] starting from which the infinite and the atemporal themselves can alone appear.

Do you distinguish between the concept of "mortality" and that of "finitude"? After all, one could imagine, if only as a mere logical possibility, a non-mortal yet nevertheless finite being. How do you understand the relation between these two concepts and how do you understand this relation to have been negotiated throughout the history of phenomenology since Heidegger?

Unlike Sartre, I take human finitude to be founded on the mortality of the human being. Sartre dissociates finitude and mortality—traditionally united—because he wants to stress the fact that death arrives in an always unexpected and premature manner, and because he considers birth and death to constitute the *external* limits of existence. In effect, he maintains that "death is a pure fact, like birth; it comes to us from without and transforms us from without. At bottom, it is in no way distinguishable from birth, and it is this identity of birth and death that we name facticity."[14]

It's easy for Heidegger to respond to this in advance: the existent, precisely because he is free, has to take charge of the contingency of his being-thrown into the world, which entails, for Heidegger, that there is no brute facticity that would limit [the existent] from without, but on the contrary what he calls a "facticity of the deliverance of *Dasein* to himself" ("*Faktizität der Überantwortung*")[15]—the existent being able to receive what befalls him only by assuming it in some way or other. This makes it so that no determination has for Heidegger the exteriority of a fact of nature, and as Merleau-Ponty, opposing himself to Sartre, also says: "Existence cannot have an exterior or contingent attribute," "[I]t cannot be anything at all without being it completely, without taking over and assuming its 'attributes' and making of them the dimensions of its being."[16] This assumption of one's own facticity constitutes the tenor of all singular existence. Taking charge of one's being-thrown into existence—birth—has as its correlate a necessary and symmetrical assumption of being toward death. It is thus starting from these two limits that the finitude of existence can be understood. Neither the birth nor the death of an existent are in the strict sense "events," since they are never lived as such by him, nor yet by others. Birth is no more a past event than death is a future event but rather, as Heidegger emphasizes, every singular being exists in a "natal manner" ["*gebürtig existieren*"] just as it exists in "a mortal manner" for the entire stretch of its life.[17]

To what extent, if at all, do you understand these concepts to be implicated in or distinguishable from a certain concept of (animal, biological) life? We know, for example, the traditional Heideggerian ontological strategy: properly speaking (i.e., in the language of fundamental ontology), animals merely perish, that is, do not bear an existing relation to their end. Animals live but do not exist and perish but do not die. Only Dasein *dies, and it dies because it bears a certain significant relation to its own death. As you know, Derrida, in a number of texts, closely and critically examined Heidegger's position on this matter, which remained, I think we can say, fairly consistent from the period of* Being and Time *on. In* The Animal That Therefore I Am, *for example, Derrida questions not whether the animal has access to something like the ontological meaning of death but rather whether we do: the "as such" of death "appears" no more to us than it does to any other living creature. Can we, under these circumstances, continue to speak of a "phenomenology" or "fundamental ontology" of death in the strict sense—that is, a phenomenology without a phenomenon?*

For all of the philosophers of the Western tradition, the difference between man [*l'homme*] and animal is understood in terms of the presence or absence of reason. The traditional definition of man remains fundamentally dualist: it supposes that reason can only be an *addition* to a "nature" man shares with the totality of living beings. The idea of a superiority of man over the animal rests on this basis, since he—man—is himself an animal *plus* something else, something that does not strictly pertain to his animality. Questioning this superiority can lead one to show that it is in reality impossible to determine in all its purity and indivisibility the frontier that separates man from the animal, and this all the more so if every discourse on man "in general" (as on the animal) has as a consequence the homogenization of differences that can serve to distinguish different types of comportment within the two "kingdoms" [*règne*] in a radical way. This is the position of Jacques Derrida, who questions the logic of philosophical discourse on the animal from Descartes and Kant to even Heidegger, whom he takes to belong to "the profoundest metaphysical humanism."[18] I've devoted a long text to the discussion of the Derridean critique of the Heideggerian position,[19] in which I show that, far from supporting metaphysical humanism by placing an abyssal difference between the being of man and that of the animal (as Derrida hastily asserts), Heidegger fundamentally, in fact, puts it in question. What Heidegger highlights is the *anthropomorphism* inherent in the metaphysical tradition as a whole. It would be necessary, in my view, to speak not, as Derrida does, of the "animal that therefore I am" but rather of the "animal that I no longer am," because it is *in his entirety* that man distinguishes himself from the animal. To think animality privatively, as Heidegger does when he declares that "the fundamental ontological constitution of 'life' is a particular problem that can only be developed by way of reductive privation starting from the ontology of *Dasein*,"[20] is therefore to remain open to the *enigma* of the animal from whom we remain separated in a radical way, despite the fact that we can in some sense live with animals (which, however, always means that we can integrate them into *our* world).

One can, of course, object that there is no possible phenomenology of death because death is the non-phenomenon *par excellence*, that because it radically escapes all presence, it is the absolute other of being. And yet, in its "ineffectiveness" it is more "present" than anything in effective life will ever be. Indeed, it is a presence so insistent and so haunting that—when one does not try to tame it in this "repetition" of death that is philosophy—it is precisely a matter of fleeing from it by distraction. Constantly present in the mode of imminence, one must therefore recognize that this absolute absence—death—has a paradoxical mode of appearing; it is not the origin of any particular phenomenalization but rather gives to the totality of phenomena their singular "tenor" of finitude by letting them be released from the depth of its dark light. This is exactly what makes a phenomenological discourse on death possible. This phenomenology confines itself to the pure experience of an always possible, imminent non-sense (the abolition of existence) and does not try to give to death a sense by integrating it into a transcendence that would relativize it. It is from this relation-to-death, from this mortality, that there is a possible phenomenology.

In Telling Time: Sketch of a Phenomenological Chronology, *you evoke Heidegger's early invocation of a phenomenological "chrono-logy" by which both you and he understand the determination of logic by temporality. Clearly, the concepts of logic and time cannot, at least not in this context, be understood according to their traditional acceptation. What kind of relation between logic and temporality do you understand the notion of a "phenomenological chronology" to articulate?*

In the text you're referring to, the "sketch" character of which needs to be emphasized, and where the infinitive in "*Telling Time*" [*Dire le temps*] must be read as an optative rather than as an imperative or constative, I started off from an indication given by Heidegger in a course from the period in which he was writing *Being and Time* where he speaks of a new philosophical discipline that would be established under the name "chronology," a name that Heidegger understands literally, in the sense of a science or discipline of time.[21] Even though the vaguely sketched project of the 1926 course was never realized, it seems to me that it is possible to take it up again and even to make use of it as a guiding thread for a reading of Heidegger's work that would be attentive to his critique of logic. What Heidegger reproaches the Western tradition for in its entirety is precisely its logicism, that is to say, a certain conception of language, a certain conception of truth, and a certain conception of being that one could call de-temporalizing, since they all accord unilateral privilege to the presently given alone (which Heidegger calls *Vorhandenheit*) and, in this way, fail to recognize the proper character of time, which "is" not but that temporalizes itself, or is constant temporalization. This detemporalization is without a doubt necessary for grasping identities like Platonic ideas, for example, without which scientific thought is not possible. This is why the "forgetting" of time will not be judged by Heidegger to be a contingent fact but, on the contrary, a "destiny." Nevertheless, it remains the case that this detemporalization, which arises in the Aristotelian school and is required for the constitution of formal logic, was not perceived as such by the inventors of logic (less so Aristotle than his students, according to Heidegger). For Heidegger, it is a matter of making this forgetting appear insofar as it is at the origin of the constitution of the idea of being that determines the very form of philosophical science.

But making time appear as the very horizon starting from which Western philosophy—without knowing it—has construed its own architectonic can only mean destroying this architectonic itself. This is why Heidegger underscores the fact that chronology, or the logic of temporality that he envisages, cannot be incorporated into the tree of philosophy as a new science. To make appear, as he later says, the very ground in which the tree of philosophy takes root in a certain way means uprooting it. The entire magnificent edifice of philosophy then begins to falter, in a manner of sorts. From a historical point of view, this obviously corresponds to the crisis the idea of "system" has been in since the end of the nineteenth century, with paradigmatic figures like Kierkegaard and Nietzsche. Heidegger, who deals with the problem of systematicity in philosophy in his 1936 course (devoted to Schelling), suggests that it is possible to give up on the idea of "system" without thereby giving up on systematicity as such, without giving up on synthesis, in understanding it otherwise than as a formal synthesis.

The part that was mine—and which isn't without its risks—is the part that led me to precipitately improvise a sketch, which is not a renunciation of construction as such but rather the acceptance of a "provisional philosophy" that doesn't build in the atemporal, that, on the contrary, finds in temporality, in finitude and death, the recourse that allows it to live in this world here without dreaming or promising a beyond. *To conserve a relation to a certain systematicity even though one has been swept up in the march of time*, that is the wager that seemed to me necessary to uphold.

I found the idea of an instantaneous synthesis that comes to the act of speech itself and the idea of a totality that gives itself only in division and by caesura as much in the philosophy of language of a Humboldt as in the poetic thought of a Hölderlin. This is without a doubt why I was led—perhaps leaving Heidegger behind here, who seems rather to propose a sigetics, an access to silence that would go through a tautological use of language—to undertake a certain rehabilitation of dialectics. Perhaps I am really even tempted by the impossible liaison of the two: to understand silence without silencing the polylogue, to find an economy of speech that nevertheless preserves in itself the moment of opposition and even takes it to its limit.

*You have also written extensively on the genesis and structure, both historical and philosophical, of Heidegger's reflections on language (*Heidegger: la question du logos *most recently). What, to your mind, constitutes the enduring relevance—the central contribution, if you will—of Heidegger's reflections on logic and language?*

I devoted my *mémoire de maîtrise*,[22] completed in 1966, to "Language and Ontology in Heidegger" (*Heidegger: la question du logos* is a late book written on the basis of works pursued since the beginning of the 1970s on the same question) in view of a doctoral thesis [*thèse de doctorat d'Etat*], which I gave up on in the end, preferring to defend a thesis under the direction of Jacques Taminiaux at the University of Louvain, a place where the phenomenological tradition has been living—consistently so—ever since the death of Husserl and the transfer of his manuscripts to Belgium. These works dealt with the status of discursivity proper to the Western mode of thought insofar as it rests on the predicative proposition and is allied to a determined conception of philosophical logic. The origin of this question must first be sought for in the Nietzschean critique of "metaphysical grammar" (which grammar led to the postulation of substrates and imaginary entities) and, finally and above all, in Heidegger's questioning of the guiding role played by the *logos apophantikos* as model of any utterance of language. It is these two attempts at "surpassing metaphysics" that led me to interrogate the relation that philosophical logic bears to traditional ontology. The principle axis of my work was therefore the analysis of the Heideggerian "destruction" of the theory of language and traditional logics, which it is a matter of understanding less as the rejection of logic and the promotion of irrationality than the redirection of traditional logic back to its foundation, namely to a broader sense of *logos* than that which confines *logos* to the structure of the predicative proposition. In this regard, what constitutes Heidegger's essential contribution is his attempt to "reform" the language of metaphysics and open up the possibility of a use of language and a "phenomenological" logic that would be attuned to the "temporality of being."

What Heidegger has, to my mind, left largely "unthought"—even though he had already himself indicated the direction to follow through his interview with his Japanese interlocutor in *Unterwegs zur Sprache*[23]—is the question regarding the confrontation between the Western logical tradition—Hegelian dialectic and phenomenological, Husserlian logic in particular—and other traditions of thought, above all the Indian tradition, which gave fundamental importance to research devoted to logic and language. In this regard, it would be particularly necessary to take an interest in the research developed in India within the framework of the "logical" (*Nyaya*) school between the third and thirteenth centuries (the *Navya-Nyaya* school or the "New Logic"). Another axis of research would have in view the possible rapprochement between the conceptions of language and "phonocentrism" proper to certain Western thinkers, such as Humboldt and Heidegger, and the works of the school of linguistic analysis (*Vyakarana*) marked by figures like the grammarians Panini (fourth century BC) and Patanjali (second century BC) and above all Bhartrihari (probably fifth century AD). I consider such work to be the prelude to the fundamental task that, in my view, should be that of the thinkers of the twenty-first century: the development, within a resolutely "postcolonial" horizon, of a dialogue between Western thought and other traditions of thought.

Translated by Tarek R. Dika

Notes

1. A degree obtained at the end of one's secondary (high-school) education. The *filière classique* or "classic stream," so called because of its emphasis on Greek and Latin.

2. Monique Dixsaut is a professor emerita of philosophy at the University of Paris I Panthéon–Sorbonne.

3. Henry Corbin was a philosopher, theologian, and professor of Islamic studies at the École pratique des hautes études Paris. He was one of the first French

intellectuals to translate Heidegger into French. See his translation of Heidegger, "Qu'est que la metaphysique?."

4. An annual national competition for high school students in nearly all subjects of study.

5. See Husserl, *L'origine de la géométrie* and Derrida, *Husserl's* Origin of Geometry.

6. Werner Marx was a professor of philosophy at the New School and the University of Freiburg and the director of the Husserl-Archives and is the author of numerous books on Hegel, Husserl, and Heidegger, including *Heidegger and the Tradition, Absolute Reflexion und Sprache*, and *Hegel's* Phenomenology of Spirit.

7. Jan Patočka was one of the most significant figures in phenomenology in the latter half of the twentieth century and is the author of numerous books, including *Plato and Europe*; *Heretical Essays in the Philosophy of History*; *Body, Community, Language, World*; and *An Introduction to Husserl's Phenomenology*.

8. Roman Ingarden was a student of the Polish logician and philosopher Kazimierz Twardowski and later a student of Husserl's and is the author of *The Literary Work of Art, On the Motives which Led Edmund Husserl to Transcendental Idealism*, and *The Ontology of the Work of Art*.

9. The interview to which Dastur refers here was conducted on May 23, 1946, by Maurice Fleurent. Merleau-Ponty, *The Merleau-Ponty Reader*, 86.

10. See Husserl, *Experience and Judgment*, §10, 41.

11. See Heidegger, *Four Seminars*, 80.

12. Patočka, "Heidegger penseur de l'humanité," 388.

13. See Merleau-Ponty, *The Visible and the Invisible*, 130–56. Heidegger, *On Time and Being*, 1–25.

14. Sartre, *Being and Nothingness*, 698.

15. Heidegger, *Being and Time*, 127, and Heidegger, *Gesamtausgabe*, vol. 2, §29, 135.

16. Merleau-Ponty, *Phenomenology of Perception*, 477.

17. Heidegger, *Being and Time*, 426.

18. Derrida, *Of Spirit*, 12.

19. Dastur, "Pour une zoologie 'privative' ou comment ne pas parler de l'animal."

20. Heidegger, *Being and Time*, §41, 238.

21. Heidegger, *Logic*.

22. Not to be confused with a thesis. As its name suggests, a *mémoire de maîtrise* is a piece of writing that demonstrates a student's competence to write an original thesis (*doctorat d'Etat*) on some subject matter, given the research he or she has conducted.

23. See also Heidegger, *On the Way to Language*.

Phenomenology and the Frontier

JEAN-YVES LACOSTE

You have characterized your work as the exploration of the "frontier zone" between philosophy and theology, where the boundaries between them are no longer meaningful. Reflecting on your work as a whole, one might further say that your theoretical task has been to investigate, by means of phenomenology, the reaches of philosophical reflection in light of what you have called the "liturgical possibility." What kind of possibility does the "liturgical" refer to and how does it relate to the frontier between philosophy and theology?

"Liturgical" is often poorly understood, as if my ambition were to produce a phenomenology of worship. The concept is the result of a strategy. We have at our disposal a discipline, the philosophy of religion, whose existence I have no objection to. Nevertheless, I have always been embarrassed that the modern philosophy of religion, schematically from Schleiermacher through to William James, relies heavily upon a concept of experience: experience as religious sentiment. This concept has the advantage of providing an easy entry into the subject but the drawback of assigning narrow limits to the relationship of man to God. What is the believer "doing" when his experience of God is not a "religious experience" (for example, reading and agreeing with a theological text without feeling the presence of God at all)? Existing "before God," *coram Deo*, is not the same as living in a perpetual "religious experience." And "liturgy," if one accepts this starting point, is nothing more than what Gerhard Ebeling called the "*coram* relationship."[1] Ebeling is a dogmatician, which I'm really not; the concept of liturgy was born out of a philosophical question, for the simple reason that it arose from an embarrassment created by the philosophy of religion. The possibility I deployed was quite unambitious: that of a relationship to the Absolute that at certain points we know is real (I limited myself to situations in which the Absolute is known as a subject offering itself in relationship). Nothing, therefore, compels us to say that "possibility is held higher than reality." The possibility that liturgy gives us to understand is a realized possibility. From this realization, I chose, in *Experience et absolu*, a paradigmatic case: the experience of "night" in John of the Cross, conceived as "non-experience" and "non-event." Subsequent work of mine has attempted to examine the presence of affection at the heart of every liturgical situation. Every reality is the possible become real. No longer in the present case, however.

The result is that the relationship between philosophy and theology becomes almost uninteresting. The philosopher of religion certainly reads theological texts and he can even find paradigms for his analyses in theology. However, no jurisprudential conflict can arise here. The introduction of a Christological paradigm into the philosophy of religion is legitimate and needs no defense. One will at least have the courtesy to admit that the smidgen of Christology in my work really doesn't claim to be a Christology. We cannot avoid this intrusion if our mother tongue is that of Christianity (or Judaism and, in a way that I do not know, Islam). We unintentionally appeal to theology very frequently—let us recall, for example, that according to Carl Schmitt, all our political concepts are secularized theological concepts. By appealing to it voluntarily we avoid naivety . . .

Talk of limits or borders loses its pertinence here. Liturgy is a possibility for man: it has the quality of the a priori. However, we only have an a posteriori knowledge of the a priori. When I conclude my descriptions, in *Experience et absolu*, with a Christological allusion, "where" do we stand? We certainly do not leap over a gap between philosophy and theology. Most important, what I said earlier neither stands nor falls with its Christological elucidation. In fact, the kenotic Christological paradigm retrospectively casts light on descriptions that are in themselves valid—I have just said that the purpose is not Christian and only Christian. One example merits scrutiny, that of Karl Rahner's theory of "anonymous Christians."[2] In proposing this concept, Rahner wanted, first of all, to make his contribution to the old theory of the salvation of unbelievers (in which I have never been interested). But what matters more to me is that he then made use of a transcendental possibility. Theology has a concept, which Rahner takes up, that of the "obediential power to the Hypostatic Union": clearly, if God made himself man, it first of all had to be a human possibility.[3] Rahner is the author of a transcendental Christology, that is to say, an a priori deduction of the "fact" of Jesus Christ. I have smaller ambitions. Even so, our aims are not too far apart. Liturgy, which is real, is necessarily possible. Not only is it possible, but it is possible for everyone. Theology speaks about God; it must also teach us how to speak to God (but does it always?). It also teaches us how to exist *coram Deo* and according to what logic. And the "we" of whom I speak is also the one philosophers talk about. When we talk about liturgy, we place ourselves in a border region. We are here and there at once—or neither here nor there. Labels no longer apply.

Still, you have written and directed numerous theological works, including Dictionnaire critique de théologie *and, most recently,* Histoire de la théologie. *Your more philosophical works themselves possess themes that are strongly theological as well. What does the investigation and reflection upon specifically theological phenomena offer to philosophy? Does the relation between them amount to a fully reciprocal exchange?*

We have to come to some agreement on the existence of "specifically theological" phenomena. Are there, first of all, problems that are of interest only to theology? That is not clear. Everything that pertains to theological inquiry also pertains to history, for example. The question of the anointing of the sick can be studied in socio-historic terms. We constantly speak of the "historical" Jesus—and even if the "historical Jesus" is, of course, the Jesus of the historian, nothing prevents the historian from admitting that it is the one and the same Jesus with whom he is dealing . . . Theological questions are, in fact, vulnerable—that is, they do not *belong* to theology. A French historian, Jacques Le Goff, wrote a *histoire du purgatoire* that has great merits but has no theological interest.[4] The Church is of interest to the sociologist, and it is sociologically interesting. And since God, finally, is also the concern of philosophers (and not just philosophers), it must be said that He is not the preserve of theologians . . .

This does not mean that there are no theological questions; it simply means admitting that there are no exclusively theological questions. The history of the Church is certainly a theological discipline, which can be written according to theological presuppositions. It highlights the contribution of the saints, it relies on a concept (also known in philosophy since the Stoics) of divine providence, etc. But who will claim that the historian who brackets any theological presupposition or theological "intellectual concern" [*intérêt de connaissance*] cannot also contribute to writing this story?

The case of the philosopher is certainly not the same as that of the sociologist or historian. If we go back to Christian antiquity, we don't find "theology." "Theology," in Greek, refers to mythology. "Philosophy," however (and always in Greek), is entitled to deal rationally with divinity. And if, for example, we asked Origen to provide a name for what he does, that name would be "philosophy." In his *Contra Celsus*—the most monumental Christian apologetic against paganism that we have—Origen develops a common Patristic theme: Jews and Christians are the true or the best philosophers. Greek philosophy is not repudiated en bloc. The Jewish and Christian experience, however, is that of the truly philosophical life and truly philosophical knowledge. It would take a long time for theology to acquire the name by which we now know it. In Thomas Aquinas, it is called "sacred doctrine" or "sacred page," *doctrina sacra* or *sacra pagina*. Aquinas, in his *Summa Contra Gentiles* for instance, is himself able to slide easily from what we would call a philosophical inquiry to one that we would call theological. Theological modernity (one particular theological modernity, in any case) was founded on the establishment of the distinction between two orders, that of the "natural" and the "supernatural." It was also rooted in the birth of universities and the encounter of the faculties of philosophy and theology within those universities. Theology as we know it was created by the academy. But the fact that it took twelve centuries to get there might suggest that it was not absolutely necessary . . .

This is not necessarily to deny the academic specificity of the theological. The philosopher may discuss the Trinity (even though there is no shortage of theologians queuing up to forbid him), but the theologian fills an "ecclesial mission" that requires him to use sources—a "believing" use, let's say—in a way that is not quite the same as that of the philosopher. Nothing is apparently more neutral than a dictionary or a history of theology: it is about the transmission of knowledge, the statement of theoretical facts, etc. However, this is a false neutrality. Developing an encyclopedic work is not a work of original thought and therefore not of theological thought. It does, however, bring into play epistemological interests that are properly committed. The level of commitment is certainly less than that of an original contribution to theology: an encyclopedia is only a minor contribution. However, one must be perceptive. And if one is, one understands that the second edition of the *Lexikon für Theologie und Kirche* bears the clear mark of Karl Rahner's theology and that if there was a third edition (under the responsibility of Walter Kasper), this was certainly in order to provide the reader with a working tool influenced by more discreet theological choices. What I would add is that we sometimes find dictionary articles that, despite the theoretical discretion appropriate to the genre, are obviously part of the corpus of their author: for instance, Bultmann's articles in Kittel's *Wörterbuch zum Neuen Testament Theologisches*.

Encyclopedic works certainly do not give rise to thought, they only give rise to knowledge . . . Theology, however, gives rise to thought (and it sometimes even thinks, purely and simply). The fact that the theological is available to us, in books, in traditions, etc., and that no barrier is placed between the philosopher and the theological text, is immensely important. According to the statutes of the medieval university, the theologian had the right to access the works of the philosopher, but the converse was not true: the philosopher was nothing more than a philosopher. Admittedly, these statutes are obsolete. There is certainly no shortage of philosophers who have no theological interests. Can philosophy, in the modern sense of the word, avoid a confrontation with theology? Nothing is less clear. We have known an intellectual situation where philosophy sustained theological texts: Christian Platonism, Christian Aristotelianism, etc. We perhaps know (or, alternatively, should have the choice of promoting) a situation in which theology, if the philosopher encounters it, provides an excess of rationality that there is no reason to deny. Theology has for a long time been under the protection of a concept, that of "mystery," which has a frightening air about it for the philosopher. Furthermore, this discourse is under the protection of faith. However, "mystery" and "faith" should not frighten them. The mysterious is not illogical: it has its own phenomenality, which we can understand. Faith is not non-rational: it is a mode in which reason is exercised. And if we accept both of these statements, then we will accept the hypothetical fertilization of the philosophical by the theological. Early in his *Phenomenology of Spirit*, Hegel speaks of the divine life as a "game of love with itself," using terms that discretely but firmly refer to Trinitarian theology.[5] Schelling not only offers a philosophy of revelation, but in *Ages of the World* he plays the same game as Hegel (he plays it quite differently, of course). More recently, we have seen the publication of essays on "Trinitarian ontology" by Clemens Kaliba, Klaus Hemmerle, and others.[6] Theology is not at all "wholly other" than philosophy. To which we can add that it is less important whether we practice philosophy or theology and that the present task (if we are to believe Heidegger) is "simply" the task of thinking.

What is the special pertinence of phenomenology for your work of re-exploring these frontier territories long abandoned as intractable wildwood?

Concepts always constitute an *organon*: an instrument. We cannot think without them. We are often the heirs of an *organon*: it is not at our disposal because we chose it but because it was given to us—by circumstance, by our teachers, and so on. That said, the choice of phenomenology is, firstly, one that I made, and, secondly, one in which no theological interest was taken into consideration. In fact, the first conceptual tools proper to theological discourse that I encountered were those of Kierkegaard, at a time in my life when Husserl and Heidegger, then Lévinas and Henry, exercised a power over me for other reasons—above all the exploration of the "continent of consciousness," both among those who spoke about consciousness and those who did not. So it is simply by chance that my phenomenological readings have shown themselves able to organize what little theology I knew or, more precisely, to give rise to theological interests. These phenomenological readings were therefore eclectic. It is a peculiarity of French universities, however, to have produced philosophers that can read Husserl just as well as Heidegger, to benefit from one and the other reading, and thus not be tied to any orthodoxy. (Not every French phenomenologist of my generation was so lucky: I have known dogmatic Husserlians and fanatical Heideggerians, Lévinasians of the strict observance, etc.) Phenomenology, as I encountered it in the wake of May '68, is what Spiegelberg has cautiously called a "movement."[7] I found myself taken with this movement. Above all, I found myself taken with it without initially seeing in it the conceptual tools that could be put to the service of theological or, more vaguely, Christian concerns.

I attended Lévinas's last seminar at the Sorbonne. He dedicated it to Henry, whom he admired immensely, and he could not avoid mentioning Eckhart a bit—but the goal was not to introduce the mystical life . . . The publication of the complete works of Heidegger began in 1977, and that event saw the appearance of the Marburg lectures, now completed, in which we find little of interest to the theologian. There were readers of Lévinas who tried to theologize his work, but they were mistaken: despite the importation (careless, no doubt) of a theological vocabulary, Lévinas had no other ambition than to organize, phenomenologically, a "first philosophy." In short, I was attracted to phenomenology for the rigor of the descriptions I found there. Not until later did I think to "use" phenomenology to describe what the classics, both big and small, had described . . .

One curious fact bears mentioning in passing. Rudolf Otto sent Husserl (born a Jew, baptized partly through routine and partly through social convention, and a devout Christian in his later years) a copy of his book *The Idea of the Holy*. The book comes from Marburg and is therefore neo-Kantian. Strangely though, Husserl saw in it a contribution to a phenomenology of religion. There is a moral there (which I did not know when I began to engage with Husserl's phenomenology): there was room—for "the master"—for a phenomenological approach to religious phenomena. Husserl, moreover, thought that the young Heidegger was working—or would work—on developing such an approach. Recent studies and publications have, in fact, taught us that Heidegger had an extensive theological education. In Husserlian terms, all phenomena are equal (the idea that some are more equal than others is a recent idea). The idea of a phenomenology of religious facts is a phenomenological commonplace. Not everyone has always recognized this.

A remark is necessary here. We speak of Husserl and Heidegger but must still observe that Heidegger took leave of phenomenology (in 1930, with the study *Vom Wesen der Warheit*).[8] The post-phenomenological Heidegger, whom William Richardson names "Heidegger II," has indeed been taken over by French phenomenology—being French phenomenology, however, it declined to make a break between a "realistic" Husserl and an "idealistic" Husserl. So I learned to decipher the continuities more than to establish a map of the discontinuities. Heidegger II has certainly had bad disciples. Husserl, in his later period, encouraged Fink, whose posthumous fragments from this period reveal actual Gnostic tendencies. Still, my contemporaries and I have approached the "aletheology" of Heidegger II as the pursuit of a phenomenological itinerary, just as we have read the *Logical Investigations* and *Ideas I* and *II* with the same interest.

It's not hard to find the reason for a fruitful engagement with phenomenology. To put it metaphorically, we must take note of the hospitable nature of phenomenology, such as it burst on the scene with Husserl. We are not dealing here with a bed of Procrustean theory, such that everything that is, and every way of being, would have to comply with its constraints on pain of losing the right to be. Husserl treats everything that appears as it appears, and as it appears from itself—a starting point that he never denied and that has a "realistic" character. Every phenomenon is a phenomenon. But "to every fundamental mode of objectity . . . there belongs a fundamental mode of evidence."[9] What, then, is the fundamental mode of evidence of the phenomena we call "religious"? We are entitled to ask this question. We are entitled to ask it, especially, as a question capable of receiving a consistent answer, or answers. Phenomenology, in this sense, must be of interest to the philosopher of mathematics—Husserl's *Habilitationsschrift*, on the philosophy of arithmetic, is pre-phenomenological, but Husserl had an enduring interest in logic and mathematics. It must also be of interest to the moralist—Scheler's theory of values is, of course, shaky, but it belongs to the "phenomenological movement." And having given these two examples, we can conclude that nothing is impossible for anyone exploring the "liturgical" or "religious" field in phenomenological terms. Phenomenology would collapse altogether if it only contained, in essence, one possible theological moment—an observation that does away with the critique of a "theological turn" suffered by phenomenology at the hands of careless believers. To answer the first question plainly, the liturgical possibility is an "anthropological" possibility, *sit venia verbo*, whose phenomenological description is unrestrictedly possible in phenomenology.

Pascal, of course, famously elected the "God of Abraham, Isaac, and Jacob" over the "God of the philosophers." The exigencies of such a decision loom large in contemporary continental thought—theological as much as philosophical. Yet against the tide of general consensus, in Experience and the Absolute *you offer a sort of rehabilitation of the "Absolute"—the most classical name of the "God of the philosophers." Why are you compelled to make such a radical rehabilitation? And would it be fair to say that,* pace *Hegel, you have sought to divorce the "Absolute" in "Absolute Knowledge" from "Knowledge," that is, from the measure of the (our) Concept(s)? How would you articulate your relation to Hegel? And yet Kierkegaard himself is a major point of reference, no less profound than implicit, in your work . . .*

We should do away with Pascal's distinction. Doing so is certainly difficult for a French person, who necessarily has a soft spot for a great thinker who was also a great stylist. Among the great thinkers of the West, Pascal is the one who, as Cartesian as he was, repudiated philosophy most brutally. But what is this repudiation worth? I wholeheartedly agree that the biblical tradition knows many things about God that Greece did not know. One of the mentors of my youth, Maxime Charles, liked to relegate the God of Aristotle to what one might call the "outdated gods" (others would call them "idols").[10] Now, does this apply to the God of the philosophers when these philosophers are also readers of the Biblical text and its Christian or Jewish commentaries? All things considered, one should say no. Concepts have a history, and there are, therefore, dead concepts—which means, playing on words, that there are as many dead gods. Does it follow that the philosopher who respects God's divinity has nothing to say about God? An almost classical polemic against the "*causa sui*" is inscribed into our memory (more than that, it's constantly present). However, the God of the philosophers, despite Heidegger, is not merely *causa sui*. Descartes himself, who bears some of the responsibility, certainly does not worship the *causa sui*, but we must not forget that he concludes his Third Meditation with a prayer of adoration.

One must go further. The eighteenth century certainly knew the reign of a God who was not that of Abraham, Isaac, and Jacob—not all concepts are created equal, and neither theism nor deism have the least idea of him of whom theology speaks—"natural theology" unquestionably tells us about a God who is *nothing more* than that of philosophers and intellectuals. The Enlightenment, however, did not have the last word in the history of philosophy. The God of whom Hegel and Schelling speak is the same as the one of whom theology speaks (and even if Hegel and Schelling claim to speak better than theology does, we need not concede them this). In spite of himself, Kierkegaard belongs to the history of philosophy, (although he would rather have played the role of "Christian thinker") and, in any case, it is clear that he also confirms the end of natural theology. And here we enter a long chapter in the history of philosophy, where Nietzsche's "God is dead" perhaps endorses the twilight of the idols, but it would not take long for Rosenzweig to make heard his own defense and illustration of the God who saves (Rosenzweig, who is totally opposed to Hegel but still the unintended heir of a breakthrough in which Hegel played a leading role).

I mention all this by way of saying that we have the right (and duty!) to demolish metaphysics (a task that appears increasingly difficult as we try to locate the birth certificate of onto-theology) but that words are worth exactly the use we make of them and that the words of philosophy are not to be feared. I had a goal in mind when I let myself speak provocatively of God as Absolute: not to pronounce the name of God. This name is certainly not unpronounceable. But does introducing God as the Absolute make a deliberate concession to metaphysics (in the Heideggerian sense)? Certainly not. It was done, quite modestly, in order to position it within a particular domain (in this case that of German idealism, specifically that of Hegel) in order to occupy it in a different way. In other words, there is a non-metaphysical thought of the Absolute. This is not the highest of the divine names. However, it is not less divine than "self-subsistent being" or "pure act of being." The use of names in this domain takes precedence over the history of these names. We are demolishing metaphysics, or are trying to do so. We are trying to think beyond what it has thought, or to think after it—it does not really matter. However, we cannot make a blank slate of it. Heidegger called it the end of philosophy and said that we had to face a post-philosophical task, that of thinking. Perhaps. But is the absoluteness of God a reality we cannot think? Concepts have a history; the concept of the Absolute has one. We probably have to conceive the absoluteness of God anew. It seemed to me, in any case, that the possibility was given to us. As I conceive the experience or non-experience of the Absolute, it is a resolutely anti-Hegelian experience (or non-experience). Is it too much of a concession to metaphysics to use one of its concepts in trying to "reconceive" it? Thought never thinks from nothing. It thinks, to follow the pattern suggested by Heidegger, in three stages: reduction, destruction, construction. It is by putting to work what we have destroyed (I do not speak of "deconstruction"—the concept was foreign to his phenomenology) that we can build. And in building, finally, we are confronted with a major historical phenomenon: not only can we not exit metaphysics as easily as we change our point of view, but we do not think post-metaphysically without thinking with metaphysics. This gives food for thought. Our problem is to grasp what it offers us . . .

The task, therefore, is to deny or overcome Pascal's alternative. I am not doing anything novel here. Montaigne's God is not that of a pure philosopher (it should also be asked what purity is at stake when we speak of a pure philosopher). Descartes wrote a theory of the Eucharist, as did Leibniz. Malebranche attempted to disentangle the inextricable relationship between "nature" and "grace." Hegel and Schelling, in their own ways and without much concern for orthodoxy, bequeathed us theologies of creation, the Trinity, etc. (We are indebted to Xavier Tilliette for his work on the Christ of philosophers, the Holy Week of philosophers, the ecclesiology of philosophers, etc.)[11] I can certainly appreciate the force of Barth's objection: if it is Christology, it is not philosophy; if it is philosophy, it cannot be theology. The objection, however, begins from the Pascalian antinomy. If we refuse it, for the simple reason that every phenomenon has the same right as any other to be welcomed and described, then we will have no trouble saying that there is only one God—of Abraham, Isaac, Jacob, philosophers, and scientists. He certainly discloses himself in a different way to the "theologian" (or to the simple Christian) than to the "philosopher," but these *different* appearances are still different appearances of the *same* thing. Since there is more than one perspective, one needs to do hermeneutical work. This work is not doomed to failure. One of my colleagues at the École normale supérieure was led from atheism to Christianity by an assiduous study of philosophical texts. I was myself fascinated by the God of the philosophers at a time when the God of the Christian faith was poorly represented in churches. There is only one God, who does not appear to the philosopher in the same way that he does to the theologian. We should therefore take heed of the emergence in Pascal of something that borders on neo-Marcionism. Philosophy is not doomed only to think the divine, a neutral *to theion*, at odds with a theology that is alone authorized to speak about God, *ho théos*.

In the end, there is no absolute knowledge, because absolute knowledge is an eschatological fact, and we live within history. And within history, we must concede to Kierkegaard that knowledge is governed by what we might call a "law of fragmentation." The title of the *Philosophical Fragments* is almost as interesting as the text; if there must be thinking, and if the work of thinking must be a demolition of German idealism, then the "crumbs" or the "fragments" are our best guarantee against a totalization of knowledge that leaves no room for a knowledge to come. There is more. Kierkegaard defines himself as neither a philosopher nor a theologian but as a "Christian thinker" with the stress on "thinker." We cannot attribute to Kierkegaard a rigorous concept of thought, one that is distinct from philosophy—but the word is there, and it is there to indicate an in-between or the flight from an alternative. Everything happens as if we have to choose between philosophy and theology (and the neo-Thomism that started to emerge during the last years of Kierkegaard's life will do much to enforce this division of labor). Do we really have to choose? The intrusion of thought in Kierkegaard, and later in Heidegger's 1931–1932 lectures, allows us not to. The God of Jewish and Christian experience certainly offers himself up to praise before he offers himself up to thought. But if we accept the basic fact that he also offers himself up to thought, then we can refuse to segregate what we think—whether it is in the camp of theology or of philosophy—and can therefore be content to think. It is for the philosopher and theologian to recognize the relevance of our work—and since I mentioned Barth, let's not forget that he knew the influence of Kierkegaard, whom he does not mention in his history of *Protestant Theology in the Nineteenth Century* but who is omnipresent in the first commentary on Romans . . .

To say that we are content to think can seem outrageous. It is "wise" to work as a theologian and only as a theologian, or as a philosopher and only as a philosopher. Such wisdom, however, leads to an impasse: By what right do we separate what Christian antiquity refused to separate? The one who tries to think, in fact, is only interested in what comes to experience for him and is only describing contents of his current or possible experience. Phenomenology, to put it frankly, cannot endorse the separation of the philosophical and theological. It cannot encourage any prejudice with regard to what it is given. The description will be different each time: the pen lying on my desk, the work of art that I enjoy, the man who is said to come from God. Still, we do not need to employ a subterfuge to say that in every instance it is phenomenality with which we are dealing. I entitled one of my books *La phénoménalité de Dieu*. This does not refer to an event in the manner of theophany. It simply meant that if God enters the field of the phenomenon (if he appears in memory, in sacramental presence, etc.), he has the right to be thought (or demands to be thought) both with respect to what links his manifestation to all manifestation as well as to what distinguishes his manifestation from any other. Thought is thinking without limits.

In an article you wrote for the Dictionnaire critique de théologie, you offer what would have to be called nothing less than an "eschatological hermeneutic" of modern philosophy: "The systems of thought through which the metaphysical fate of the West has been carried out have been numerous, but they all have in common at least either the realization of the eschaton *in history (Hegel), or a rigorous discrediting of the eschatological problem (Nietzsche). And they implicitly consent to a reign of death over man (and over the access to meaning)."*[12] *What, exactly, does this mean?*

If anything is certain it is that these two words, "nihilism" and "eschatology," must be pronounced in every investigation into modern Western philosophy. From the standpoint of theology, the resurgence of the eschatological problem (which had been completely overshadowed in the nineteenth century) began with the book by Johannes Weiss, *Die Predigt Jesu vom Reiche Gottes* (1892). From the perspective of philosophy, it was thanks to the thesis of Hans Urs von Balthasar,[13] on the one hand, and, on the other, Jacob Taubes's book *Occidental Eschatology*. This resurgence was a major event, and one can thus say that the "department of eschatology" is now working "overtime."[14] Which eschatology, however? If we ask Hegel to provide us with a starting point, it will be a matter of a "realized" eschatology, an end that promises no future other than its own perenniality. But if that is the starting point, then the philosophy of the end of history is defenseless against a philosophy of the eternal return of the same. Writing a genealogy of nihilism is not an easy thing. In a tribute to Henri de Lubac, reprinted in *Le monde et l'absence d'œuvre*,[15] I dared to suggest that the theory of "pure nature" bore a considerable share of responsibility. One slightly surprising example is provided by the theory of "limbo"—the *limbus infantium*. According to that theory, unbaptized children who die are not allowed into the Kingdom of God. They are doomed to live (forever) at the fringes of hell, where they enjoy a natural beatitude. And for them this natural beatitude is enough, for the simple reason that no "natural desire to see God" is implanted in them. While the theory is somewhat kitschy it still has its supporters. Unfortunately, these supporters do not see that an eternity lived in limbo would inevitably be a figure of a Hegelian "bad infinity": a repetitive eternity, doomed to give rise to boredom, is as hellish as possible. There is only a small step from here to Nietzsche, who is the most violent thinker of what we might call the "anti-historical." He is the one who consistently denies the once and for all character of "history of salvation" and the cross. He is, therefore, the declared opponent of any eschatology. Nihilism (understood as the devaluation of the highest values and death of a God in whom we would have assigned the status of value) does not affirm that there is nothing or that there is nothing more than the reign of Nothing. It affirms the impossibility of the final word. Nothing more, nothing less.

What does an eschatology that is resistant to the onslaught of Nietzsche involve? I have just suggested that it is primarily a criticism of any realized eschatology. There is room in Hegel for every article of the Christian confession of faith, except one: Hegel does not expect "the resurrection of the dead and the life of the world to come." Now, can we refrain from making room for "being that is not yet"? Phenomenology, especially Husserlian phenomenology, focuses primarily on primary experiences. Husserl was developing a philosophy that started from the bottom—which does not prevent it from having the ambition to rise, and to rise up toward God. Phenomenology, however, has never believed that everything is given when the most basic evidences are given. And if there is a privileged philosophical experience, it is quite simply one of wonder before that which was not there and now gives itself to intuition. Despite the *Crisis*, one does not need to take Husserl for a philosopher of history, let alone a philosopher of realized history. It is necessary, in any case, to take account of the means that he gives us to overcome nihilism. Overcoming nihilism can be done very simply, in the practice of the reduction, which we can accept here in its first two canonical forms (I have never used a transcendental reduction). To bracket—that is, not to preoccupy oneself with what is outside the immanent field of consciousness, to concern oneself therefore with the essential, or *eidos*—is not a procedure of negation. It is to affirm that things are and to say that without falling into the sterile debate that opposes "realism" and "idealism" (what Husserl later called his "transcendental idealism" is, let us be clear, not what was traditionally called idealism). In common experience, no one asks if what he perceives has a being external to consciousness. We dream, relive our memories, perceive, wait, we give ourselves to a work of conceptualization, etc., and the only thing that interests us is the content and the how of the appearing. There is no place whatsoever for a reign of Nothing or a devaluation of the highest values, especially for an eternal return of the same. Phenomenology enjoys whatever is given to it. It also patiently awaits whatever will be given to it. And as long as we show any interest at all in Husserl's research on time, from *On the Phenomenology of the Consciousness of Internal Time* to the C-manuscripts to the Bernau manuscripts,[16] we find that the life of consciousness forbids the eternal return of the same, as the practice of the reduction forbids the advent of nihilism. There can be no nihilist phenomenology. But phenomenology can welcome the eschaton: it is enough for it to be given, although it comes here and now, of course, only in the form of anticipations or as a "micro-eschatology."[17]

In light of this, how do you understand the significance of eschatology for philosophy—a task clarified further as phenomenological? Is there, in other words, an irreducibly eschatological dimension to the practice of philosophy in general and phenomenology in particular?

Phenomenology is a matter of intuition and description, it speculates only because of a lack of anything better (if there is a lack of "originary intuitions"), and if it constructs, it can only be in strict fidelity to its intuitive data. However, I fully concede that we can practice phenomenology in an eschatological horizon (though not all would say so). This concession is not made to a totalizing thought that, based on this or that anticipation, would speak backward from the end: that is what Hegel did and what phenomenology cannot do. And here phenomenology returns us to hermeneutics. "We must choose between absolute knowledge and the hermeneutics of testimony."[18] This sentence of Ricoeur ought to be inscribed in golden letters on the front page of every text. When it comes to eschatology, the phenomena that we are talking about are phenomena given to us within the horizon of a history—whether it's a matter of the experience of mystics or of texts presented as divine speech.

Turning now to the relation between phenomenology and metaphysics: Is their relation still a question worth asking, and does it have a determinant sense? Do you, as other contemporary phenomenologists do, hold that phenomenology is or can in some sense be "post-metaphysical"? Or is phenomenology (transcendental or not) more implicated in "metaphysics" than some of its practitioners would like to believe?

Both are possible. Husserl's phenomenology can be regarded as the height of the theoretical efforts of the West. It can also pass for a post-metaphysical enterprise. For those working in the perpetual back and forth between Husserl and Heidegger, however, the questions lose some of their weight. There is certainly no critique of metaphysics in Husserl. Moreover, his language is often that of metaphysics. The turn to Descartes, finally, may be regarded as a concession to metaphysics. Heidegger, for his part, denounced the onto-theological constitution of metaphysics (and one often has the impression that Husserl, when he speaks of God, does so in onto-theological terms . . .), but Derrida sees in Heidegger a metaphysician. Let us repeat, for the sake of clarity, that we are still unable to write a history of metaphysics. The crucial moment in the history of onto-theology has been known for some years now: the turning point came in Suárez. The questions, however, outnumber the claims. Does Neoplatonism belong to the history of onto-theology? Is Latin philosophy and theology metaphysical, as Heidegger claimed? We are still exploring a terrain that is only partially mapped. In the course that he taught at Marburg in 1927, when finishing *Being and Time*, Heidegger described Thomas Aquinas as the first modern and outlined a critique of onto-theology as a foray into the work of Aquinas.[19] Can we say this categorically? Fortunately, most of the texts of Heidegger are now accessible to us, and we can avoid naive readings. Here again, let us say that the concept of limit—either metaphysical thinking or post-metaphysical thought—is not really at work. Whether we like it or not, we are the heirs of metaphysics. We may desire an exodus, but the whole idea of an accomplished rupture would be a misconception. It would be rash of us to believe that metaphysics belongs to our past. Maybe we are still metaphysicians. And even: perhaps there is a moment of eternal truth in metaphysics . . .

The priority of the affective-corporeal dimension in your own work seems, at the very least, to resemble and radicalize a certain development that took place in history of phenomenology: viz., the displacement of Husserl's more or less epistemic determination of intentionality by Heidegger's existential determination of intentionality. Is it nevertheless right to see a tension in your work between the desire to retain a Husserlian conception of consciousness, on the one hand, and a Heideggerian radicalization by way of a "pre-theoretical" affectivity, on the other? How do these relate?

First of all, let's be clear that the pre-theoretical dimension is as crucial for Husserl as for Heidegger. The theory of ante-predicative evidence is certainly not constructed, in Husserl, to counter Heidegger. But for both philosophers, whatever is given to us is given first of all as a silent grasping or apprehension. From this perspective *Experience and Judgment* is one of the keystones of phenomenology: Husserl was always concerned with the theory of judgment (and Heidegger was concerned with it in his doctoral thesis). But in working through the problem of evidence—understood as experience of the truth—he could not fail to perceive that things make themselves available to us before we talk about them and in any case, independently of whatever we say about them. And here it is not a choice between a Heideggerian form of phenomenology and a Husserlian style of phenomenology. The "life world" as conceptualized in the later works of Husserl, is not the "world" described by Heidegger. "Life," moreover, is not "existence" (a term that Husserl abhorred). But in both oeuvres, knowledge is silent before being assumed in the element of discursivity. I fully accept that with, it is true, the impression of accepting a fundamental truth.

The issue of affective knowledge, however, arises differently. Husserl developed a strong philosophy of corporeality, and we know that Heidegger never speaks of either the body or flesh. Husserl, conversely, speaks about "affection" merely to denote the impact of the external upon us, without ever implementing a clear theory of affectivity. And on this point, we cannot avoid finding theoretical enrichment in *Being and Time* (and an over-enrichment in Henry). However we describe it, knowledge involves affect; even the most "disinterested" knowledge, viz. *theôria*, according to Heidegger (quoting Aristotle), has its affective tone. However, is it necessary for what affects us to tally up exactly with what we know? In *Être en danger*, I sketched out a theory of the constitution of the object in which I reserve the name of object for whatever appears to me without affecting me, simply because, when it appears to me, I am affected by something other than it. A fit of anxiety or a memory distracts me and the rose bush that once appeared to me as a "thing of beauty" is no longer here except in the mode of an object.[20] I am always present as a consciousness that is both affective and affected. But the affecting function of what I perceive is put out of play: I perceive without being affected by what I am perceiving.

What concepts do you use to talk about this affected "I"?

Here, my debt to Husserl is undeniable. On the one hand, is the subject (the metaphysical subject, which we owe to Descartes) to be laid to rest? Not if one accepts the idea of a constitution of objectity in a perception without affection; corresponding to objectity is what may be called a quasi-subject whose only task is representation. It follows, nevertheless, that we cannot abandon either the concept of subjectivity or that of intentionality. Denying them is, in a sense, naive. The purpose of this naïveté is respectable, preventing the self from occupying so strong a position that the other is only the other, or that intentional content is only intentional content. This is not what Husserl wanted. Consciousness, according to Husserl, is, from the beginning, decentered to the extent that it is intentional. Intentionality is centripetal (something is given to me), but it is also centrifugal (I am given over to it). Reading the summary of phenomenology that Heidegger proposed in the lecture course on the *History of the Concept of Time: Prolegomena* should be enough to persuade us of that. And it should be enough to persuade us that, although the concept of intentionality (like that of consciousness [*Bewusstsein*]) is missing from Heidegger, the existent truly exists in an authentically intentional and, obviously, conscious manner. Is it necessary to choose between intentionality and care? Maybe not. The appearance of a "tension" here, in my opinion, is nothing more than the expression of an alliance.

In Expérience et absolu *(1994) it is the kenotic saint or "holy fool" who provides the paradigm for liturgical dwelling, whereas subsequently (*Le monde et l'absence d'œuvre, *2000) you seem more concerned with quotidian ways of access to a realm at least analogous to the liturgical or the eschatological-like, such as the moment of rest or the work of art. How do you conceive of the relation between aesthetic or "sabbathic" experience and the properly liturgical realm itself?*

"Liturgical" phenomena are not the only ones that merit my interest. First of all, they are interesting because of what they give to be understood; they are also interesting in that they belong to a class of phenomena, call them "aberrant" phenomena. What kind of aberrance? Let's say that they violate the standard logic of being-in-the-world. We can exist *coram Deo*. In the same way, we can experience "rest," or unintentional joy, and others besides. But if permission is uncontestable (if we can, we certainly may . . .),[21] what we are permitted in these cases is an experience, or an existential content of experience, that is just about insignificant. Liturgical experience, the experience of rest, etc., all these experiences do not reveal, and probably conceal, the exact sense of what "to exist" means. Should one, however, concede everything to the Heideggerian *Daseinsanalytik*? I do not believe so. In *Note sur le temps* I simply attempted to position myself against the main thesis of *Being and Time*. Heidegger says that "the essence of existence is care," and if "carelessness" appears in the text then it is in the shape of a fallen [*déchue*] experience. However, a positive reading of "carelessness" is possible, which introduces a non-Heideggerian interpretation of temporality and which has its own phenomenological richness. To exist, in a way, is also to violate the common laws that govern existence. We can do more than exist. Heidegger himself knew that; in the "later," post-phenomenological texts he describes experiences that are no longer commensurate with the existent but now with "mortals": see *Gelassenheit*, *Das Ding*, etc.[22] But if we stick to the book of 1927, we must recognize that it has no shortage of partiality (or, to put it more politely, that it is partial). And in this respect, the propositions I made on behalf of aberrant phenomena come down to refusing what must surely appear to us as a theoretical narrowing of what I ended up calling, in *Être en danger*, "life."

In Heidegger no phenomenon is forbidden to appear. Duly noted. Some phenomena, however, are kept silent or discrete to the point of insignificance but that, upon careful scrutiny, often seem much more significant than insignificant. The standard logic of being-in-the-world can be subverted. And liturgy is not the only thing that subverts it.

In La phénoménalité de Dieu: Neuf études *you say that God is* connaissable comme aimable *(knowable through being loved) . . .*

The purpose of the study is simply to elucidate a well-defined case of affective knowledge [*connaissance affective*]. To do this, it was necessary to avoid a disjunction between "faith" and "reason," which, it should be clear to everyone, is as ruinous as that between the "God of the philosophers" and the "God of Abraham, Isaac, and Jacob." Can we know [*connaître*] God without loving Him? If one brackets the case, mentioned in the New Testament, of the "faith of demons" (we bracket it out because the demons do not understand [*connaissent*] the basis of being-in-the-world), the idea of a God that one would, first of all, know in order then to love places suspicion on the knowledge in question. Knowing [*Connaître*] is not knowledge [*savoir*]. Knowledge [*Le savoir*] is propositional, knowing [*la connaissance*] involves me fully ("personally," in Polanyi's epistemology),[23] and this includes my entire affective life. There are more everyday examples than the knowledge of God. Can we "know" the Bach of the *Art of Fugue* or the *Musical Offering* without feeling coming into play and in some way "sympathizing" with the work? Everyone will agree with these examples. Bach demands to be loved on pain of not being known at all. Consequently, can the work of reason alone be a work of the knowledge of God? Knowledge of God—our knowledge—is inscribed in the overall logic of existence. The knowledge of God is in this sense only one case. It is, however, a special case. We can be interested in God, from a purely theoretical interest, without loving Him. But if we can do so, it is because our interest is only "theoretical" and does not have the richness of the Greek *theôria*. Whoever talks about *theôria* can cross over to the Latin and talk about *contemplatio* or, with Bernard of Clairvaux, *consideratio*. And once this crossing is made, it becomes clear that God is not an object of supreme knowledge [*savoir*] (we have known this for a long time!) and that his appearance, however it appears to us, is only ever adequately welcomed by those who love the One who appears to them.

The adverb "adequately" is obviously carelessly used if taken in its Husserlian sense. We have no knowledge [*connaissance*] of God that will ever adequately place him at our disposal. Therefore, whatever the aberrant nature of the experiences in which we come face to face with God, these experiences are limited—the limits of the world, limitations of the flesh, etc. Neither in theory nor in experience is this particularly dramatic. One of the greatest of the divine names is the Infinite: thanks to Duns Scotus we can talk about it somewhat precisely. Another divine name that one must appeal to is the Eternal. We are neither infinite nor eternal in the world. The paradox is that in the world God nonetheless gives Himself to be known and that our knowledge, infinitely non-comprehensive, can claim validity. Bérulle speaks of man as "a nothingness capable of God."[24] Both Eastern and Western theology understand the absolute future of man with the help of the concept of "divinization." Divinization cannot happen in the world. In the "world," taken in its strict sense, in fact, man is "without God," *athéos* (Ephesians 2:12). We do not, however, have to choose between the alternatives of atheism or comprehensive knowledge. Finite knowledge of God (and it will be eternally finite) is a knowledge that one can call "adequate" in a cautious way. It does not lie. God gives himself to us as God. We must be satisfied with that. But within this finite knowledge (which is always forced to admit to an unknowing) our beatitude can be found—sometimes in a paradoxical mode, as in the apologue on "perfect joy" that appears as the conclusion of my *Note sur le temps*. One point, in any case, deserves emphasis: the awareness of our finitude is fundamentally more acute in the liturgical experience than in the phenomenon of being-toward-death . . .

There seem to be significant implications for the theorization of subjectivity latent in your account of the phenomenality of God. How would you describe them?

We must first understand: neither man nor God is subjects, even if man can experience a quasi-subjecthood. Speaking about divine subjectivity, on the other hand, hardly seems possible: speaking about it leads one to conceive of God in the image of man and probably toward an abstract monotheism. If we adopt a Christian, that is to say, Christological, point of view, we must certainly say that there is room "in" God for a human subjectivity. If we adopt such a view, however, one will need to go further, and in a more fruitful direction, and say that there is room in God for human affectivity: if the spirituality of the "[sacred] heart of Christ" has anything to teach us, even though we seem a long way from any piety, it is that. That said, subjectivity, such as we can describe it, is ours. (How could it be otherwise?) And since this is the case, I add that consciousness is not a static a priori but lives according to the rhythm of what is given to it and adapts to what is given to it. Talking about the phenomenality of God therefore requires that we bind subjectivity to a language we would not bind it to if we were simply talking about non-divine phenomena. The phenomenology of Lévinas, in his monomaniacal focus on a single appearance, that of the Other, explored an area that I think Husserl explored badly—because Husserl explored intersubjectivity without taking note of the irruption, in the proper sense, of the Other into the field of my consciousness. The phenomenology of Lévinas, however, does not provide the means to thematize the appearance of one who appears as loveable—because the Other, in Lévinas, always appears as the one who enjoins me not to kill him. To every being its proper phenomenality, and to every phenomenality the welcome that it demands from us. So, subjectivity needs to be conceived in a more flexible way. We still have to learn what Gurwitsch[25] suggests to us about the field of consciousness, which is that it is always and everywhere. But is any theme ever uniformly posed? Is the work of subjectivity the same when the field of consciousness is taking shape around the theme of "God," "the Other," or "a pen on my desk?" I don't think so. The fidelity of consciousness to what is given to it is first in relation to the modalities of reception reserved for the given. Husserl's work on passive and active syntheses is still relevant here. Consciousness synthesizes. It does so in the dual mode of receptivity and spontaneity. But whatever it synthesizes, the given is given from itself, and in order for the gift to be received as such, without distortion, it will always be necessary to accept that *quidquid cognoscitur ad modum cogniti cognoscitur* ["whatever is known is known according to the manner of the knower"].[26] The tradition could not think it. Phenomenology can. And the implications latent in my work are perhaps latent for good reason: it is a matter of phenomenological truisms. (This does not mean that every phenomenology observes these prescriptions . . .)

Does your affirmation of finitude and embrace of the fragmentary, which you've been referring to, amount to a rejection of what Husserl, in the Crisis, *defined as the unique* telos *of Western rationality? Or is it, alternatively, a way of rethinking reason?*

The *Crisis*, for its French translator, is the apogee of the West's theoretical paranoia. I wouldn't go that far. The wisest course may be to draw attention to a ubiquitous concept in Husserl, that of science. Whenever we use the term "science" our immediate reference is provided by mathematics or logic. But let us exercise caution. The German calls it *Wissenschaft* and in that language any more or less cognitive work is a *Wissenschaft*. The essay published in 1911 as *Philosophie als strenge Wissenschaft* (*Philosophy as a Rigorous Science*; in French, *La philosophie comme science rigoureuse*) makes it clear that Husserl's ambitions were considerable: nothing less than the organization of an arch-discipline. I say "discipline," however, in order to avoid using the term science. The *Crisis* is concerned with scientific knowledge. It is a question, however, of reconnecting the world of science to the world of life. The paradigmatic discipline, then, is one that can carry out a critique of scientific reason, because it knows how and why science is constituted. I completely accept that. It remains the case, though, and this is not insignificant, that I know too little of what is called "exact" science to dare to propose any criticism of scientific reason whatsoever and that my work is devoted above all to knowing [*la connaissance*], as distinct from propositional knowledge [*savoir propositionnel*]. But if anything is certain it is that such knowing loses much of its substance when it is integrated into a science. We can attempt a phenomenological approach of social facts: Alfred Schutz has produced analyses of them that command respect.[27] We can lay the phenomenological foundations of geometry (both Husserl himself and Oskar Becker have done so).[28] Phenomenology, more generally, can help the sciences understand themselves. But when the sciences are not in play and we are happy with just knowing [*connaissance*], thus begins the rule of the fragmentary. This rule is not that of the illogical. It is, simply, that of a logic of the particular—of the experience that Aristotle defined as "knowledge of *kath'hekaston*." For my part, there is no question of giving up the ambitions of philosophy, the universality of truth, etc. It is a question, in fact, of evidence more than of truth, or of the true as evidently given. If one is to follow Fink (in the *Sixth Cartesian Meditation* and the posthumous fragments published by Ronald Bruzina), the transcendental reduction frees the self from its humanity, a work of "dehumanization" (*sic*). I flatly deny this. Philosophy is a human affair. Heidegger has taught us to recognize that a specifically Greek experience was at work in Plato and Aristotle. The same Heidegger has taught us to see the experience that is at work in first Latin and then modern philosophy. In any case, the philosopher can never be defined as an intellect devoid of flesh outside of history. Truth is not truth-for-me, in the Californian sense of the expression. But it is still formulated from evidence granted to humans. It is unlikely that dolphins, which Robert Spaemann said might be persons, do philosophy.[29] The alien creatures described in C. S. Lewis's trilogy do not seem to do it either. [30] To our great embarrassment, philosophy is our business. That is why we need not be frightened when faced with the juxtaposition of fragments. Not everyone has the chance to do metaphysics or take advantage of absolute knowledge. (And Husserl, it must be said, never dreamed of an absolute knowledge.)

In your 2010 Richard Lectures at the University of Virginia, From Theology to Theological Thinking, *you called for a transition from "theology" to "theological thinking," which involves a profound dialogue with philosophy. Do you advocate in these lectures a sort of philosophically informed theology, a relaunching, after Heidegger, of "philosophical theology"?*

I confess my absolute reticence (I am "continental") vis-à-vis what the English-speaking world calls "philosophical theology": whatever has been published under this label always leaves me unsatisfied. What I proposed in my Richard Lectures was, in fact, only a hypothesis that I am not really able to establish completely. "Theological thinking" means that theology can and must think. This also means that it may not. If we merely understood "thinking" as intellectual work, then all the theological disciplines would be works of thinking, regardless of whether they concerned canon law, the history of Christian doctrines, or biblical philology. By "thinking," however, I understand, with Heidegger, that which we are still not doing—but what we need to do finally to escape nihilism, and to escape it more fiercely than we can by using the ammunition provided by Husserl's phenomenology. There is, however, one reservation. According to Heidegger thinking is always to come. A careful reading of the history of theology, however, convincingly demonstrates that theology could not only be a conceptual calculus or prelude to a systematization but that it has known centuries in which it deserved, I believe, to receive the title of "thinking." Emmanuel Martineau, commenting on Saint Bernard in homage to Etienne Gilson (one of my predecessors as Richard Lecturer), spoke about "spirituality" in relation to Bernard, which is trivial, but observed that spirituality may contain within it an overcoming of metaphysics.[31] The paradox, then—that which, in any case, I would like to clarify—would be that of a theology capable of thinking, of going beyond philosophy, even before philosophy concerns itself with what "thinking" means. Heidegger leaves us thinking as a task and is content to speak in a mysterious way about what thinking means. The point I address to Heidegger, from here, is this: Was theology, at least in its pre-Scholastic form, not thinking long before us?

Translated by K. Jason Wardley

Notes

1. Gerhard Ebeling was a Lutheran theologian and a student of Rudolf Bultmann, a New Testament scholar heavily influenced by Heidegger. For his account of the "*coram* relation[ship]," see, for example, *Luther*, 220–24.

2. Rahner, *Karl Rahner in Dialogue*, 207–15.

3. Rahner, *Foundations of Christian Faith*, 218.

4. Goff, *Naissance du purgatoire*.

5. Hegel, *Phenomenology of Spirit*, 19.

6. Kaliba, *Die Welt als Gleichnis des dreienigen Gottes* and Klaus Hemmerle, *Thesen zu einer trinitarischen Ontologie.*

7. Spiegelberg, *The Phenomenological Movement.*

8. Heidegger, *Vom Wesen der Warheit*, in *Gesamtausagabe*, vol. 9.

9. Husserl, *Formal and Transcendental Logic*, § 60, 160.

10. Maxime Charles was a priest of the archdiocese of Paris, a chaplain to the Sorbonne from 1944–1959, and the founder of the Centre Richelieu in 1945.

11. Xavier Tilliette is a Jesuit, historian, philosopher, and an influential interpreter of Schelling. He is the author of a massive oeuvre on a wide variety of philosophical and theological topics. See in particular, *Le Christ de la philosophie*; *La Semaine sainte des philosophes*; *Le Christ des philosophes*; *Les philosophes lisent la Bible*; *L'Église des philosophes, de Nicolas de Cuse á Gabriel Marcel*; and *Philosophies eucharistiques, de Descartes á Blondel.*

12. Lacoste, "Béatitude. B. Théologie systématique," in *Dictionnaire critique de théologie*, 181.

13. Balthasar, *Apokalypse der Deutschen Seele.*

14. See Balthasar, "Some Points of Eschatology," 255–77.

15. Lacoste, "Le désir et l'inexigible: pour lire Henri de Lubac," in *Le monde et l'absence d'œuvre.*

16. The Bernau manuscripts on time-consciousness can be found in *Husserliana*, vol. 33. For an overview of the Bernau manuscripts, see Zahavi, "Time and Consciousness in the Bernau Manuscripts."

17. Kearney, "Epiphanies of the Everyday," 3–20; "Sacramental Imagination and Eschatology," 55–67.

18. Ricoeur, "The Hermeneutics of Testimony."

19. Martin Heidegger, Geschichte der Philosophie von Thomas von Aquin bis Kant (Winter Semester 1926/27).

20. Lacoste, *Être en danger*, 51.

21. Lacoste expressed the phrase in parentheses in English.

22. Heidegger, *Country Path Conversations*; *Feldwege-Gespräche*, in *Gesamtausgabe*, vol. 77; *What Is a Thing?*; *Die Frage nach dem Ding*, in *Gesamtausgabe*, vol. 41.

23. Polanyi, *Personal Knowledge.*

24. See Bérulle, *Opuscules de Piété*, particularly opuscules X, 92, and XXX, 142.

25. Gurwitsch, *Field of Consciousness* and *Marginal Consciousness.*

26. The Latin phrase comes from Thomas Aquinas, himself developing an Aristotelian maxim. See Aquinas, *Summae theologiae.*

27. Schutz, *The Phenomenology of the Social World.*

28. Becker, "Contributions toward a Phenomenological Foundation of Geometry and Its Physical Applications."

29. Spaemann, *Persons*, 248.

30. Lewis, *Out of the Silent Planet*, *Perelandra*, and *That Hideous Strength.*

31. Martineau, "Étienne Gilson et la problème de la théologie."

The Collision of Phenomenology and Theology

EMMANUEL FALQUE

What, to your mind, distinguishes—historically and philosophically—the various generations of French phenomenology from one another?

We may certainly speak of a second generation of French phenomenologists, and perhaps also a third, if we count among the first Emmanuel Lévinas, Michel Henry, and Paul Ricoeur; among the second Jean-Luc Marion, Jean-Yves Lacoste, Jean-Louis Chrétien, and Didier Franck; and among the third Claude Romano, myself, and others. In reality, a difference in context marks the distance between these different generations. The first generation, which developed in the aftermath of World War II, remained closely tied to the works of Husserl and their availability in French translation. This original context had more to do with transmission than critique, though the latter soon came in the work of Michel Henry, for example, whose treatment of "auto-affection" called intentionality into question, or in Emmanuel Lévinas's work on counter-intentionality.

The second generation, which emerged in the 1970s in France, came about in a time of crisis, or at least opposition. As the human sciences and Marxism were flourishing, the French phenomenologists constituted a secret resistance, opposing the reduction of Being to beings in the ontic sciences, on the one hand, and also opposing a type of Christianity lost in the horizon of the world, after having renounced its true identity, on the other hand. This generation established a real relation to the history of philosophy and tried to draw resources directly from that tradition. Against the hegemony of the human sciences, they reopened the philosophical question of "meaning" and even questioned texts themselves. They were no longer content to think "on the margins." Without ever renouncing rigorous and strong thinking, they believed that they could say something new. Catching others in its wake, this generation renewed French philosophy and philosophical research more generally, though it remained highly dependent on the idea of overcoming metaphysics—an idea that has itself been overcome these days.

The third, which formed in the eighties in France, developed in a novel situation, characterized less by opposition than by the desire for comprehension. A new mode of tolerance and a certain type of relativism typified that time period, with the abolition of the death penalty, for example, and the arrival of socialism in France (though phenomenology has always claimed to be apolitical, and rightly so.) This generation, which was less ideological, was also more distant from the "masters." For them, Husserl, Heidegger, and even Jean Beaufret already belonged to the history of philosophy. The rapport with phenomenology was no longer a question of identity (over-and-against Marxism or the human sciences, for instance). It was more a way of *entering into* the history of philosophy and studying relevant texts. Jean-Luc Marion's influence here has been considerable. All who have worked with him are indebted to him for this approach, which takes philosophy seriously in its history, even within the context of contemporary issues.

From the ecclesial point of view, and for phenomenologists who consider themselves Christian, the Second Vatican Council and its reception also mark a considerable turning point. Following the opening speech of John XXIII calling for a conceptual system that "meets the needs of the present day," and what Jean-Paul II called the "new evangelization,"[1] there is now a completely different way of understanding the status of apologetics. Another sort of rapport with non-Christians becomes possible, based on tolerance rather than condemnation. Put differently, this generation was no longer satisfied with simple philosophical reflection. It appealed to experience, whether religious or not, in order to flesh out conceptual understanding. Kant's dictum bears repeating: "Intuition without concept is blind, concept without intuition is empty."[2] The time has now come when the force of conceptualization, developed by a number of contemporary philosophers and Christian phenomenologists, joins together with the richness of experience.

More humble, perhaps, but less ambitious, this third generation of phenomenology agrees to remain provisional [*tâtonnante*], to focus on description rather than analysis, to trace the contours of experience rather than establish its structures. These days in France, this "turn" is more and more apparent—not simply and exclusively the famous "theological turn in French phenomenology" but the turn to a "phenomenology of the limit," practiced between the limits of the possible and conceivable, at least from the point of view of common experience. The ordinary becomes a fecund place [*le lieu de la fécondation*]; it becomes a site for the description of an experience that is apparently insignificant, inasmuch as it is shared in common. Rather than exclude, the third generation wants to include. Better, this generation accepts a certain form of perspectivism that, far from denying the concept and uniqueness of truth, recognizes that truth has value only to the extent that it is constituted by a community.

The question of experience is, indeed, what most concerns the latest generation of phenomenologists. Phenomenology now emphasizes the practical more than the theoretical. Whether their focus is Christianity, art, literature, politics, psychiatry, or film, contemporary phenomenologists are aware that they can no longer content themselves with philosophy alone. Contemporary phenomenology faces the prospect of merely "spinning its wheels" if it cannot find sustenance outside itself.

Nothing is more inconsequential to this new generation than knowing whether or not their discourse remains within metaphysics or the so-called onto-theology. The characterization of metaphysics from such a perspective [*par un tel prisme*] has now become obsolete, especially since it corresponds to nothing in the history of philosophy, except for a certain Scotist notion of the prism of thought. (In reality this idea comes from Thomas of Erfurt, who was the subject of Heidegger's *habilitation*.)[3] The problem is no longer about the boundary but more about the matter itself. Whether one is inside or outside of metaphysics is not all that important. All that counts is the validity of the concepts forged to deal with what is being considered, whether those concepts have to do with language, the body, experience, literature, etc. In this sense, phenomenology can no longer be content with itself.

The boundary between phenomenology and analytic philosophy, for example, is less hermetically sealed today than it has been, particularly in the recent works of Claude Romano and Jocelyn Benoist. The importance of phenomenological work in the fields of psychiatry (e.g., Natalie Depraz) and literature (e.g., Jérôme de Gramont) is also clear. As for me, I seek out—and hope to find—in theology, mysticism, patristic and medieval philosophy, and the Bible itself something that renews the fecundity of thought. The first generation of phenomenologists (e.g., Max Scheler, Edith Stein, Theodor Lipps, Hannah Arendt, and Ludwig Binswanger) are of considerable importance here. What has been called (perhaps wrongly) the "realist turn" in phenomenology in the 1920s still has more to teach us! Thought must have (real) content if it is not to remain purely abstract. In this sense Maurice Merleau-Ponty would become an essential point of reference among this later generation, in opposition to older thinkers, who frequently saw his work only as a poetic form of thought. For Merleau-Ponty, there truly was an emphasis on description, which is too often forgotten.

How do you understand your place in contemporary phenomenology?

For me, the point is not to leave phenomenology behind or to situate myself elsewhere. To be a phenomenologist is *not* to be beholden to a particular school, much less a particular ideology. It has to do with focusing on "the thing itself." That is to say, being a phenomenologist means being preoccupied with the lived experience [*vécu*] aimed at by consciousness, or by the flesh, and not just the totality of beings in their supposed exteriority. In this sense, I remain a phenomenologist in that I pay attention to those acts proper to subjectivity rather than objects that simply exist. Nevertheless, the methods of phenomenology are not always adequate to reach what is intuited. My work, *Les noces de l'Agneau*, on "the body and the Eucharist," points out some of phenomenology's limits: the hypertrophy of flesh in the body, the excess of passivity in activity, and the abundance of sense in non-sense. The real problem is not whether one recognizes oneself as standing within a particular current of thought. Rather, the problem has to do with recognizing that phenomenology has not yet, or not always, deployed concepts that are adequate for talking about the whole of reality. By focusing on the "flesh," for example, or on the *Leib*—in Husserl or Merleau-Ponty's sense (i.e., the "lived body")—one forgets the sense of *Leib* as "organic body," the *Körper* itself, as Nietzsche conceived it. There is a certain Docetism in contemporary phenomenology, which stems from a widespread imposition of the "lived body" in opposition to the "extended body." Yet between the "extended body" and the "lived body," I have coined the concept of "expanded body" ["*corps épandu*"] (*Les noces de l'Agneau*). It involves focusing on the organic body, which is properly human and does not ignore the life of our organs and our interior chaos. The mute and silent experience of our own body cannot always be expressed in its proper sense. Perhaps it is necessary to accept the absence of meaning, or at least a lack of all intentionality.

Hence, there is a second limit to the way phenomenality is conceptualized today: as a means to understanding the excess of meaning in what is meaningless, a constant effort to recover what Kant called "the confused mass of sensations," or the "area about which one is unable to speak," to quote Heidegger on Nietzsche.[4] In reality, since the origin of phenomenology, intentionality has been privileged, even when it is overturned by counter-intentionality (Lévinas) or transformed in auto-affectivity (Henry). There is, frankly, little or no place for chaos or pandemonium in phenomenology today, except perhaps Maurice Merleau-Ponty's "brute nature" or life in "the savage state."

So there is still a primacy given to weakness over force, or passivity over activity. Certainly, a phenomenological treatment of passive syntheses, of the demand of the face of the other, or of the excess of intuition in intention is necessary. Yet it cannot simultaneously conceal the vital force necessary for any subject to heal from an illness, for example. We can no longer advocate the welcome of the other, which is certainly essential, if we do not at the same time consider the vitality responsible for the existence of the subject (though without necessarily advocating a sort of heroism of the ego, which is a commonly held view). In a phenomenological investigation treating a theological object, for example, it is appropriate to find God and the Holy Spirit defined as "force" (or "strength") and not exclusively as "gift." This is the price to pay to find a mode of conceptuality, intensely present in thinkers from centuries past like Spinoza and Nietzsche, and that modern authors like Gilles Deleuze, Antonin Artaud, or Georges Bataille call for us to rediscover. It is not about passing from one tradition to another but forging a way through the concepts and authors in order to try to say, to try to describe things as they give themselves, and even within (and not just beyond) the limits within which they give themselves, remaining faithful to the primary imperative of phenomenology: the "return to the things themselves," as a description of an act of consciousness and an assumption of lived experience. Phenomenology remains "descriptive" not because it is content to examine itself but because it turns to other considerations—art, literature, poetry, cinema, architecture, psychiatry, and (why not?) also theology. My triptych—*Le passeur de Gethsémani* (1999), *Le Métamorphose de la finitude* (2004), and *Les noces de l'Agneau* (2011)—attempts to base itself on experiences and constitutive existentials of human existence in order to give meaning and philosophical content to theological dogmas, without reducing either: anguish and death for *Gethsémani* (Good Friday), birth for the Resurrection (Holy Saturday), the body and eros for the Eucharist (Maundy Thursday). The *theological triduum* (Eucharist, suffering and death, and resurrection) is rooted first of all in a *philosophical and phenomenological triduum* (eros and body, anguish and death, birth and rebirth), even as the latter (theology) is a means of transforming the former (philosophy).

Do you recognize yourself in the label "theological turn"?

Certainly the boundary between philosophy and theology seems displaced, but there is a new fecundity engendered by the intersection of disciplines that must be considered seriously and radically. By remaining on the "threshold" ["*seuil*"] of theology (Blondel, Ricoeur, Lévinas), by separating it out as a corpus (Marion), or by passing from theology to philosophy indiscriminately (Henry, Chrétien), the boundaries are not all that well established, as I see it. "The more one theologizes, the better one philosophizes." This formula from the introduction to *Dieu, la chair et l'autre* is an essential principle for me.[5] It has less to do with separating philosophy and theology in their disciplines, or with confusing them because of their shared affiliations; rather, it has to do with daring to practice both philosophy *and* theology at the same time, at least while studying them both, and claiming for oneself the intersection between them in the unity of one's own person. In actuality, nothing is more traditional. Thomas Aquinas was not a theologian and *then* a philosopher but a theologian *and* a philosopher. It was the same author, philosopher *and* theologian, who wrote a unified work, *Summae Theologiae*, with three parts: *Prima Pars* (the Trinity, creation), *Secunda Pars* (human action, morality, virtue, etc.), and *Tertia Pars* (Christology). There is no sense in studying the second philosophical part independent of the two other theological parts. Thomas Aquinas's gesture is important and still has more to teach us today. It is precisely when I know *when and where* I am theologizing that I also know *when and where* I am philosophizing.

It works the same way today when one examines theological objects in the context of phenomenology. As I see it, the difference between philosophy and theology is not about specific content (there can be a phenomenology of prayer, liturgy, or Eucharist, for example) but rather about the point of departure (starting from man or God) and the modality (possibility or reality).

The famous "theological turn in French phenomenology" should not be viewed with suspicion but rather recognized and taken as given, though only in a certain sense. Such a turn does not indicate a confusion of genres—quite the contrary. Paradoxically, it is because the theological practice of phenomenology is not endorsed, or even claimed, that it becomes open to attack. So Dominique Janicaud's critique has motivated the concerned parties to defend themselves—as if one must remain exclusively philosophical in the eyes of other philosophers (all the while practicing theology without wanting to admit it). To the contrary, paradoxically, by being conscious of oneself as a theologian, one remains fully philosophical.

If finitude, for example, has a very considerable importance in my work, it is precisely because the horizon of the limit, or "man as such" ["*l'homme tout court*"], is that which primarily defines phenomenology and the philosophical approach as such, at least in their beginnings. The metamorphosis of finitude, or the resurrection, will be put in action by the theologian but not by the philosopher. This is neither a confusion of genres nor a "masked advance."[6] The position here is explicit, and all the more effective and convincing, inasmuch as it enriches, and thrives on, the two fields of philosophy *and* theology.

Based on the famous statement of the principle of principles in Ideas I, *Husserl claims that phenomenology must be "presuppositionless," and Heidegger wants to adhere to a "rigorous methodological atheism." For your part, you bring together "manifestation and revelation," "phenomenology and Theophany," especially in chapter two of* Dieu, la chair et l'autre, *where you rely on John Scotus Eriugena. How do you understand the relation between the requirements of the phenomenological method and the claims of theophany?*

It is obvious that there is a link between phenomenology and theophany, at least in the context of theology. God is manifestation, "the one who appears (*phainesthai*)" or "the one who self-manifests," as you have pointed out in reference to my analysis of John Scotus Eriugena. Yet, in the context of philosophy, one cannot so easily connect phenomenology and theophany. That there is a theological practice possible for phenomenology does not mean that we have to give in to phenomenology's hegemonic tendencies—quite the contrary. The danger of phenomenology consists precisely in its desire to annex every discipline, including theology, without realizing that not every discipline belongs to phenomenology. The paradox is this: one becomes better at the theological practice of phenomenology when one is also a theologian, not allowing oneself to be a philosopher pure and simple. In this sense, every theophany is a wellspring for phenomenology in that the manifestation of God is one of the modes of appearing *par excellence*. But phenomenology is not, for all that, theophany, since the divine is not the primary object of the phenomenologist—at least inasmuch as he is, and recognizes himself to be, a philosopher first and foremost.

The "pre-emption of the infinite over the finite," which is actually Cartesian and has been asserted more or less explicitly by a number of contemporary phenomenologists, does not go without saying for me. For what is primary is not the "infinite" or the "finite" but "finitude" itself (i.e., the blocked [*bouché*] horizon of our existence). That initial starting point, which is certainly Heideggerian but also Husserlian, is too often forgotten.

It seems to me that whole segments of contemporary phenomenology confuse the finite and finitude, viewing the sum total of finite things as a second determination of finitude, which in no way corresponds to the initial determination of what I call "finitude as such" or "man as such."

As your question about the double prerequisite of "presuppositionlessness" (Husserl) and "rigorous methodological atheism" (Heidegger) indicates, there are no grounds for authorizing the phenomenologist to override the principle of principles—that is, the phenomenon "as it gives itself" and "within the limits in which it gives itself." The famous statement of the "principle of principles" is not only methodological, as is commonly believed, but also philosophical. "The absence of any presupposition," to which I have referred and that remains faithful to Husserl and Heidegger, necessarily keeps philosophy at the horizon-limit of our existence, independent of any image of God. The real error of the "theological turn"—if there is a charge to be made—consists not in the usurpation of theology by philosophy, which is a lesser sort of evil, but in philosophy surpassing [*dépassement*] its own proper boundaries or limits.

To affirm, for example, as I have in *Métamorphose de la finitude*, that there is no "drama of atheistic humanism" is not simply to take a position opposed to Henri de Lubac, which would not make much sense anyway. Rather, it has to do with understanding that the times have changed. Being able to live and content oneself with "humanity as such" is also a human possibility, the very possibility that Christ inhabits in his incarnation. In becoming man, the God-man assumes all the dimensions of man, including being satisfied with being human, not in opposition to God but independent of him. Every non-theism is not atheism or anti-theism, as Maurice Merleau-Ponty pointed out—*contra* Henri de Lubac—in a lecture at the Collège de France (*Éloge de la philosophie*). Being a philosopher—or better, a phenomenologist—does not require the annexation of theophany into phenomenology, but it does require phenomenology to stick to the horizon of "man as such," even if revelation (and also, in this instance, theophany) has a means of transforming the structure of man as such through the resurrection or "the metamorphosis of finitude."

Certainly, the movement of this conversion is, in this instance, explicitly theological, even as it puts pressure on and inverts a philosophical horizon. Yet the leap of faith does not deny the structure of philosophy; quite the contrary, it assumes it. That is to say, in recognizing that the anterior structure is not theological, even if it might become so by being transformed through the power and action of God, one recognizes its antecedent as purely philosophical. The distinction between the genres of theology and philosophy rests on the recognition of each genre. It is too often forgotten that theophany and philosophy have been too immediately joined. One remains a philosopher in assuming the theological position, as a theologian; and one remains a theologian in assuming the philosophical position, as a philosopher. "Manifestation" is one thing, and "revelation" is another in that one speaks of man on the one hand and God on the other. The two are better connected the less they are confused. Such is the paradox of the gap between disciplines that must be maintained in order to cross them.

Are you not taking away with one hand (the absence of a direct link between theology and phenomenology, at least from the point of view of philosophy) what you give with the other (a possible link between phenomenology and theology in the context of theology)?

Your excellent question leads me to add some detail, or to say something about my own evolution regarding the relation between phenomenology and theology proper. If my *Les noces de l'Agneau*, seems to be outside of phenomenology, it is not because it tries to discard phenomenology definitively—quite the contrary. It has more to do with adopting another attitude or with taking a different path. Until recently, phenomenologists have only adopted other perspectives in order to examine theology from the side of phenomenology. The objects of theology itself have become objects for philosophy, as I try to show in my book, *Le combat amoureux*. Incarnation (Michel Henry), prayer (Jean-Louis Chrétien), Eucharist (Jean-Luc Marion), and liturgy (Jean-Yves Lacoste) are some of the ways of treating God, and even the sacraments, philosophically. The question remains, essential and never asked, of a "return shock" of theology onto phenomenology. We can no longer content ourselves with treating the objects of theology philosophically, without questioning the meaning and repercussions of theology itself for phenomenology.

Such a "return shock" of theology onto phenomenology does not mean that it is the job of theologians to practice phenomenology—quite the contrary. It has more to do with recognizing that theology ought to criticize phenomenology in order to show the latter's insufficiencies. This is part of my purpose in *Les noces de l'Agneau*. The return to the "organic body," or better toward the "expanded body" against the hypertrophy of the "lived body," comes in reality from theology itself. God is not made flesh only (*Leib*) in becoming incarnate on earth. The incarnate God is certainly defined by the "life of his body," and this is how I understood the meaning of his resurrection in *Métamorphose de la finitude* following *Passeur de*

Gethsémani. Yet God also, and primarily, becomes "body" (*Körper* or *Leib*, in the organic sense of the term), and this is the proper way to speak of God's "incarnation," which is in reality an "in*corp*oration." Christianity still suffers from a form of Docetism that should be definitively repudiated and that phenomenology all too often transmits. The incarnate Christ had "members like us," "bones like us," "hair like us," "organs like us," and so forth, as Tertullian argues in his *De carne Christi* against the Gnostics (Valentians in particular). These sorts of things must now be considered by phenomenology, as a "return shock" of theology onto phenomenology. No longer only "flesh" but also "body." No longer exclusively "lived in his bodily self-awareness" ["*kinesthèses*"] but the "life of organs," even in their interior chaos and space, about which we cannot say anything.

One can see how theology itself, and your theological career, have affected and changed your view of phenomenology. Of all the French phenomenologists, your approach seems most fully theological—at least from an institutional point of view. Your approach is not, however, restricted to theology, as a discipline. In studying the tradition, particularly patristic and medieval philosophy, you find tools to examine phenomenology itself. Can you explain how your knowledge of medieval philosophy and theology influences your conception of phenomenology and theology?

You have here touched on an essential point in my work. The entirety of my phenomenological and theological work supports the study of tradition and, in particular, the corpus of patristic and medieval philosophy. Historians of medieval philosophy sometimes reproach me for being too much of a phenomenologist, and phenomenologists reproach me for being too much of a historian, to say nothing of those theologians who wonder whether I write in the context of philosophy or theology. In addition to the necessity of skipping over the historical contexts, or at least loosening them in order to look at them differently, the "phenomenological practice of medieval philosophy" suffers from the danger of "anachronism," which I warned against from the beginning in the introduction to *Dieu, la chair et l'autre*. In that work, I do not ask medieval thinkers to respond to my questions. They have enough to do with their own questions, and I with mine! Rather, in light of the way that they respond to their own queries, I can know how to respond to mine. The contexts are different, the responses also, and the questions even more so. Still, in the middle of this difference, a certain experience of consciousness is commonly sought after so that, in either case, some relation with God can be shared. If the fathers and medieval thinkers are not phenomenologists, they can be "read phenomenologically," in the sense that a community of experience can be found there.

John Scotus Eriugena, for example, did not invent the Heideggerian definition of the phenomenon. Yet, by defining theophany as "*theophania*"—from the Greek, although he wrote in Latin and even translated Denys the Areopagite into Latin—Scotus already makes "manifestation" (*phainesthaï*) the central component of a theology that converges with phenomenology (though in a unique way). Meister Eckhart did not himself discover the "reduction." Still, with his idea of "detachment" (*Abgeschiedenheit*), Eckhart in some way puts "the world" and even "the subject itself" in brackets in order to find what exists as a pure conversion, which is thus a reduction radicalized to the extreme. Similarly, there is "flesh" for Irenaeus (*sarx, caro*), which reveals something about the "visibility of Adam"; or the "body" for Tertullian (*soma, corpus*), which reveals its "solidity" ["*consistance*"]; or the "conversion of the senses" for Bonaventure, which retrieves the meaning of "to touch," examined as a certain type of phenomenality. Such examples can be multiplied to infinity and are chosen with some circumspection in my work. I might also mention the "communion of saints" and "intersubjectivity" in Origen; or "angelic otherness" and the emergence of a "relation with the other" in Thomas Aquinas; or the question of "haecceity" and "the singular relation to the other" in Duns Scotus.

In reality, the examples are less important than the path taken. What matters is, as you have pointed out, the dual, reciprocal fecundity of phenomenology and medieval philosophy. It is especially true in the medieval epoch that philosophy and theology are not separated, particularly in the monastic and scholastic traditions. If it is no longer a question of denying their eventual—and even necessary—separation, then this gesture has something to teach us, precisely because it contains within it a description of a life of communal and unified experience rather than a simple separation of concepts, as subtle as it is. One is not a philosopher *or* a theologian in the Middle Ages but a philosopher *and* a theologian. This is exactly the kind of experience that we need to rediscover today.

You started out with a work on Saint Bonaventure: Saint Bonaventure et l'entrée de Dieu en théologie. *In this work, it is certainly "experience" that is the source of your reflections. Yet the essay remains very conceptual. To speak of experience does not imply, for you, a renunciation of abstraction but a deepening of the necessary work of conceptualization. So, for example, you try in that work to show how the Trinity can be thought of as a gift, thereby closely linking phenomenology and theology. Can you tell us how you understand yourself and see yourself as an heir to the Franciscan tradition, as you seem to claim?*

The first thing I want to emphasize is the fact that I do not deny anything in that first essay, though some details of my thoughts on the matter have since changed. What is important to me in that book is the blow it delivers to Martin Heidegger, according to whom any theology is only able to slip into the "bed of philosophy," thereby reducing itself. To the contrary, there is certainly an "entrance of God into theology" that is not identical to the "entrance of God into philosophy," in the sense that defining God as Trinity does not primarily identify God with a concept.

However, and this is where my approach may have changed, one cannot simply show that a thinker escapes onto-theology and thereby imagine that he is outside "metaphysics," as if the term always designates a corpus or attitude against which one has to guard. At the risk of oversimplifying, the boundaries have now moved. I am not, or am no longer, in agreement with all the "philosophies of the leap" that act as if it is necessary to define a pure discourse as a-philosophical, non-philosophical, or something other than philosophical in order to let God be God and remain himself. The greatness of God consists not in denying our humanity or our human reason but in descending and inhabiting his *kenosis* in order to transform it. My disagreement with Heidegger's view (more Protestant than Catholic) stems from the alleged prerogative of a theology, which, historically, corrupted itself with philosophy. There is no such understanding in either Saint Bonaventure's or Thomas Aquinas's approaches. For the Franciscan (Bonaventure), theology takes over philosophy while relying on it; and for the Dominican (Aquinas) the servant understands it as an honor to be able to "live" in the master's house. It is only by transforming "service" into "servitude," through a certain misunderstanding of Thomas Aquinas, that anyone is expected to be the master (theology) or the servant (philosophy). My book on Bonaventure proposes, therefore, to step outside of the rivalry, even if it still bears the marks of certain previous preoccupations, like the overcoming of onto-theology in particular, which I now consider to be outdated.

The second point I want to make, which is absolutely essential, has to do with the difference that must be maintained between Denys the Areopagite and Saint Bonaventure and thus also between two possible forms of phenomenology, which are more complementary than contradictory. It is Denys (in *Mystical Theology*) who first proposes a phenomenology and theology of "excess" in the "saturation" of a phenomenon that overflows and dazzles us. This approach is essential and has, in fact, been inherited by Hans Urs von Balthasar. God can never be reduced to the measure of man. He gives himself where he wants to, when he wants to, and how he wants to, reversing, as it were, the ordinary structures of experience. Where Bonaventure differs from Denys, and thus where phenomenology and theology differ, lies in the fact of developing what we have called "an ontology of poverty" rather than an "apocalypse of glory." "The humility of God is so great," as Bonaventure says in his *Collationes in Hexaemeron*, "that reason fails."[7] The failure of reason before God does not prove God's grandeur but God's smallness—not God's glory on Mount Tabor but his incarnation in Bethlehem. Of course these two perspectives are not opposed. Nonetheless, by focusing too much on what is revealed, one misses the meaning of the incarnate. The particularity of Christianity relative to Judaism lies not only in the *kabôd* or the "weight of glory" but also in kenosis or the humility of the flesh.[8] The Franciscan influence is important here in that it holds the mystery of birth as primary and thus God as a child [*Dieu enfant*]. The reduction here is "anthropological" not in the sense of God being reduced to the measure of man—of which Hans Urs von Balthasar has wrongly accused Karl Rahner—but in the sense of God choosing to make *himself* the measure of man in his kenosis. Phenomenology inherited from Bonaventure starts with "man as such" and "finitude as such" out of consideration for the human in which the divine conceals and keeps itself.

The third and final point I would like to make regarding your question is a bit more personal. Certainly, the Franciscan view—and my work on Bonaventure bears witness to this—remains essential for me precisely because it supports a "phenomenology of the limit," which I claim for myself and which the resurrection transforms and inhabits. Additionally, Thomas Aquinas himself, a Dominican and not a Franciscan, has also served as a reference point for me. An important study, which I have devoted to him, "Limite théologique et finitude phénoménologique chez Thomas d'Aquin," aims to show how the beatific vision does not appear to dismantle the limit of creaturehood but rather to offer that limit to the Creator in order that he might reside there. God is not opposed to the "limit" of man but wants it and even desires it because God created us as such. God calls us only to love our limitation and to hope that it will be transformed, not in order to break it (in accordance with the Protestant or Bultmannian perspective) but in order to transform it and reorient it. Our whole being is "waiting for his body" in the resurrection, according to both the Bonaventurian and Thomist perspectives, precisely because our limited being looks for and attends to its limits so that God might fully inhabit it.

This is exactly the point where, in my thought process, the Ignatian goal appears to complete the double Franciscan and Dominican perspective. In fact, there is in the *Spiritual Exercises* an "attachment to the created," an elegy to the use of the senses, an attention to the conduct of thoughts, a taking account of the affects, an importance given to the formation of images, or a conversion of the creature in its face-to-face encounter with the Creator, which informs our thought as well as our mode of existence. Aside from all mystical detachment or flight from the world, Ignatius of Loyola gives unprecedented weight to man's relation to God, including even the recesses of a tormented soul alternating between consolation and desolation and a body taken up in the ambiguity of its passions. If there is "chaos" and even "animality" in man, which I have shown in *Les noces de l'Agneau*, God himself meets us there not to deny or ignore such aspects of human existence but to transform them in his divine Trinity.

This way of thinking, the unity of which has been fully expressed not only from the position of phenomenology and from the position of theology but also related to its spiritual anchorage, allows us to pose a concluding question about the first part of your triptych and your relationship with Paul Ricoeur. The dedication page of Le passeur de Gethsémani, *which you have not yet mentioned, refers to an experience of anguish and death. Can you tell us more about this and indicate how this essential relation with "the life-world" somehow sets you at a distance from the hermeneutic perspective?*

You are right to emphasize the importance of this starting point, which can be seen in my philosophical *Triduum* (now published as a single volume in France). The first part of the triptych on "angst and death," which corresponds to an experience and idea of "Good Friday" (*Le passeur de Gethsémani*), precedes (at least from the point of view of its origin) the second part on "the birth and resurrection," which responds to "Easter Sunday" (*Métamorphose de la finitude*). The third part is on "the body and Eucharist," which coincides with "Maundy Thursday" (*Les noces de l'Agneau*). The first book is rooted in the painful experience of the death of two loved ones: one by suicide, the other by car accident. Because there is, for me, no philosophy outside experience, or thinking outside of life—for one nourishes the other—this double tragedy caused me to examine the deepest and most intimate parts of my Christianity. Can one so easily reckon belief in the resurrection of the dead without first considering the gravity and the finitude of life? Can one affirm, following Heidegger in *Being and Time*, that "anxiety toward death" has definitively ruled out believing because "the anthropology developed in Christian theology—from Paul to Calvin's *meditation future vitae*—has always already viewed death together with its interpretation of life"?[9]

That death is not primarily a passage, or an accomplishment, or a diversion from our life here and now, is indeed the great lesson of those magnificent pages of *Being and Time*. Our "Being toward the end" refers to a "true end," even though death, which would be the last word for Heidegger, can also become, in a reversal worked by God, penultimate, or even the primary moment for the believer (entry into the resurrection). It is therefore necessary to understand our own death, and the death of Christ, in light of the death of the common man, "the death of everyone," as Charles Péguy said so well in the *Dialogue de l'histoire et de l'âme charnelle*. The tendency toward heroism all too often perverts Christianity, which establishes the death of Christ as something so exemplary that it appears wholly foreign to us; thus his resurrection becomes, if not something totally indifferent to us, at least independent of us. If he who dies does not also take on himself the ordinary occurrence of my death, then his resurrection would never take charge of mine because my death would no longer be like his. The first part of the triptych, *Le passeur de Gethsémani*, has an obvious existential dimension. It was the first book published, and the first written, probably in ignorance (which should be stated publicly!), inasmuch as those reflections were first forged out of my own desire [*au cœur de l'intime*] to weigh everything in the balance of my own human existence.

You are right to emphasize both my closeness to and distance from the hermeneutical position of Paul Ricoeur. In the first chapter of my book *Passer le Rubicon*, entitled "Is Hermeneutics Fundamental?"—in an earlier form presented in Paris at the fiftieth anniversary of the Enrico Castelli colloquium, at which, I recall, you were both present—I did put some distance between my position and the hermeneutics of the text.[10] The issue here is not to denounce but to differentiate. One can only be amazed at the extent to which "the hermeneutics of the text," based as it is on *sola Scriptura*, has innervated Catholic theology. One cannot reproach Paul Ricoeur for having developed it—to the contrary. It was fitting for him to remain in conformity with his own tradition and confession—namely, Protestantism. Yet today we can begin to develop, following the fundamental return to the signification of the text produced by Ricoeur's hermeneutics, a hermeneutic that can be "Catholic" not exclusively in the confessional sense but also and above all in the sense of a theoretical position [*au sens . . . positionnel*]. Thus I have developed a "(Catholic) hermeneutic of the body and voice," analogous to Paul Ricoeur's "(Protestant) hermeneutic of the meaning of the text" and Emmanuel Lévinas's "(Jewish) hermeneutic of the body of the text." It is essential, here, not to criticize. The confessions are different and so are the perspectives. So it is altogether fitting to take a different position. The "table of the word," according to the Second Vatican Council, cannot and must not be separated from the "table of the body." So also "the body of the text" and "the text of the body" must not be separated. Gabriel Marcel's or Maurice Merleau-Ponty's phenomenology of "incarnate being" may in this sense counterbalance the hermeneutics of the text, which, while necessary, does not say everything there is to say about Christianity, much less Catholicism.

"The pure and, so to speak, still mute experience, which now it is the issue to bring to the pure expression of its own sense" (as Husserl says)[11] makes theology fertile, inasmuch as theology then reminds phenomenology that the Word, in the person of Christ, expires in the flesh so that it may no longer speak only in the body: "He opened for us a new and living way through the curtain (that is, by his flesh)," according to the Epistle to the Hebrews (Hebrews 10:20). Paul Ricoeur grasped this point well, especially at the end of his life, when he looked at the disappearance of his own body as that which gives both hope and misery. The existential and final voice of the hermeneut shows how any "attempt at interpretation" is first and foremost embodied: he confessed in a note written on the vigil of his death: "I read on an art book cover: 'Watteau (1684–1721)' [. . .]. The dates of the birth and death of the artist frame the dates of production of each work as an event of life; but these framed dates are simultaneously the moments where the work exempts itself from the time of life and is reinscribed in the immortal—'angelic'—time of the work, the transhistorical time of the reception of the work by other living beings who have their own time."[12]

Translated by Adam Wells

Notes

1. John Paul II, *Redemptoris Missio.*

2. Kant, *Critique of Pure Reason*, A51/B75.

3. For Falque's use of this metaphor in this context—developing Marion's use in the opening pages of *On Descartes' Metaphysical Prism*—see the introduction to the first part of his *God, the Flesh and the Other.*

4. See Nietzsche, *The Will to Power*, 307.

5. Falque, *Dieu, la chair et l'autre*, 37; Falque, *God, the Flesh and the Other*, 16; Falque, *Passer le Rubicon*, 9–25, 187–89.

6. For Falque's use of this image, which defines a critical moment in which his position is clarified in relation to the "second generation," particularly Marion, see his essay "*Lavartus pro Deo.*"

7. Bonaventure, *Les Six Jours de la creation*, 242.

8. With "weight of glory" Falque is referring to Saint Paul's expression in 2 Corinthians 4:17, which is often noted to lie in continuity with the classic Old Testament concept of the *kabôd* or glorious presence of the covenant God, which derives from the Hebrew term signifying something heavy.

9. This quotation from *Being and Time* (*Sein und Zeit*, *Gesamtausgabe* 2, §49, 249n1) corresponds to 408n6 of the Stambaugh English translation, which offers a more accurate translation of this passage than the Macquarrie-Robinson edition. Note that the Martineau French translation, which Falque quotes here, has "la *théologie* élaborée dans la théologie chrétienne . . . " (emphasis added). See Heidegger, *Être et temps*.

10. This event, the Enrico Castelli Jubilee Symposium, took place on January 7, 2011, at the Institut catholique de Paris.

11. Husserl, *Cartesian Meditations*, 38.

12. Ricoeur, *Living Up to Death*, 59–61.

Attempting to Think Beyond Subjectivity

JEAN-LOUIS CHRÉTIEN

CAMILLE RIQUIER: *Your philosophical formation was first made in the school of phenomenology. Can it be said that phenomenology therefore gives to your path of thinking its unity of inspiration? Is Heidegger your great teacher, even more than Husserl, and perhaps against him?*[1]

The life of the mind is composed entirely of encounters, of having to report them and to be accountable to them [*d'avoir à y répondre, comme à en répondre*]—up to our very last breath, where only our formation is interrupted, which does not form us for time alone. But for this we need a language or some languages. My greatest debt is owed to those who have passed them on to me. Learning Latin and Greek, which does not happen at a young age without anguish, has given to me a sense of the weight of every word and of the rigor of syntax. And it is through translating also that one's own language is discovered. I have truly been established [*institué*] by my teachers [*instituteurs*], for it is necessary to have learned one's language well in order to know that learning it is never finished and to be continually taught by it. Without that there is little more than barbaric stammering and the confusion of misunderstanding. Philosophically, an early encounter with Henri Maldiney introduced me, in an unforgettable way, to the thought of Heidegger, not through lessons on what Heidegger thought but through the demand it places on ways of seeing and on choices of words. Saint Augustine says that we have no human master in matters of the truth, for no one is lord over it, but only instructors who arouse, direct, and focus our attention.[2] This released me from the strictly Marxist-Leninist education I received in my family, inflated in its own certainties, but that leaves on certain dimensions of the real a critical regard that I do not renounce. Heidegger has taught me to read the philosophers, especially the Greeks, whom I have taught for most of my life. I only read Husserl after reading him, and I ultimately read Husserl following him, but with the recognition that the unique probity of Husserl's vision, its perpetual deepening, cannot but inspire. The unity of a philosophical itinerary, however, is not found in the list of its filiations and debts (about which I can only speak in the plural, for every voice is polyphonic); it is ahead of itself, located in that which does not cease to call out to it. (It is therefore teleological but a teleology that we cannot master and that we discover little by little under new and surprising forms, sometimes despite ourselves.) I will add that the incessant reading of Plato (before immersing myself in the immense Platonic tradition), begun very early, and then Kierkegaard, the first Christian thinker that I found myself reading closely (whatever the incommensurability of their status), led me to reflect, first inchoately, on thought's written forms of expression—and then it led me to some doubts about the false transparency of the exhibition of theories in the language of the university, where a ready-made language, anonymous and more feeble, claims to stand over a stronger language, unique in its kind. Is a language that leaves nothing to be thought by claiming to say everything in the mode of univocal explanation truly a language of thought? The flavor enhancers in TV dinners always have the same taste and conceal the fact that there is no flavor left there at all or that it has been completely neutralized.

C.R.: *From your very first books, your writing is divided between poetry and philosophy. What links do you establish between them within your own meditation on the word [*parole*]? Is it wrong to say that the second is a reflection on the first or that it at least finds its source there?*

Do we have to substantivize and hypostasize writing [*écriture*] and add to it a possessive adjective? In classical French that is only done for Holy Scripture [*Écriture*] and, rightly, without a possessive adjective. Regarding your question, I have commented on other poets, and I have described in *Répondre*, the diverse moves of response in epic, lyric, or tragic poetry, but it would be pedantic to give a commentary on my own collections. The modes of speech [*parole*], being responses to the same call, are irreducibly plural. You will see that my poetry has always remained strictly profane. But I'll stop here (self-commentary is the entrance to degradation). In any case, I have never conceived or imagined that my philosophical works were second to my poetry or that my poetry illustrated my theses. The sole figure, to my knowledge, for whom your question would be pertinent is Saint John of the Cross, in "Dark Night of the Soul" for example, but he has biblical poems like the "Song of Solomon" for a model, and I do not know the response he would have given to your question. This magisterial example is *sui generis*. And what do you do with Lucretius?

C.R.: *By making yourself attentive to numerous acts of speech [*parole*], such as, for example, response, promise, prayer, etc., the very task of description seems to invite you to leap over disciplinary boundaries, like those between philosophy and literature in your latest work,* Conscience et Roman. *Do these boundaries nevertheless exist, or is it truly the role of the philosopher to contest them?*

Let me take your question as an occasion to say that the guiding theme of all of my writings has been a phenomenology of speech [*parole*] as the place where all meaning comes to light and is received [*se recueille*]. This word is that of finitude, since even the word [*parole*] of God only comes to us in the words of men. I do not consider the response one act of speech [*parole*] among others, for every word is responsive, to the world, to others, to God, and this is even the case for the monologue, which is ultimately always a dialogue. In its incarnation as voice, the word [*parole*] actualizes the entire body for meaning. The human body is the bearer of speech [*porte-parole*],[3] even when we fall silent, which is also one of the essential modes of speech. If speech is responsive, we only speak out of being affected, which does not imply necessarily that every meaning [*sens*] is affective. The Greeks posited awe for the world at the source of philosophy, but there are other fundamental affects. I pursued this meditation on the affect through the responses we give to it in, for example, *La Joie spacieuse*, *De la fatigue*, or *L'Effroi du beau*. This composes the unity of my path amid the great diversity of its themes.

Regarding your question, I will respond in two steps. First of all, the literary forms of philosophy itself are inexhaustibly diverse, without for all that shattering the unity of its essence: the poem (Parmenides, Lucretius), the dialogue (Plato, Saint Augustine, Malebranche), the commentary on a philosophical work (Late Antiquity, the Middle Ages), the aphorism or fragment (Pascal, Nietzsche), the lecture, the treatise, the journal article, the doctoral thesis (which changes over time: Ravaisson's was fifty pages), and so on.[4] Sometimes it is in a genre all to itself, as we can consider the *Phenomenology of Spirit* to be Hegel's or certain books of Kierkegaard, not to mention Nietzsche's *Zarathustra*. A composition's literary form does not by itself determine its membership in philosophy or its exclusion from it. But it is always good to meditate on the philosophical meaning of the choice of form. Second, and this is a totally different question, there is nothing in human culture that philosophy cannot contemplate and from which it cannot learn something. To examine the form of space in Cezanne's paintings is neither to become a painter nor simply an art historian. To contemplate evil in Milton or Dante is not to substitute poetry for philosophy. The hermeneutical dimension of my work and its *longue durée* perspective led me to support my descriptions by writings of all kinds, but this falls under a methodological intention and does not lead toward a sinking into undifferentiated confusion. But assuredly, just as an epistemologist ought to appropriate the procedures of science, if you pose a philosophical question about the modern novel, you cannot ignore the formal and stylistic analysis developed in the critical literature, for without it you will not reach the very thing that is the object of your question. A sharp eye is not born from pretentious ignorance.

C.R.: *What is the relationship for you between philosophy and theology, the difference between which is rarely thematized in your work?*

This question does not allow a simple response, for in reality it contains many different questions. The word "theology" (and "theologian") has distinct meanings through history. The word can be traced back to Greek antiquity, but initially the *theologoi* are the mythographical poets like Homer and Hesiod. If you understand by "theology" a rational and argumentative elaboration of propositions about the divine, the gods, or God, it presupposes philosophy and as a matter of fact it rightfully takes philosophy as its starting point. In this sense there is a theology of Aristotle and the Stoics (who show that materialist theologies exist). Every "religion" (and the unity of such a concept is much more obscure and problematic than it seems) critically interrogates itself but does not, for that reason, contain a theology, if you ascribe a strong meaning to the *logos*. In this sense, the first theologian of biblical faith is Philo, thoroughly learned in Greek philosophy. The very concept of *faith*, strictly monotheist, is much more precise than "belief," since it implies the revelation of the unique God and the firm knowledge of his Word [*Parole*], a life lived according to hope, which is a life lived according to the promise of God. In this sense, the Greeks did not have "faith" in Zeus or Apollo, even if they affirmed their existence and their power. Many beliefs varied from one city to another, just as the historians tell us that the Eastern religions only sought to articulate a unified and coherent "doctrine" [*dogmatique*] in reaction to Christian missionaries in the nineteenth century. Whatever the case may be, it is the concept of Revelation that by its very definition creates a discontinuity and a boundary [*frontière*] since it proposes that God is manifest to us in order to give us, through the human voice of his witnesses, a definitive knowledge of himself, which our reason would not have been able to attain by its own powers. To speak of the meaning of the being of God or of the divine is not to take leave of philosophy, which has always done that, and atheism itself is a theological thesis. Even the philosophy called "analytic" includes theological investigations. But basing oneself on the unique authority of the Word [*Parole*] of God recognized as such is certainly to enter into another space than that of philosophy. Some of my books explicitly and expressly fall under revealed theology: *Sous le regard de la Bible* indicates this by its very title. To cross a boundary is to recognize its existence, not to negate it as such! By contrast, to show historically the philosophical fecundity of the biblical faith through its consequences, such as is manifested in our tradition, opening up new questions, contesting false assumptions [*évidences*], is another task that has occupied me in other *philosophical* books.

C.R.: *Since* Symbolique du corps *(2005) you have been interrogating the origins of modern subjectivity by conducting a "genealogy of figures of interiority, and of the way in which they become subjectivity."*[5] *Does this not invite us to distinguish interiority from subjectivity? What period must we return to in order to attend to the birth of "interiority"? Who are the principal figures here?*

My primary purpose along these lines is to attempt to think beyond subjectivity. This is a recent term, hardly more than a couple of centuries old. As soon as it appears, it reigns supreme, along with the will, understood in new ways, to the point that most people cannot even imagine that we would not be able to take it for a foundation, and the simple hypothesis almost seems sacrilegious, tearing man away from his foundations. The contemporary crisis of human identity, where individualism is exacerbated so much that we no longer know who we are, leads to a multiplication of works on this theme, especially on the very term of the *subject*. Quite often we look to our ancestors only, the forerunners of our thought. My aim is rather to emphasize the rupture and to look on this side of subjectivity for resources that can take us beyond its era, without it being a matter, clearly, of turning back but rather of creating some distance and putting things in perspective, which allows us to get away from being like a hamster in a cage running in place on its wheel. As for the distinction between the exterior and interior, it is given by the life of our body itself, by affectivity, by internal speech [*parole*] and other phenomena. It is grasped not only by philosophy or its concepts but also by schemata that organize actions and practices and also arouse specific affects. In *Symbolique du corps* I studied what can be called in the Christian tradition the "spiritual senses," for which touch, vision, hearing, etc., open up onto orders of irreducible phenomenality, and which run beyond material things. In a book I am currently writing, I study the architectures of the self (like Saint Teresa of Avila's "interior castle," but there are many others), which present different schemata and are no less decisive. There is no interiority without interiorization, no more than without manners of speaking [*diction*] or the figuration of interior space, all of which make it knowable and, in this sense, constitute it for us. *Conscience et Roman* approaches all this by starting from the other side of the rupture or rift, that of the modern "subject."

C.R.: *The idea of the "heart" that is employed in your neologism, "cardiognosie,"*[6] *from* Conscience et Roman, *appears to be more and more central in your work. What meaning does it possess for you and what importance do you give to it, particularly in your latest books?*

The term "heart," which we must separate from all sentimentality and schmaltz, designates in biblical language the center of the human person, ipseity itself, and includes both intellect and will. It remains alive and meaningful as long as the Jewish or Christian faith survives. Witness, for example, its importance in Pascal. Its presence in my writings comes from the works that I study and also from its relative philosophical neutrality, for it is not in itself connected to the definition of the soul in Plato, Aristotle, or other such thinkers, and its historical character is not of the same nature. In this sense it is invaluable for description.

MARC CERISUELO: *It is with Balzac that the central notion of "cardiognosie" truly appears in* Conscience et Roman. *In Stendhal, despite the massive insinuation of the narrator into the inner self of the characters, this power of "reading into hearts is most of the time an unaccomplished or illusory desire that one barely touches"*[7] *How does the Balzacian approach allow a true examination of the secret of hearts?*

The neologism "*cardiognosie*," which I forged after biblical Greek, is substituted for that standard but too vague notion of the omniscience of the narrator and specifies its purpose: the intimacy of a character's thought and desire, impossible to know de jure and not only de facto (like the simultaneous knowledge of events that occur in many places of the world, necessarily fictional in the past but possible today). This *cardiognosie* has numerous degrees: partial or total knowledge of what the character is himself aware, knowledge of what escapes him, of what he hides from himself. How does Balzac exemplarily incarnate this project? First because he explicitly sees in the novel a major place for the knowledge of man, then because he himself constructs the theory of its practice by introducing the concept of "speciality" (the intuitive vision of the soul of the other and of the laws that govern it), which is equivalent to what I call "*cardiognosie*," and finally because of the architectonic sweep of his project, as the very title of the *Comédie humaine* indicates, which he erects in the face of Dante, with everything that that implies (including the displacement of theological poetry by the novel). Henry James has perhaps better than anyone discerned Balzac's project, and he saw in his own way this unique dimension, which, once opened, cannot be closed.

M.C.: *A reading of the two volumes of* Conscience et Roman *reveals a singular relation to literary theory. On the one hand, and contrary to other philosophers who approach literature, your investigation is very rigorous: your work is founded almost as much on the knowledge of the secondary literature as on direct contact with the works themselves. On the other hand, your approach is explicitly philosophical and proposes if not to overcome at least to displace the horizon of reading. From the perspective of the representation of psychical life in the novel, how do you situate the originality or proper status of your contribution if one compares your book to* Transparent Minds *(1978), a classic work dedicated to the subject by the American scholar Dorrit Cohn?*

I have acknowledged my debt to the magisterial work of Dorrit Cohn many times. Its English title, *Transparent Minds*, indicates straightaway its question and its paradox: the mind or consciousness of the other is only accessible to us through its manifestations (actions, gestures, or words), it can be transparent to us voluntarily or involuntarily, and bringing about such a transparency is for her the proper task of fiction (according to the title of a recent work of hers),[8] even if this is through a biography or historical work. With her help, I begin from the same law (on which she has certainly not been the first to focus but which she has orchestrated) and move toward another perspective. In this vein, my debt is really to Georges Poulet, who, in his very diverse works, describes in a way that is both structural and subtly differentiated the proper activity of consciousness, as well as to Erich Auerbach, who, by the stylistic analysis of passages, highlights radical transformations in the relation to external or internal reality, directly from its way of being articulated. *Conscience et Roman* takes a *longue durée* approach: peculiar to the modern novel is its activity of uniting the depths of realism, in the multiform and always more acute description of every aspect of society and the actual material world, with the depths of the fantastic. For passing into the consciousness of another, to the point of perceiving in him more than he perceives in himself, is more fantastical than a magic carpet or an enchanted sword. But this is not a matter of a monstrous juxtaposition, for each inhabits the other: the described real tends more and more to become the singularly real and idiosyncratic, the imaginary world of what consciousness perceives and what affects it—very much like fantasy, which allows us to journey (in my opinion) into the intimacy of consciousnesses, establishes a miraculous "experiment of thought" or even an eidetic variation, which discovers real traits of psychological life, its movements, its strata, its lawfulness, often with more penetration that philosophies. As far as "literature" goes, a concept that is as late as it is obscure (as Jacques Rancière has shown): insofar as it only signifies written culture, I do not use it or hypostasize it, for I do not consider it phenomenologically. Rather, I want to maintain a generic approach, here the novel.

M.C.: *The organization of your thought puts strong emphasis on the double path that connects the history of the novel and the history of the representation of consciousness: namely, the one that is content, from Lucian to Lesage,*[9] *with an artificial uncovering of the "interior" (a term to be understood in all the extensions of its meaning ever since the image of a house with a removable roof prevailed in this tradition); and the one that in the novel of the nineteenth and twentieth centuries leads from the "real" exposition of interiority to the constitution of subjectivity. You do not attempt to highlight the causes of this radical transformation but rather its meaning and modalities. How has the novel become so exceptionally good [*est-il devenu le "surdoué"*] at unveiling our secret intentions?*

Phenomenology methodologically uses fiction and thought experiments in order to uncover essential laws, but its role does not consist in building houses of etiological cards, bringing into play all at once hypotheses falling under religious, social, national, or economic history, domains that are themselves in constant renewal from one generation to the next. The *conditions* of the modern novel can be brought to light—that without which it could not have emerged—but its causes cannot be. Among these conditions, there are some Christian ones: the equal dignity of every human person, the importance of quotidian life, within which my salvation or ruin is decided, the examination of conscience and the scrutinization of my deepest intentions . . . The novel takes possession of this unlimited depth of interiority, obtained or constituted by centuries of doctrines and practices, and, in the strict sense of the word, renders it *profane* by eliminating its center and source, God himself (there are exceptions, Dostoevsky or Bernanos, but this is precisely what makes them unique). This profanation becomes the site of a new sacrality, that of subjectivity. Beckett will knowingly deride it. The transparent consciousness of the novel acts on our perception of ourselves and others; it is the summit of psychologism in its exacerbated exploration where what appears as powerfully penetrating becomes superficial and conventional thirty years later, a movement characteristically modern. The *chansons de geste* did not attempt to renew our knowledge of man, no more than did the picaresque novels, but the modern novel has at its heart a project of exploration and unmasking, which determines its growing arrogance [*qui fait sa fierté croissante*]. But the unique strength of this genre that dissolves the difference among genres and integrates wherever it can something from all the others (poetry, theater, philosophical dialogue, etc.) is to be able (and in a certain manner possessing it as a duty) to carry out ceaselessly its own self-critique, liberating itself from its own petrifactions and laughing at its own conventions. In this way it becomes the most virulent critic of its postulate of transparency, turning it against itself, as I have shown particularly in relation to Victor Hugo, Faulkner, and James, who acknowledge a principle obscurity.

M.C.: *While volume 1 of* Conscience et roman, La Conscience, *openly multiplies its approaches (Stendhal, Balzac, and Hugo for the nineteenth century, Woolf, Faulkner, and Beckett for the twentieth) while focusing on interior monologue, in sotto voce La Conscience gives to the reader the impression of an expansion of commentary—certainly focused on the employment of free indirect style*[10]*—which is henceforth solely focused on the works of Flaubert and James. This calls for a two-fold question: first, and* cum grano salis, *did you not have the impression of reproducing, quasi-mimetically, a certain Jamesian "manner" in the tireless and ever more precise recovery of the treatment of the subject? More generally, on a methodological plane, do we not witness, in the second volume, an excrescence of commentary to the detriment of a more "rhetorical" approach?*

This difference between the two volumes (which nevertheless form a single work, though they can be read separately) is completely intentional. I abhor superficial thinking, as Merleau-Ponty said: the spirit is only reached by a slow immersion in the letter, which resists our arbitrary nature, and where each word has its own weight. The first volume puts to the test the relevance of the question through the great diversity of authors studied

(I had originally hoped for more). Within distinct traditions, Flaubert and James are unanimously recognized as founders of aspects of the twentieth-century novel; even more, if the interior monologue can be easily isolated, the revelatory power of free indirect style, which has porous boundaries and a perpetual irregularity about it, requires a larger context in order to be brought to light. The analysis of forms of space (the near and the far, the theoretical mode of representation where consciousness is represented by places, above all in James), the recurrence of certain stylistic traits (Flaubert's "*comme*" for example), can only make available all their meaning within the horizon of the entire novel. The part on James is more developed, in fact, both because he is notoriously more difficult and because, if there are certain good studies in French, we are still suffering a deficiency that I wanted to fill. My sole desire is to direct readers to the works themselves with a little more clarity and with some directions in order to take the paths for themselves. There again, so the saying goes, God is in the details [*Dieu est dans le detail*]. And only this degree of development can highlight what the novel brings about in a singular way toward our vision of consciousness, whereas the synthetic condensation of the thought of the novelists into theses with a philosophical appearance impoverishes or distorts it. The commentary, as far as written works go, is a matter of patient attention and humility before that which is greater and richer than we are. My project is not meta-theoretical, like Ricoeur's in *Time and Narrative*, which, with his typical equilibrium, gives a critical appraisal of interpretations more than sticking with the thickness of the letter (I mean in what he says about novels). As for mimeticism, I admit it, making my case worse, for I have always followed the rule that a certain stylistic appropriation of what one comments on is necessary. We cannot comment on Saint Bernard with the same language as we would use for Plato or Kant. At the beginning of the part on Flaubert, I demonstrate that I am not alone in this. There is something savage (save in polemic) in the fact that a quotation is like a meteorite, a body radically foreign to the speech [*parole*] that welcomes it and calls for it, gratefully giving to it a fugitive hospitality. This final word seems to me more appropriate than "mimeticism." [For this guest] we must prepare a room and get out the clean sheets, for to quote is an honor that we receive, not one that we confer.

Translated by W. Chris Hackett

Notes

1. This interview, "Essayer de penser au-delà de la subjectivité," appeared in *Critique* 790 (March 2013): 241–52. It is the centerpiece of a special issue dedicated

to "le patient questionnement de Jean-Louis Chrétien." The product of a written correspondence between Chrétien and Marc Cerisuelo and Camille Riquier in July 2012, it centers on Chrétien's most recent work, the two-volume *Conscience et Roman*, for which Chrétien became the first recipient of the Prix du Cardinal Lustiger, sponsored by the Académie française.

2. Augustine, *De magistro*, 1193–220.

3. The primary meaning of "*porte-parole*" is "spokesperson," or one who officially represents an entire group or body. Chrétien is playing on the parts of this phrase as well, for "porte" can mean "gate" or "door" and also as a verb, to "carry" or "bear."

4. Felix Ravaisson was a philosopher and archeologist, an important precursor to Bergson, and the author of *De l'habitude,* which was his doctoral thesis, and other works.

5. See Chrétien, *Conscience et roman*, vol. 1, *La conscience au grand jour*, 7–39.

6. In the wake of modern psychology, contemporary French has come to distinguish between two words, "*gnose*" and "*gnosie*." The former term corresponds to the English term "gnosis" and has the sense of an esoteric salvific knowledge that is only achievable by an inner circle of initiates, etc. The latter term, "*gnosie*," is unique to modern psychology and concerns the capacity for an individual to recognize the form of an object by means of one of the five senses (see the technical term "gnostic" or "gnosic function"). It seems that in English there is no consensus: some authors use the term "gnostic" while others use "gnosic" when referring to this capacity. Merleau-Ponty uses this adjectival form of the term, "*gnosique*," instructively (for this context) in *Phénoménologie de la perception*, 88. The English translation by Paul Kegan translates *gnosique* as "gnosic." See *Phenomenology of Perception*, 85.

7. Chrétien, *Conscience et roman*, 1:93.

8. Cohn, *The Distinction of Fiction*.

9. Lucian of Samosata was a Greek rhetorician and satirist commonly understood as one of the earliest novelists. Alain-René Lesage was a French novelist and dramatist.

10. *Le style indirect libre*, "free indirect style," or "free indirect discourse," is a kind of third-person narration that embeds a character's speech or thoughts. By blending elements of third- and first-person speech, it allows a third-person narrative to utilize the point of view of the first person. Flaubert made this technique famous in 1857 with *Madame Bovary*, and it has since become widespread.

Acknowledgments

The authors would like to thank the Johns Hopkins University Humanities Center, the University of Michigan Society of Fellows and Department of Comparative Literature, the University of Virginia Department of Religious Studies, the Australian Catholic University School of Philosophy, and the École normale supérieure (rue d'Ulm), institutions whose generous support made this project possible. We would also like to thank Hent de Vries and Kevin Hart for their encouragement throughout. Helen Tartar, whom we lost too soon, enthusiastically supported this project from the very beginning. Thomas Lay and Eric Newman graciously saw it through each step of the way. Our copy editor, Ziggy Snow, and our translators (Nils Schott, Larry McGrath, Chris Fenwick, Adam Wells, K. Jason Wardley, and Scott Davidson) were indispensable. Many thanks to Jean Leclercq and Grégori Jean for compiling the "interview" with Michel Henry. Finally, we would like to thank our interviewees for participating in what we hope will open a new window into the historical and philosophical significance of contemporary French phenomenology.

Bibliography

Alquié, Ferdinand. *La critique kantienne de la métaphysique*. Paris: Presses Universitaires de France, 1968.

———. *La découverte métaphysique de l'homme chez Descartes*. Paris: Presses Universitaires de France, 1950.

———. *Qu'est que comprendre un philosophe*. Paris: Table Ronde, 2005.

———. *Le rationalisme de Spinoza*. Paris: Presses Universitaires de France, 1981.

Aquinas, Thomas. *Basic Writings of Saint Thomas Aquinas*. Translated by Anthony C. Pegis. Indianapolis: Hackett, 1997.

———. *Commentary on Aristotle's* Metaphysics. Translated by Richard J. Blackwell and Richard J. Spath. Notre Dame, IN: Dumb Ox Books, 1999.

Aristotle. *The Complete Works of Aristotle*. 2 vols. Edited by Jonathan Barnes. Princeton, NJ: Princeton University Press, 1984.

Armogathe, Jean-Robert. *La nature du monde: Science nouvelle et exégèse au XVIIe siècle*. Paris: Presses Universitaires de France, 2007.

———. *Theologia cartesiana. L'explication physique de l'Eucharistie chez Descartes et dom Desgabets*. The Hague, Netherlands: Martinus Nijhoff, 1977.

Augustine, Saint. *The Confessions*. Translated by Henry Chadwick. Oxford: Oxford University Press, 2008.

———. *De magistro*: *Patrologia Latina*. Vol. 32. Edited by J.-P. Migne. Paris: 1845.

Barbaras, Renaud. *Le désir et la distance. Introduction à une phénoménologie de la perception*. Paris: Vrin, 1999.

———. *Introduction à une phénoménologie de la vie*. Paris: Vrin, 2008.

Barth, Karl. *Protestant Theology in the Nineteenth Century*. Translated by Brian Cozens and John Bowden. London: SCM Press, 2001. Originally published as *Die protestantische Theologie im 19. Jahrhundert* (Zürich, Switzerland: Theologischer Verlag, 1952).

Balthasar, Hans Urs von. *Apokalypse der Deutschen Seele: Studien zu einer Lehre von letzten Haltungen*. 3 vols. Einsiedeln, Switzerland: Johannes Verlag, 1937 1939.

———. "Some Points of Eschatology." In *Explorations in Theology*. Vol. 1, *The Word Made Flesh*, 255–77. Translated by A. V. Littledale and Alexander Dru. San Francisco: Ignatius Press, 1989.

Balzac, Honoré. *La Comédie humaine*. 7 vols. Edited by Pierre Citron. Paris: Seuil, 1965.

Becker, Oskar. "Contributions toward a Phenomenological Foundation of Geometry and Its Physical Applications." Translated by Theodore Kisiel. In *Phenomenology and the Natural Sciences*, ed. Joseph Kockelmans and Theodore J. Kisiel, 119–43. Evanston, IL: Northwestern University Press, 1970.

Benoist, Jocelyn. *Autour de Husserl: l'ego et la raison*. Paris: Vrin, 1994.

———. *Concepts: Introduction à l'analyse*. Paris: Éditions du Cerf, 2010.

———. *Éléments de philosophie réaliste*. Paris: Vrin, 2011.

———. *L'idée de phénoménologie*. Paris: Beauchesne, 2001.

———. *Les limites de l'intentionalité: Recherches phénoménologiques et anaytiques*. Paris: Vrin, 2005.

———. *Représentations sans objet: aux origines de la phénoménologie et de la philosophie analytique*. Paris: Presses Universitaires de France, 2001.

———. *Sens et sensibilité. L'intentionalité en context*. Paris: Éditions du Cerf, 2009.

Benoist, Jocelyn, and Michel Espagne, eds. *L'itinéraire de Tran Duc Thao*. Paris: Armand Colin, 2013.

Bergson, Henri. *Essai sur les données immédiates de la conscience*. Paris: Felix Alcan, 1889.

Bernard, Saint. *De Consideratione*. In *Sancti Bernardi opera*, III: *Tractatus et opuscula*. Edited by J. Leclercq and H. M. Rochais. Rome: Editiones cistercienses, 1963.

Bérulle, Pierre de. *Opuscules de Piété*. Edited by Miklos Vetö. Grenoble, France: Millon, 1997.

Boethius. *The Theological Tractates*. Translated by H. F. Stewart and E. K. Rand. London: William Heineman, 1918.

Bonaventure, Saint. *Les Six Jours de la creation*. Paris: Desclée-Cerf, 1991.

Boutroux, Émile. *The Contingency of the Laws of Nature*. Translated by Fred Rothwell. Chicago: Open Court, 1916.

Brague, Rémi. *Aristote et la question du monde: essai sur le contexte cosmologique et anthropologique de l'ontologie*. Paris: Presses Universitaires de France, 2001.

———. *The Legend of the Middle Ages: Philosophical Explorations of Medieval Christianity, Judaism, and Islam*. Chicago: University of Chicago Press, 2009.

———. *The Wisdom of the World: The Human Experience of the Universe in Western Thought*. Translated by Theresa Fagan. Chicago: University of Chicago Press, 2004.

Brentano, Franz. *Psychology from an Empirical Standpoint*. Edited by Linda L. McAlister. London: Routledge, 1973.

Buytendijk, Frederik Jacobus Johannes. *Allgemeine Theorie der menschlichen Haltung und Bewegung*. Berlin: Springer, 1956.

Canguilhem, Georges. *La connaissance de la vie*. Paris: Vrin, 1952.

———. *Le normal et la pathologique*. Paris: Presses Universitaires de France, 2013.

Cassirer, Ernst. *The Philosophy of Symbolic Forms*. 3 vols. Translated by Charles W. Hendel. New Haven, CT: Yale University Press, 1955–1957.

Cavaillès, Jean. *Méthode axiomatique et formalisme. Essai sur le problème du fondement des mathématiques*. Paris: Hermann, 1938.

———. *Sur la logique et la théorie de la science*. Paris: Presses Universitaires de France, 1947.

———. *Transfini et continu*. Paris: Hermann, 1947.

Celan, Paul. *Die Niemandsrose*. Frankfurt am Main, Germany: S. Fischer, 1963.

Chrétien, Jean-Louis. *Conscience et roman*. 2 vols. Paris: Éditions de Minuit, 2009, 2011.

———. *De la fatigue*. Paris: Éditions de Minuit, 1996.

———. *L'effroi du beau*. Paris: Éditions du Cerf, 1987.

———. *La joie spacieuse: Essai sur la dilatation*. Paris: Éditions de Minuit, 2007.

———. *Répondre: Figures de la réponse et de la responsabilité*. Paris: Presses Universitaires de France, 2007.

———. *Sous le regard de la Bible*. Paris: Bayard, 2008.

———. *Symbolique du corps: la tradition chrétienne du Cantique des Cantiques*. Paris: Presses Universitaires de France, 2005.

Cohen, Hermann. *Kants Theorie der Erfahrung*. Berlin: Dümmler, 1871.

Cohn, Dorrit. *The Distinction of Fiction*. Baltimore, MD: Johns Hopkins University Press, 1999.

Courtine, Jean-François. *Phénoménologie et théologie*. Paris: Criterion, 1992.

———. *Suarez et le système de la métaphysique*. Paris: Presses Universitaires de France, 1990.

———. *Transparent Minds*. Princeton, NJ: Princeton University Press, 1978.

Dastur, Françoise. *Heidegger: La question du logos*. Paris: Vrin, 2007.

———. *La Mort: Essai sur la finitude*. Paris: Hatier, 1994; Paris: Presses Universitaires de France, 2007.

———. "Pour une zoologie 'privative' ou comment ne pas parler de l'animal." *Alter*, Revue de Phénomenologie, 3 (1995): 281–318.

———. *Telling Time: Sketch of a Phenomenological Chronology*. London: Athlone, 2000.

David, Alain, and Jean Greisch. *Michel Henry, l'épreuve de la vie, Actes du Colloque Michel Henry*. Arles, France: Sulliver, 2005.

Derrida, Jacques. *The Animal That Therefore I Am*. Translated by David Wills. New York: Fordham University Press, 2008.

———. *The Gift of Death*. Translated by David Wills. Chicago: University of Chicago Press, 2007.

———. *Husserl's* Origin of Geometry*: An Introduction*. Translated by John P. Leavey Jr. Lincoln: University of Nebraska Press, 1989.

———. *Of Spirit*. Translated by Geoffrey Bennington and Rachel Bowlby. Chicago: University of Chicago Press, 1989.

———. *On Touching: Jean-Luc Nancy*. Translated by Christine Irizarry. Stanford, CA: Stanford University Press, 2005.

———. "Violence et Métaphysique." *Revue de Métaphysique et de Morale* 3–4 (1964): 425–73.

———. *La voix et le phénomène*. Paris: Presses Universitaires de France, 1967.

Desanti, Jean-Toussaint. *Les Idéalités mathématiques. Recherches épistémologiques sur le développement de la théorie des fonctions de variables réelles*. Paris: Éditions du Seuil, 1968.

———. *La philosophie silencieuse ou critique des philosophies de la science*. Paris: Éditions du Seuil, 1975.

Descartes, René. *Regulae ad directionem ingenii*. In *Oeuvres de Descartes*, vol. 10. Edited by Charles Adam and Paul Tannery. Paris: Vrin, 1975.

———. *Passions of the Soul*. In *The Philosophical Writings of Descartes*, vol. 1. Translated by Rober Stoothoff. Cambridge: Cambridge University Press, 1985.

Dionysius the Areopagite, Pseudo-. *The Complete Works*. Translated by Colm Luibheid and Paul Rorem. London: SPCK, 1987.

Ebeling, Gerhard. *Luther: Einführung in sein Denken*. 4th ed. Tübingen, Germany: Mohr/Siebeck, 1981.

Espagne, Michel, ed. *L'école normale supérieure et l'Allemagne*. Transfer: Deutscher-Französische Kulturbibliothek, vol. 6. Leipzig, Germany: Leipziger Universitätsverlag, 1996.

Falque, Emmanuel. *Le combat amoureux: Disputes phénoménologiques et théologiques*. Paris: Hermann, 2014.

———. *Dieu, la chair, et l'autre*. Paris: Presses Universitaires de France, 2008.

———. *God, the Flesh and the Other: From Irenaeus to Duns Scotus*. Translated by W. Chris Hackett. Evanston, IL: Northwestern University Press, 2014.

———. "*Lavartus pro Deo*: Jean-Luc Marion's Phenomenology and Theology." In *Counter-Experiences: Reading Jean-Luc Marion*, edited by Kevin Hart, 181–200. Notre Dame, IN: University of Notre Dame Press, 2007.

———. "Limite théologique et finitude phénoménologique chez Thomas d'Aquin." *Revue des Sciences Philosophiques et théologique* 92, no. 3 (2008): 527–56.

———. *Métamorphose de la finitude: Essai philosophique sur la naissance et la résurrection*. Paris: Éditions du Cerf, 2004.

———. *The Metamorphosis of Finitude: An Essay on Birth and Resurrection*. Translated by George Hughes. New York: Fordham University Press, 2012.

———. *Les noces de l'Agneau: Essai philosophique sur le corps et l'eucharistie*. Paris: Éditions du Cerf, 2011.

———. *Passer le Rubicon. Philosophie et theologie: Essai sur les frontieres*. Brussels: Éditions Lessius, 2013.

———. *Passeur de Gethsémani. Angoisse, souffrance et mort: lecture existentielle et phénoménologique*. Paris: Éditions du Cerf, 1999.

———. *Saint Bonaventure et l'entrée de dieu en théologie*. Paris: Vrin, 2002.

———. *Triduum philosophique*. Paris: Cerf, 2015.

Fink, Eugen. *De la phénoménologie*. Translated by Didier Franck. Paris: Éditions de Minuit, 1974.

———. *Sixth Cartesian Meditation: The Idea of a Transcendental Theory of Method*. Translated by Ronald Bruzina. Bloomington: Indiana University Press, 1995.

Flaubert, Gustave. *Madame Bovary*. Translated by Margaret Mauldon. Oxford: Oxford University Press, 2008.

Franck, Didier. *Chair et corps: Sur la phenomenologie de Husserl*. Paris: Éditions de Minuit, 1981.

———. "La chair et le problem de la constitution temporelle." In *Phénoménologie et métaphysique*, edited by Jean-Luc Marion and Guy Planty-Bonjour, 125–59. Paris: Presses Universitaires de France, 1984.

Freud, Sigmund. "Das Unbewußte." *Internationale Zeitschrift für Ärtzliche Pyschoanalyse* 3, no. 4 (1915): 189–203.

Gibson, J. J. "The Theory of Affordances." In *Perceiving, Acting, and Knowing*, edited by Robert Shaw and John Bransford, 67–82. New York: Wiley, 1977.

Ginzburg, Carlo. *Occhiacci di legno. Nove riflessioni sulla distanza*. Milan: Giangiacomo Feltrinelli, 1998.

Goff, Jacques Le. *Naissance du purgatoire*. Paris: Gallimard, 1981.

Goldstein, Kurt. *Der Aufbau des Organismus: Einführung in die Biologie unter besonderer Berücksichtigung der Erfahrungen am kranken Menschen*. The Hague, Netherlands: Nijhoff, 1934.

———. *Human Nature in the Light of Psychopathology*. New York: Schocken Books, 1963.

———. *The Organism: A Holistic Approach to Biology Derived from Pathological Data in Man*. New York: American Book Company, 1939.

Gondek, Hans-Dieter, and László Tengelyi. *Neue Phänomenologie in Frankreich*. Berlin: Surkhamp, 2011.

Greisch, Jean. *Ontologie et Temporalité. Esquisse d'une interprétation intégrale de Sein und Zeit*. Paris: Presses Universitaires de France, 2002.

Gurwitsch, Aaron. *Field of Consciousness*. Pittsburgh: Duquesne University Press, 1964.

———. *Marginal Consciousness*. Translated by Lester E. Embree. Athens: Ohio University Press, 1985.

Hegel, G. W. F. *Phenomenology of Spirit*. Translated by A. V. Miller. Oxford: Oxford University Press, 1976.

Heidegger, Martin. *Being and Time*. Translated by John Macquarrie and Edward Robinson. New York: Harper & Row, 1962.
———. *Being and Time*. Translated by Joan Stambaugh. Albany: SUNY Press, 2010.
———. *Contributions to Philosophy: Of the Event*. Translated by Richard Rojcewicz and Daniela Vallega-Neu. Bloomington: Indiana University Press, 2012.
———. *Country Path Conversations*. Translated by Bret W. Davis. Bloomington: Indiana University Press, 2010.
———. *Être et temps*. Translated by Emmanuel Martineau. Paris: Authentica, 1985.
———. *Four Seminars*. Translated by Andrew Mitchell and François Raffoul. Bloomington: Indiana University Press, 2003.
———. *Gesamtausgabe*. 102 vols. Edited by Friedrich-Wilhelm von Hermann. Frankfurt am Main, Germany: Vittorio Klostermann, 1975–2013.
———. *History of the Concept of Time: Prolegomena*. Translated by Theodore Kisiel. Bloomington: Indiana University Press, 2009.
———. "Hölderlin and the Essence of Poetry." In *Elucidations of Hölderlin's Poetry*. Translated by Keith Hoeller. Amherst, NY: Humanity Books, 2000.
———. *Logic: The Question of Truth*. Translated by Thomas Sheehan. Bloomington: Indiana University Press, 2010.
———. "Mein Weg in die Phänomenologie." In *Festgabe Hermann Niemeyer zum achtzigsten Geburtstag am 16 April 1963*. Tübingen, Germany: Privatdruck, 1963.
———. *On the Way to Language*. Translated by Peter D. Hertz and Joan Stambaugh New York: Harper and Row, 1971.
———. *On Time and Being*. Translated by Joan Stambaugh. Chicago: University of Chicago Press, 1972.
———. "Phenomenology and Theology." In *Pathmarks*, edited by William McNeil, 39–63. Cambridge: Cambridge University Press, 1998.
———. "Qu'est que la metaphysique?" Translated by Henry Corbin. *Bifur* 8 (1931): 1–27.
———. *Qu'est-ce que la métaphysique*. Translated by Henry Corbin. Paris: Gallimard, 1938.
———. *Sein und Zeit*. Tübingen, Germany: Max Niemeyer, 2006.
———. *Unterwegs zur Sprache*. Edited by F. W. von Hermann. Frankfurt am Main: Vittorio Klostermann, 1985.
———. *What Is a Thing?* Translated by W. B. Barton Jr. and Vera Deutsch. Chicago: H. Regnery, 1967.
———. "Zeit und Sein." In *Zur Sache des Denkens*. Tübingen, Germany: Max Niemeyer, 1969.
Hemmerle, Klause. *Thesen zu einer trinitarischen Ontologie*. Einsiedeln, Switzerland: Johannes Verlag, 1976.
Henry, Michel. *L'amour les yeux fermés*. Paris: Gallimard, 1976.

———. *Auto-donation. Entretiens et conférences*. Montpellier, France: Prétentaine, 2002.
———. *La barbarie*. Paris: Grasset et Fasquelle, 1987.
———. *C'est moi la vérité. Pour une philosophie du christianisme*. Paris: Seuil, 1996.
———. *De la phénoménolgie*. Vol. 1. Paris: Presses Universitaires de France, 2003.
———. *Du communisme au capitalisme. Théorie d'une catastrophe*. Paris: Odile Jacob, 1990.
———. *Entretien avec O. Salazar-Ferrer*. Clichy, France: Editions de Corlevour, 2010.
———. *Entretiens*. Arles, France: Sulliver, 2005.
———. *L'essence de la manifestation*. Paris: Presses Universitaires de France, 1963.
———. *Généalogie de la psychanalyse. Le commencement perdu*. Paris: Presses Universitaires de France, 1985.
———. *Incarnation. Une philosophie de la chair*. Paris: Seuil, 2000.
———. *Le jeune officier*. Paris: Gallimard, 1954.
———. *Marx. T.1 Une philosophie de la réalité humaine. T.2 Une philosophie de l'économie*. Paris: Gallimard, 1976.
———. *Material Phenomenology*. Translated by Scott Davidson. New York: Fordham University Press, 2008.
———. *Phénoménologie de la vie*. Vol. 3. *De l'art et du politique*. Paris: Presses Universitaires de France, 2004.
———. *Philosophie et phenomenologie du corps. Essai sur l'ontologie biranienne*. Paris: Presses Universitaires de France, 1965.
———. *Voir l'invisible. Sur Kandinsky*. Paris: Bourin, 1988.
Höfer, Josef, and Karl Rahner, eds. *Lexikon für Theologie und Kirche*. 2nd ed. 14 vols. Frieburg im Breisgau, Germany: Herder, 1957–1968. 3rd ed. 11 vols. Edited by Walter Kasper. Frieburg im Breisgau, Germany: Herder, 1993–2001.
Housset, Emmanuel. *Husserl et l'idée de Dieu*. Paris: Cerf, 2011.
Hume, David. *An Enquiry Concerning Human Understanding and Other Writings*. Edited by Stephen Buckle. Cambridge: Cambridge University Press, 2007.
Husserl, Edmund. "L'archie-originaire Terre ne se meut pas." Translated by Didier Franck. *Philosophie* 1 (1984): 1–30.
———. *Cartesian Meditations: An Introduction to Phenomenology*. Translated by Dorion Cairns. The Hague, Netherlands: Martinus Nijhoff, 1970.
———. *Crisis of the European Sciences and Transcendental Phenomenology: An Introduction to Phenomenological Philosophy*. Translated by David Carr. Evanston, IL: Northwestern University Press, 1970.
———. *Experience and Judgment: Investigations in a Genealogy of Logic*. Translated by James S. Chuchill and Karl Ameriks. Evanston, IL: Northwestern University Press, 1973.

———. *Formal and Transcendental Logic*. Translated by Dorion Cairns. The Hague, Netherlands: Martinus Nijhoff, 1969.

———. *Husserliana: Edmund Husserl Gesammelte Werke*. 42 vols. The Hague, Netherlands: Martinus Nijhoff; New York: Springer; Dordrecht, Netherlands: Kluwer Academic Publishers, 1950–2014.

———. *Husserliana Dokumente* III/1–10. Edited by Karl Schuhmann and Elisabeth Schuhmann. Dordrecht, Netherlands: Kluwer Academic Publishers, 1994.

———. *The Idea of Phenomenology*. Translated by William P. Alston and George Nakhnikian. The Hague, Netherlands: Martinus Nijhoff, 1964.

———. (*Ideas I*) *Ideas: General Introduction to Pure Phenomenology*. Translated by W. R. Boyce Gibson. New York: Collier, 1931.

———. (*Ideas II*) *Ideas Pertaining to a Pure Phenomenology and to a Phenomenology Philosophy. Second Book: Studies in the Phenomenology of Constitution*. Translated by Richard Rojcewicz and André Schuwer. Dordrecht, Netherlands: Kluwer, 1989.

———. (*Ideas III*) *Ideas Pertaining to a Pure Phenomenology and to a Phenomenological Philosophy. Third Book: Phenomenology and the Foundation of the Sciences*. Translated by T. E. Klein and W. E. Pohl. Dordrecht, Netherlands: Kluwer, 1980, 2001.

———. *Ideen zu eienter reinen Phänomenologie und phänomenologischen Philosophie*. In *Jahrbuch für Philosophie und phänomenologische Forschung*. Halle, Germany: Max Niemeyer, 1913.

———. *Logical Investigations*. 2 vols. Translated by J. N. Findlay. London: Routledge, 1970, 1976, 1977, 2001.

———. *Logische Untersuchungen*. 2 vols. Halle, Germany: Max Niemayer, 1900–1901.

———. *On the Phenomenology of Internal Time-Consciousness*. Translated by John B. Brough. Dordrecht, Netherlands: Kluwer, 1991.

———. *L'origine de la géométrie. Traduction et introduction par Jacques Derrida*. Paris: Presses Universitaires de France, 1962.

———. "Philosophie als strenge Wissenschaft." Logos 1 (1911): 289–341.

———. *Psychological and Transcendental Phenomenology and the Confrontation with Heidegger (1927–1931)*. Edited by Thomas Sheehan and Richard E. Palmer. Dordrecht, Netherlands: Kluwer Academic Publishers, 1997.

Ingarden, Roman. *The Literary Work of Art*. Translated by Ruth Ann Crowley and Kenneth R. Olson. Evanston, IL: Northwestern University Press, 1973.

———. *On the Motives which led Edmund Husserl to Transcendental Idealism*. The Hague, Netherlands: Martinus Nijhoff, 1976.

———. *The Ontology of the Work of Art*. Translated by Raymond Meyer and John T. Goldthwait. Athens: Ohio University Press, 1989.

Janicaud, Dominique. *La phénoménologie dans tous ses états*. Paris: Gallimard, 2009.

Janicaud, Dominique, Françoise Dastur, and Eliane Escoubas. "Entretien." In *Phénoménologie française et phénoménologie allemande*, edited by E. Escoubas and B. Waldenfels, 185–217. Paris: Harmattan, 2000.

Janicaud, Dominique, Jean-François Courtine, Jean-Louis Chrétien, Jean-Luc Marion, Michel Henry, and Paul Ricoeur. *Phenomenology and the "Theological Turn": The French Debate*. New York: Fordham University Press, 2000.

———. *Le tournant théologique de la phénoménologie française*. Paris: Eclat, 1992.

John Paul II. *Redemptoris Missio*. Rome: Libreria Editrice Vaticana, 1990. *Mission of the Redeemer*. Boston: Pauline Books & Media, 1991.

Jonas, Hans. *Le Phénomène de la vie. Vers une biologie philosophique*. Paris: De Boeck, 2001.

Kaliba, Clemens. *Die Welt als Gleichnis des dreienigen Gottes*. Salzburg, Austria: Müller, 1952.

Kant, Immanuel. *Critique of Pure Reason*. Translated by Norman Kemp Smith. New York: Palgrave, 1929.

Kearney, Richard. "Epiphanies of the Everyday: Toward a Micro-Eschatology." In *After God: Richard Kearney and the Religious Turn in Continental Philosophy*, edited by John Panteleimon Manoussakis, 3–20. New York: Fordham University Press, 2006.

———. "Sacramental Imagination and Eschatology." In *Phenomenology and Eschatology: Not Yet in the Now*, edited by Neal DeRoo and John Panteleimon Manoussakis, 55–67. Farnham, England: Ashgate, 2009.

Kearney, Richard, and Joseph Stephen O'Leary, eds. *Heidegger et la question de Dieu*. Paris: Grasset, 1981.

Kierkegaard, Søren. *Philosophical Fragments*. Translated by Howard V. Hong and Edna H. Hong. Princeton, NJ: Princeton University Press, 1985.

Kittel, Gerhard, ed. *Wörterbuch zum Neuen Testament Theologisches*. 5 vols. Stuttgart, Germany: W. Kohlhammer, 1933–1979.

Kojève, Alexandre. *Introduction à la lecture de Hegel*. Edited by Raymond Queneau. Paris: Gallimard, 1947.

Lachelier, Jules. *Du Fondement de l'induction suivi de psychologie et métaphysique*. Paris: Alcan, 1896.

Lachièze-Rey, Pierre. *Le Moi, le Monde et Dieu*. Paris: Boivin, 1938.

Lacoste, Jean-Yves. "Le désir et l'inexigible: pour lire Henri de Lubac." In *Le monde et l'absence d'œuvre*, 23–54. Paris: Presses Universitaires de France, 2000.

———, ed. *Dictionnaire critique de théologie*. Paris: Presses Universitaires de France, 2011.

———. *Être en danger*. Paris: Éditions du Cerf, 2011.

———. *Experience and the Absolute: Disputed Questions on the Humanity of Man*. Translated by Mark Raftery-Skeehan. New York: Fordham University Press, 2004.

———. *Expérience et absolu: Questions disputées sur l'humanité de l'homme*. Paris: Presses Universitaires de France, 1994.

———. *From Theology to Theological Thinking*. Translated by W. Chris Hackett. Charlottesville: University of Virginia Press, 2014.
———. *Histoire de la théologie*. Paris: Seuil, 2009.
———. *Le monde et l'absence de l'œuvre et autres études*. Paris: Presses Universitaires de France, 2000.
———. *Note sur le temps: essai sur les raisons de la mémoire et de l'espérance*. Paris: Presses Universitaires de France, 1990.
———. *La phénoménalité de Dieu: Neuf études*. Paris: Éditions du Cerf, 2008.
Laugier, Sandra. *L'Anthropologie logique de Quine: l'apprentissage de l'obvie*. Paris: Vrin, 1992.
———. *Why We Need Ordinary Language Philosophy*. Chicago: University of Chicago Press, 2013.
———. *Wittgenstein: le mythe de l'inexpressivité*. Paris: Vrin, 2010.
Lebrun, Gerard. *La patience du concept: essai sur le discours hégélien*. Paris: Gallimard, 1972.
Lévinas, Emmanuel. *Autrement qu'être ou au-dela de l'essence*. Leiden, Netherlands: Martinus Nijhoff, 1974.
———. *De l'existence à l'existant*. Paris: Vrin, 2002.
———. "Is Ontology Fundamental?" Translated by Peter Atterton. *Philosophy Today* 33, no. 2 (1989): 124–25.
———. *Le temps et l'autre*. Paris: Presses Universitaire de France, 2011.
———. *Totalité et infini*. Leiden, Netherlands: Martinus Nijhoff, 1961.
———. *Totality and Infinity*. Translated by Alphonso Lingis. Pittsburgh: Duquesne University Press, 1969.
Lewis, C. S. *Out of the Silent Planet*. London: Bodley Head, 1938.
———. *Perelandra*. London: Bodley Head, 1943.
———. *That Hideous Strength*. London: Bodley Head, 1945.
Libera, Alain de. *Archéologie du sujet: Naissance du sujet*. Paris: Vrin, 2007.
———. *Archéologie du sujet: La quête de l'identité*. Paris: Vrin, 2008.
———. *Archéologie du sujet: Le sujet de l'action*. Paris: Vrin, 2013.
———. *La Mystique rhénane. D'Albert le Grand à Maître Eckhart*. Paris: Le Seuil, 1994.
———. *La Référence vide. Théories de la proposition*. Paris: Presses Universitaires de France, 2002.
Macksey, Richard, and Eugenio Donato, eds. *The Structuralist Controversy: The Languages of Criticism and the Sciences of Man*. Baltimore, MD: Johns Hopkins University Press, 2007.
Marion, Jean-Luc. "Avant-Propos." In *Phénoménologie et métaphysique*, edited by Jean-Luc Marion and Guy Planty-Bonjour, 7–14. Paris: Presses Universitaires de France, 1984.
———. *Being Given: Toward a Phenomenology of Givenness*. Translated by Jeffrey L. Kosky. Stanford, CA: Stanford University Press, 2002.
———. *Certitudes négatives*. Paris: Grasset and Fasquelle, 2010.

———. *Dieu sans l'être*. Paris: Fayard, 1982; 2nd ed. Paris: Presses Universitaires de France, 2010.

———. "Du fondement de la distinction entre théologie et philosophie." *Budhi: A Journal of Ideas and Culture* 13, no. 1–3 (2009), http://journals.ateneo.edu/ojs/index.php/budhi/issue/view/34.

———. *Étant donné. Essai d'une phénoménologie de la donation*. Paris: Presses Universitaires de France, 1997, 2013.

———. *L'idole et la distance. Cinq études*. Paris: Grasset, 1977.

———. "Metaphysics and Phenomenology: A Relief for Theology." *Critical Inquiry* 20, no. 4 (1994): 582–83.

———. "Métaphysique et phénoménologie: une relève pour la théologie." *L'avenir de la métaphysique, Bulletin de litterature ecclésiastique* (1991–1992): 21–39.

———. *On Descartes' Metaphysical Prism: The Constitution and Limits of Onto-theo-logy in Cartesian Thought*. Translated by Jeffrey L. Kosky. Chicago: University of Chicago Press, 1999.

———. *Le phénomène érotique*. Paris: Grasset, 2003.

———. "The Phenomenological Origins of the Concept of Givenness." In *The Reason of the Gift*. Translated by Stephen E. Lewis, 19–35. Charlottesville: University of Virginia Press.

———. *Reduction and Givenness*. Translated by Thomas A. Carlson. Evanston, IL: Northwestern University Press, 1998.

———. *Réduction et donation. Recherches sur Husserl, Heidegger et la phénoménologie*. Paris: Presses Universitaires de France, 1989.

———. "Remarques sur l'utilité en théologie de la phénoménologie." *Archivo di filosofia* 79, no. 2 (2011): 11–22.

———. *Sur l'ontologie grise de Descartes. Science cartésienne et savoir aristotélicien dans les Regulae, Librairie Philosophique*. Paris: Vrin, 1975.

———. *Sur la théologie blanche de Descartes. Analogie, création des vérités éternelles*. Paris: Presses Universitaires de France, 1981.

Martineau, Emmanuel. "Étienne Gilson, 1884–1978." In *Étienne Gilson et nous: la philosophie et son histoire*, edited by Marie-Thérèse d'Alverny and Monique Couratier, 61–72. Paris: Librairie philosophique J. Vrin, 1980.

———. "Prudence et considération. Un dessein philosophique de saint Bernard de Clairvaux." In *Les Études philosophiques* 1, 23–45. Paris: Presses Universitaires de France, 1980.

Marx, Karl. *Capital*, vol. 3. Translated by David Fernbach. London: Penguin, 1991.

Marx, Werner. *Absolute Reflexion und Sprache*. Frankfurt am Main: Vittorio Klostermann, 1967.

———. *Hegel's* Phenomenology of Spirit: *Its Point and Purpose: A Commentary on the Preface and Introduction*. Translated by Peter Heath. New York: Harper and Row, 1975.

———. *Heidegger and the Tradition*. Translated by Theodore Kisiel. Evanston, IL: Northwestern University Press, 1971.

Merleau-Ponty, Maurice. *Éloge de la philosophie* (Paris: Gallimard, 1953). Translated by John Wild, James Eddie, and John O'Neill as *In Praise of Philosophy and Other Essays*. Evanston, IL: Northwestern University Press, 1970.
———. *The Merleau-Ponty Reader*, edited by Ted Toadvine and Leonard Lawlor. Evanston, IL: Northwestern University Press, 2007.
———. *Phénoménologie de la perception*. Paris: Gallimard, 1945. Translated by Paul Kegan as *Phenomenology of Perception*. London: Routledge, 2005.
———. *The Visible and the Invisible*. Translated by Alphonso Lingis. Evanston, IL: Northwestern University Press, 1969.
———. *Le visible et l'invisible*. Edited by Claude Lefort. Paris: Gallimard, 1964.
Nabert, Jean. *L'Expérience intérieure de la Liberté*. Paris: Presses Universitaires de France, 1923.
Nietzsche, Friedrich. *Thus Spoke Zarathustra*. Edited by Adrian Del Caro and Robert Pippin. Cambridge: Cambridge University Press, 2006.
———. *The Will to Power*. Translated by Walter Kaufmann and R. J. Hollingdale. New York: Random House, 1968.
Otto, Rudolf. *The Idea of the Holy*. Translated by John W. Harvey. Oxford: Oxford University Press, 1958. Originally published as *Das Heilige: Über das Irrationale in der Idee des Göttlichen und sein Verhältnis zum Rationalen* (Breslau, Germany: Trewendt & Granier, 1917).
Patočka, Jan. *Body, Community, Language, World*. Translated by Erazim Kohák. Peru, IL: Open Court, 1999.
———. "Heidegger penseur de l'humanité." *Epokhè* 2 (1991): 383–86.
———. *Heretical Essays in the Philosophy of History*. Translated by Erazim Kohák. Peru, IL: Open Court, 1999.
———. *An Introduction to Husserl's Phenomenology*. Translated by Erazim Kohák. Peru, IL: Open Court, 1999.
———. *Le monde naturel et le mouvement de l'existence humaine*. Translated by E. Abrams. Dordrecht, Netherlands: Kluwer, 1988.
———. *Papiers Phénoménologiques*. Translated by Erika Abrams. Paris: J. Millon, 1995.
———. *Plato and Europe*. Translated by Petr Lom. Stanford, CA: Stanford University Press, 2002.
Péguy, Charles. *Dialogue de l'histoire et de l'âme charnelle*. Paris: Gallimard, 1972.
Pichot, André. *Expliquer la vie, de l'âme à la molecule*. Versailles: Quae, 2011.
———. *Histoire de la notion de vie*. Paris: Gallimard, 1993.
———. *Petite Phénoménologie de la connaissance*. Paris: Aubier, 1991.
Polanyi, Michael. *Personal Knowledge: Towards a Post-Critical Philosophy*. Chicago: University of Chicago Press, 1958.
Rahner, Karl. *Foundations of Christian Faith*. Translated by William V. Dych. New York: Crossroad, 1978.
———. *Karl Rahner in Dialogue: Conversations and Interviews, 1965–1982*. New York: Crossroad, 1986.
Ravaisson, Felix. *De l'habitude*. Paris: Fournier, 1838.

Richardson, William. *Heidegger: Through Phenomenology to Thought*. The Hague, Netherlands: Martinus Nijhoff, 1974.

Richir, Marc. *Phénomènes, temps, et être I. Ontologie et phenomenology*. Grenoble, France: Jérôme Millon, 1987.

———. *Recherches phénoménologiques I, II, III*. Brussels: Ousia, 1981.

———. *Recherches phénoménologiques IV, V*. Brussels: Ousia, 1983.

———. *Le Rien et son apparence*. Brussels: Ousia, 1979.

Ricoeur, Paul. "The Hermeneutics of Testimony." In *Essays on Biblical Interpretation*, edited by Lewis S. Mudge, 119–54. Philadelphia: Fortress Press, 1980.

———. *Living Up to Death*. Translated by David Pellauer. Chicago: University of Chicago Press, 2009. Originally published as *Vivant jusqu'à la mort* (Paris: Seuil, 2007).

———. *Time and Narrative*. 3 vols. Translated by Kathleen Blamey and David Pellauer. Chicago: University of Chicago Press, 1984–1988.

Romano, Claude. *Au cœur de la raison, la phénoménologie*. Paris: Gallimard, 2010.

———. *L'Aventure temporelle: trois essais pour introduire à l'herméneutique événementiale*. Paris: Presses Universitaires de France, 2010.

———. *Event and Time*. Translated by Stephen E. Lewis. New York: Fordham University Press, 2013.

———. *Event and World*. Translated by Shane Mackinlay. New York: Fordham University Press, 2009.

Sartre, Jean-Paul. *Being and Nothingness*. Translated by Hazel E. Barnes. New York: Washington Square Press, 1993.

———. *L'être et le néant*. Paris: Gallimard, 1943.

Schelling, Friedrich Wilhelm Joseph von. *The Ages of the World*. Translated by Jason M. Wirth. Albany: State University of New York Press, 2000.

Schutz, Alfred. *The Phenomenology of the Social World*. Translated by George Walsh and Frederick Lehnert. Evanston, IL: Northwestern University Press, 1967.

Sellars, Wilfrid. *Empricism and the Philosophy of Mind*. Cambridge, MA: Harvard University Press, 1997.

Simon, Claude. *Leçon de choses*. Paris: Éditions de Minuit, 1975.

Simondon, Gilbert. *L'individu et sa genese physico-biologique*. Grenoble, France: Millon, 1995.

———. *Du mode d'existence des objets techniques*. Paris: Aubier, 1989.

Spaemann, Robert. *Persons: The Difference between "Someone" and "Something."* Translated by Oliver O'Donovan. Oxford: Oxford University Press, 2007.

Spiegelberg, Herbert. *The Phenomenological Movement: A Historical Introduction*. 2 vols. The Hague, Netherlands: Nijhoff, 1960.

Spinoza, Baruch. *A Spinoza Reader*: Ethics *and Other Works*. Edited by Edwin Curley. Princeton, NJ: Princeton University Press, 1994.

Stirner, Max. *The Ego and Its Own*. Edited by David Leopold. Cambridge: Cambridge University Press, 1995.

Straus, Erwin. *Phenomenological Psychology*. New York: Basic Books, 1966.

———. *Phenomenology of Memory*. Pittsburgh: Duquesne University Press, 1970.

Stumpf, Carl. *Tonpsychologie*. 2 vols. Leipzig, Germany: Verlag von S. Hirzel, 1883–1890.

Suárez, Francisco. *Disputationes metaphysicae*. Hildesheim, Germany: G. Olms, 1965.

Tanner, Kathryn. "Theology at the Limits of Phenomenology." In *Counter-Experiences: Reading Jean-Luc Marion*, edited by Kevin Hart, 201–35. Notre Dame, IN: University of Notre Dame Press, 2007.

Taubes, Jacob. *Occidental Eschatology*. Translated by David Ratmoko. Stanford, CA: Stanford University Press, 2009. Originally published as *Abendländische Eschatologie* (Berlin: Matthes & Seitz Verlag, 2007).

Tertullian. *La chair du Christ* (*De carne Christi*). Vols. 1–2. *Sources Chrétiennes*. Paris: Cerf, 1976.

Thao, Tran Duc. *Phenomenology and Dialectical Materialism*. Translated by R. S. Cohen. Dordrecht, Netherlands: D. Reidel, 1986.

Tilliette, Xavier, SJ. *Le Christ de la philosophie*. Paris: Cerf, 1991.

———. *Le Christ des philosophes: Du Maître de sagesse au divin Témoin*. Namur, Belgium: Culture et Verité, 1993.

———. *L'Église des philosophes, de Nicolas de Cuse á Gabriel Marcel*. Paris: Cerf, 2006.

———. *Les philosophes lisent la Bible*. Paris: Cerf, 2001.

———. *Philosophies eucharistiques, de Descartes á Blondel*. Paris: Cerf, 2006.

———. *La Semaine sainte des philosophes*. Paris: Desclée, 1992.

Travis, Charles. *Objectivity and the Parochial*. Oxford: Oxford University Press, 2010.

———. *Occasion Sensitivity: Selected Essays*. Oxford: Oxford University Press, 2008.

———. *Perception: Essays after Frege*. Oxford: Oxford University Press, 2013.

———. *Thought's Footing: A Theme in Wittgenstein's* Philosophical Investigations. Oxford: Oxford University Press, 2006.

Valéry, Paul. "Choses tues." In *Œuvres*, vol. 2. Edited by Jean Hytier, 478–79. Paris: Gallimard, 1970.

———. "Tel quel." In *Oeuvres*, vol. 2, 560. Paris: Gallimard, 1970.

Vioulac, Jean. *L'époque de la technique. Marx, Heidegger et l'accomplissement de la métaphysique*. Paris: Presses Universitaires de France, 2009.

Vries, Hent de. *Minimal Theologies*. Translated by Geoffrey Hale. Baltimore, MD: Johns Hopkins University Press, 2005.

Waldenfels, Bernhard. *Phänomenologie in Frankreich*. Berlin: Surkhamp, 1983.

Weiss, Johannes. *Die Predigt Jesu vom Reiche Gottes*. Göttingen, Germany: Vandenhoeck & Ruprecht's, 1892.

Weizsäcker, Viktor von. *Der Gestaltkreis. Theorie der Einheit von Wahrnehmen und Bewegen*. Frankfurt, Germany: Suhrkamp, 1997.

Wittgenstein, Ludwig. *On Certainty*, edited by G. E. M. Anscombe and G. E. Moore. New York: Harper, 1969.

———. *Philosophical Investigations*. Translated by G. E. M. Anscombe. Oxford: Blackwell, 1953.

———. *Philosophical Remarks*. Translated by Rush Rhees. Chicago: University of Chicago Press, 1975.

———. *Tractatus Logico-Philosophicus*. Translated by D. F. Pears and B. F. McGuinness. London: Routledge, 1961.

Wolfson, Harry Austryn. *The Philosophy of the Church Fathers: Faith, Trinity, Incarnation*. Cambridge, MA: Harvard University Press, 1956.

Zahavi, Dan. "Time and Consciousness in the Bernau Manuscripts." *Husserl Studies* 20, no. 2 (2004): 99–118.

Contributors

Renaud Barbaras is professor of philosophy at the University of Paris I Sorbonne–Panthéon. He has written many books on the phenomenology of perception and the phenomenology of life, including *The Being of the Phenomenon: Merleau-Ponty's Ontology*; *Introduction á une phénoménologie de la vie*; *La vie lacunaire*; and, most recently, *Dynamique de la manifestation*.

Jocelyn Benoist is professor of philosophy at the University of Paris I Sorbonne–Panthéon. He is the author of *Representations sans object: aux origines de la phénoménologie et de la philosophie analytique*; *Sens et sensibilité: l'intentionalité en context*; and, most recently, *Le bruit du sensible*.

Jean-Louis Chrétien is professor of philosophy at the University of Paris IV. He has written nearly thirty books on the history of philosophy, phenomenology, theology, poetry, and literature, including *The Call and the Response*; *The Unforgettable and the Unhoped For*; and *The Ark of Speech*.

Jean-François Courtine is professor of philosophy at the University of Paris IV. He has written numerous books on the history of metaphysics and phenomenology, including *Suárez et le système de la métaphysique*; *La cause de la phénoménologie*; and *Archéo-Logique: Husserl, Heidegger, Patočka*.

Françoise Dastur taught philosophy at the University of Paris I Sorbonne–Panthéon, the University of Paris XII Val de Marne, and is currently professor emerita at the University of Nice Sophia-Antipolis. She has written widely on the history of phenomenology, including *Heidegger and the Question of Time*; *Telling Time: Sketch of a Phenomenological Chronology*; and *Death: An Essay on Finitude*.

Emmanuel Falque is Doyen of the Faculty of Philosophy at the Institut catholique de Paris. He is the author of *The Metamorphosis of Finitude*; *God, the Flesh, and the Other*; and, most recently, *Le combat amoureux: Disputes phénoménologiques et théologiques*.

Michel Henry was one of the most prominent phenomenologists of the last century. He has published widely on phenomenology, psychoanalysis, art, and theology, including *The Essence of Manifestation*; *Material Phenomenology*; and *I am the Truth: Toward a Philosophy of Christianity*.

Jean-Yves Lacoste is Honorary Professor of Philosophy at Australian Catholic University and Life Member of Clare Hall, University of Cambridge. He is the general editor of the *Encyclopedia of Christian Theology* and has published numerous books on religious phenomena, including *Experience and the Absolute* and, more recently, *Être en danger*; *From Theology to Theological Thinking*; and *L'Intuition sacramentelle et autres essais*.

Jean-Luc Marion is emeritus professor of philosophy at the University of Paris IV and the University of Chicago and is a member of the Académie française. He is the author of numerous books on the history of philosophy, phenomenology, and theology, including *Descartes' Metaphysical Prism*; *Being Given: Toward a Phenomenology of Givenness*; and *God without Being*.

Claude Romano is professor of philosophy at the University of Paris IV. He is the author of *Event and World*; *Event and Time*; *There Is: The Event and the Finitude of Appearing*; and *Au cœur de la raison, la phénoménologie*.

Index

Abelard, P., 60
Abraham, 195, 197, 205
Aertsen, J., 36
aesthetic, aesthetics, aestheticism, 15, 47, 68, 74, 90, 92, 99, 119, 124, 126, 135, 204
Alain. *See* Chartier, É.-A.
Alquié, F., 41, 43, 63
Althusser, 32, 41, 43
Apollo, 231
Aquinas, T., 11, 36–37, 51–53, 60, 191, 202, 210, 216, 221–23
Archives Husserl de Paris of the École normale supérieure, 4, 24, 45
Arendt, H., 213
Aristotle, 10–11, 25, 34, 41–42, 51–52, 64, 73–75, 95, 160, 169, 179, 184, 195, 203, 208, 231, 233
Armogathe, J.-R., 41, 63
Artaud, A., 215
Aubenque, P., 32, 50, 64
Auerbach, E., 234
Augustine, St., 10–11, 48, 60, 228, 230, 238
Austin, J., 12–13, 99, 102, 104, 108
Austrian philosophy, 29
Bachelard, G., 175
Baden School, 38
Badiou, A., 2
Balthasar, H. von, 58, 135, 199, 210, 222–23
Balzac, H., 21, 233–34, 236
Barbaras, R., 3, 18–20, 23, 145–75
Barth, K., 58, 197–98
Bataille, G., 215
Beaufret, J., 26, 40, 42, 46, 53, 58, 64, 212
Becker, O., 208, 210
Beckett, S., 236
Being and Time: Macquarrie-Robinson English translation, 39, 227; Stambaugh English translation, 39, 227
Benoist, J., 2, 4, 6–7, 11–15, 22–23, 26, 30–31, 34–36, 38–39, 55, 97–116, 213
Benvenuto, S., 143
Bergson, H., 2, 52, 142, 146, 164, 171, 176, 238
Bernanos, G., 236
Bernard of Clairvaux, St., 32, 205, 209, 237
Bernau manuscripts, 200, 210, 255
Bernet, R., 4, 25, 27

Bérulle, P. de, 206, 210
Bethlehem, Israel, 223
Bhartrihari, 186
Binswanger, L., 213
Biran, M. de, 127, 137
Blondel, M., 216
Boethius, 23
Bogdan, M., 142–43
Böhme, J., 33
Bolzano, B., 39, 114, 116
Bonaventure, St., 221–23, 226
Boston College, 53
Bourgeois, B., 147, 174
Bourin, F., 122
Boutroux, É., 119, 142
Bouveresse, J., 11, 100, 115
Brague, R., 25, 34, 38, 40–41, 43, 63
Brandom, R., 12, 92
Brentano, F., 28, 39, 75
Breton, S., 41, 50, 53, 63
Brohm, J.-M., 143
Bruzina, R., 208
Bultmann, R., 191, 209, 223
Buytendijk, F., 73, 95

Calle-Gruber, M., 144
Calvin, J., 224
Campbell, R., 170, 175
Camus, A., 176
Canguilhem, G., 163, 175
Cartesian movement, Cartesianism, 43, 75–76, 195, 217
Cassirer, E., 70, 92, 95
Castelli, E., 225, 227
Cavaillès, J., 24, 46, 64
Cavell, S., 12, 69
Celan, P., 41–42
Centre d'études cartésiennes, 43
Centre Husserl, 24
Centre national de la recherche scientifique (CNRS), 24, 45, 121
Centre Richelieu, 210
Cerisuelo, M., 233–36, 238
Certeau, M. de, 35
Cezanne, P., 231
Charles, M., 195, 210
Chartier, É.-A. (aka Alain), 119,142
Chicago, Illinois, 45
Chrétien, J.-L., 21–23, 31, 58, 211, 216, 219, 228–38
Clauberg, J., 51, 64
Cohen, H., 67, 92, 95
Cohn, D, 234, 238
Colette, J., 4, 27
Collège de France, 115, 218
Collingwood, R., 35
Concours Général, 176
Corbin, H., 37, 39, 176, 186
Courtine, J.-F., 3–4, 7, 22, 24–39, 45–46, 50, 98
Cusano, S., 143

Dante, 231, 234
Dastur, F., 4, 20–21, 23, 27, 30–31, 39, 147, 174, 176–87
David, A., 143
Davidson, D., 66
Davidson, S., 142
Deleuze, G., 2, 41, 145–46, 215
Denys the Areopagite, 221–23
Depraz, N., 213
Derrida, J., 2, 4, 23, 26–27, 29, 31, 36, 41, 44–48, 53, 57–58, 62, 107, 174, 177, 180, 182–83, 187, 201
Desanti, J.-T., 46, 64, 145, 174, 178, 187
Descartes, R., 5, 41–45, 50, 52, 63, 76, 121, 127–30, 134, 138–40, 151, 153, 182, 195, 197, 201, 203
Descombes, V., 11
Dhermy, T., 142–44
Didier, F., 7
Dika, T., 1–23, 186
Dionysus, 130
Dixsaut, M., 176, 186
Docetism, 214, 220
Donato, E., 22
Dostoevsky, 236
dualism, 127, 151, 165, 168

Ebeling, G., 188, 209
Eckhart, M., 136, 138, 193, 221
École des hautes études en sciences sociales, 63
École normale supérieure (ENS), 24, 26, 40–43, 45, 63, 97–99, 146, 174, 187, 197

École normale supérieure de Saint-Cloud, 145
École pratique des hautes études, 143, 186
Éditions Gallimard, 122
English, J., 4, 27, 100
Enrico Castelli Colloquium, 225
Enrico Castelli Jubilee Symposium, 227
Epiméthée of Presses Universitaires de France, 46
Erasmus, 60
Eriugena, J., 217, 221
Escoubas, É., 4, 27, 31, 39
Espagne, M., 24, 38
essentialism, 94–95
Evans, G., 73
existentialism, 32, 74, 176

Falque, E., 4, 7–11, 21, 23, 211–27
Faulkner, W., 236
Fédier, F., 42, 53, 63
Fichte, J., 8, 33, 60, 174
Fink, E., 26, 38, 177–78, 194, 208
Flaubert, G., 236–38
Fleurent, M., 187
Fonds Michel Henry, 117, 119
Foucauldian archealogy, 4, 33
Foucault, M., 33–35, 145
Franciscan philosophy, 221–23
Franck, D., 4, 7, 22, 24–26, 31, 38, 45–46, 48, 97–98, 211
Free University of Brussels, 38
Frege, G., 102, 110, 114
Freud, S., 122, 129–30

Gadamer, H.-G., 66, 93, 178
Galibert, T., 143
Garelli, J., 4, 27, 31, 147, 174
Gaspar, 135
Gaudé, I., 143
Gibson, J., 83, 95
Gilson, E., 209
Ginzburg, C., 35
Giovannangeli, D., 4, 27
Goethe, J., 135
Goff, J. Le, 190, 209
Goldstein, K., 73, 95, 163–64, 175
Gondek, H.-D., 27–31
Göttingen Lectures, 25
Gramont, J. de, 213
Granel, G., 4, 27, 31
Gregorian University, 59
Greisch, J., 4, 27, 53, 64, 143
Guenancia, P., 26
Gurwitsch, A., 207, 210

Haar, M., 4, 27
Habermas, J., 6
Hackett, C., 1–23, 38, 119, 237
Hadot, P., 60
Hegel, G., 6, 9–10, 20–21, 25, 31, 33, 51, 58, 60, 91–92, 141, 143, 174, 177, 180, 186–87, 192, 195–97, 199–201, 209, 230
Hegel, philosophy of, Hegelian theory, Hegelianism, 6, 10, 90, 92, 119, 147, 177, 186, 199
Heidegger, M., 3–7, 12–13, 20, 25–30, 34–35, 37–39, 40–51, 53, 56–58, 62–64, 65, 74–75, 81, 89, 91, 93–94, 99, 102, 117–18, 120–22, 124–25, 137, 141, 143, 145–46, 148, 153–57, 160, 166, 175, 176–87, 192–96, 198, 201–5, 208–10, 212–13, 215, 217–18, 222, 224–25, 227, 228–29
Heidegger, philosophy of, Heideggerianism, 6, 25–26, 33–35, 37, 43, 59, 81, 88–89, 99–101, 105–6, 120, 122, 147, 156, 169, 182, 186, 204, 221
Heideggerian hermeneutics, 13
Heideggerian phenomenology, 6–7, 12, 16, 30, 180, 202
Hemmerle, K., 192, 210
Henry, A., 117
Henry, M., 3–4, 16–18, 23, 26, 28–29, 31–32, 34, 45, 48, 54, 57–58, 99, 117–44, 148, 173–75, 193, 203, 211, 215–16, 219
Hesiod, 231
Hölderlin, F., 177, 185
Homer, 231
Honnefelder, L., 36
Housset, E., 57
Hugo, V., 236
Humboldt W. von, 185–86
Hume, D., 14, 70, 84–88, 96
Humean empiricism, 67
Humean type, 14, 68

Husserl-Archives, 174, 187
Husserl, E., 3–9, 11–17, 20, 23, 25–29, 34, 38, 44–48, 52–54, 56–58, 64, 65, 67–74, 76–77, 80–91, 93–96, 98, 100–2, 104, 114, 117–18, 120–21, 126–27, 134, 137, 140, 146–49, 151–54, 158, 160, 174, 177–80, 185, 187, 193–94, 200–3, 207–10, 211–12, 214, 217–18, 226–27, 229
Husserl, philosophy of, Husserlianism, 4, 25, 28, 49, 55, 81, 91, 94, 101, 106, 137, 178, 186
Husserlian phenomenology, 6–7, 11–13, 16, 26, 34, 92, 107, 120, 140, 180, 200
Hyppolite, J., 119

idealism, 12–13, 15, 32–33,74, 77, 102, 114, 117, 119, 150, 153, 174, 177, 194, 196–97, 200
Ignatius of Loyola, 37, 224
Imbert, C., 11
Ingarden, R., 178, 187
Institut catholique de Paris, 63–64, 227
Institut d'histoire des sciences at the Sorbonne, 175
Irenaeus, 221
Isaac, 195, 197, 205

Jacob, 195, 197, 205
James, H., 21, 57, 234, 236–37
James, W., 99, 188
Janicaud, D., 1, 3–4, 9, 22–23, 25, 27, 29–32, 39, 45, 58, 216
Jean, G., 117–19
Jesus, 190
John of the Cross, St., 189
John Paul II, Pope, 212, 226
John XXIII, Pope, 212
John, St., 136, 230
Jonas, H., 3, 19, 158, 163–65
Joyce, J., 57

Kaliba, C., 192, 210
Kandinsky, W., 122, 134–35
Kant, I., 8, 23, 33–34, 40–41, 47, 51–52, 63, 74, 84–88, 90, 92, 95–96, 98, 119–20, 151, 180, 182, 193, 212, 214, 226, 237
Kant, philosophy of, Kantianism, 2, 4,15, 55, 67, 90, 92, 106, 126, 142, 152
Kasper, W., 191
Kearney, R., 53, 64, 210
Kegan, P., 238
Kierkegaard, S., 52, 133, 138, 184, 193, 195–98, 229–30
King's College, 116
Kittel, G., 191
Kojève, A., 119, 141, 143
Koyré, A., 33

Labrusse, S., 143
Lacan, J., 41
Lachelier, J., 119, 142
Lachièze-Rey, P., 119, 143
Lacoste, J.-Y., 4, 7–11, 23, 188–210, 211, 219
Lacoue-Labarthe, P., 177
Lagneau, J., 119, 142
Lask, E., 29
Laugier, S., 102, 116
Le Thor, France, 64
Lebrun, G., 91
Leclercq, J., 117–19
Lefort, C., 29
Leibniz, G. von, 34, 41, 52, 147, 197
Les Éditions de Minuit, 46
Lesage, A.-R., 235, 238
Lévinas, E., 5–8, 22, 29, 31, 34, 53–54, 57–58, 98–99, 107, 146, 153, 160–62, 175, 179, 193, 207, 211, 215–16, 225
Lévy, B., 41, 63
Lewis, C. S., 208, 210
Libera, A. de, 32, 35, 39
Lipps, T., 213
Lubac, H. de, 199, 218
Lucian of Samosata, 235, 238
Lucretius, 230
Lycée Honoré-de-Balzac de Paris, 63
Lycée Louis Pasteur (Neuilly-sur-Seine), 63
Lyon, France, 177
Lyotard, J.-F., 145–46

Macksey, R., 22
Maldiney, H., 31, 228
Malebranche, N., 41, 197, 230
Mandache, B., 142–43

Manent, P., 41, 63
Marburg, Germany, 28
Marburg lectures, 38, 193
Marburg School, 28, 55, 95, 193, 202
Marcel, G., 225
Marion, J., 4–5, 7–11, 16–17, 22–23, 25–28, 31–32, 36, 38–39, 40–64, 98, 107, 211–12, 216, 219, 226
Marquet, J., 33
Martineau, E., 32, 39, 41, 43, 209–10, 227
Marx, K., 122, 131–32, 140
Marx, W., 177, 187
Marxism, 41, 63, 122, 131–33, 145–46, 211–12, 229
McDowell, J., 12, 14–15, 66–67, 70, 72, 82
McGrath, L., 95
Meinong, A., 39
Merleau-Ponty, M., 18–19, 24, 26, 28–31, 35, 57, 65, 70, 73, 78, 82, 93, 98, 101, 145–48, 152–57, 160, 164, 172, 174–75, 177–81, 187, 214–15, 218, 225, 236, 238
metaphysics, 2, 4–5, 7–8, 10–11, 19–21, 23, 25, 31, 33, 35–37, 40, 46, 49–54, 59–62, 65, 93, 98–99, 101–3, 105–6, 109, 114, 119, 126, 139, 147, 151, 162, 165, 168, 171–72, 182–83, 185–86, 196–97, 199, 201–2, 208–9, 212–13, 222
Metzger, A., 84, 96
Milton, J., 231
Montaigne, M. de, 197
Mount Tabor, 223
Munich, Germany, 134
Munier, R., 164, 175

Nabert, J., 119, 142
Natorp, P., 29, 67, 92, 95
naturalism, 118
neo-empiricism, 88, 92
neo-Hegelianism, 3, 6, 15, 22
neo-Kantianism, 8, 14–15, 22, 29, 67, 70–71, 74, 91–92, 95, 193
neo-Marcionism, 197
neoplatonism, 41, 202
New School, 177, 187
Newton, I., 87
Nice, France, 45
Niemeyer, P., 25–26
Nietzsche, F., 25, 34, 51–52, 74, 90–91, 106, 116, 119, 130–31, 133, 176, 184–85, 196, 199–200, 214–15, 226, 230
nihilism, 61, 123, 133, 199–200, 209

O'Leary, J., 53, 64
Origen, 191, 221
Otto, R., 193

Panini, grammarians of, 186
Paris, France, 38, 53, 59, 119, 144, 177, 210, 225
Parmenides, 230
Pascal, B., 195, 197, 230, 233
Patanjali, grammarians of, 186
Patočka, J., 29, 148, 150, 152, 156, 170, 174–75, 177–78, 180, 187
Paul, St., 224, 226
Peacocke, C., 73
Péguy, C., 225
Philo, 231
Pichot, A., 163, 175
Planty-Bonjour, G., 38
Plato, 20–21, 25, 176, 179, 208, 229–30, 233, 237
Platonism, platonic, 20, 37, 89, 184, 192, 229
Polanyi, M., 205, 210
post-Heideggerian phenomenology, 27–28, 32, 34, 99
post-Husserlian phenomenology, 32, 148, 152–53
post-Kantianism, 32–33, 90, 117, 177
post-Wittgensteinian philosophy, 66, 70
poststructuralism, 29
Poulet, G., 234
Presses universitaires de France, 46, 122
Procrustean theory, 9, 194
Proust, M., 57
psychologism, 76, 118, 236
Putnam, H., 12, 99

Queneau, R., 144

Rahner, K., 58, 189, 191, 209, 223
Rancière, J., 235
Ravaisson, F., 230, 238
Renaudot Prize, 141

Renaut, A., 41, 43, 63
Rhineland, Germany, 32
Richard Lectures, 208–9
Richardson, W., 89, 96, 194
Richir, M., 27–28, 31, 38, 147, 174
Rickert, H., 38
Ricoeur, P., 24, 31, 45, 53, 58, 174, 177–78, 201, 210, 211, 216, 224–27, 237
Rilke, R., 164, 166–68
Riquier, C., 228–33, 238
Robinson, E., 39
Rodis-Lewis, G., 43
Roëls, C., 42, 63
Romano, C., 2–4, 7, 11–12, 14–15, 23, 48, 57, 64, 65–96, 211, 213
romanticism, 74
Rome, Italy, 59
Rosenzweig, F., 33, 196
Russell, B., 71

Saint-Denis, France, 174
Sartre, J.-P., 119, 146, 176, 178–79, 181, 187
Scheler, M., 194, 213
Schelling, F. von, 31, 33, 60, 184, 192, 196–97, 210
Schleiermacher, F., 9, 188
Schmitt, C., 189
Schmutz, J., 50
Schopenhauer, A., 119, 126, 130
Schott, N., 115
Schutz, A., 208, 210
Scotus, D., 36, 51, 206, 221
Searle, J., 71
Second Vatican Council, 212, 225
Sellars, W., 12, 14–15, 95
Serres, M., 41
Simon, C., 29, 39
Simondon, G., 163, 175
Sorbonne. *See* University of Paris IV–Sorbonne
Sources Chrétiennes, 32, 39
Southwest School, 28
Spaemann, R., 208, 210
Spiegelberg, H., 193, 210
Spinoza, B., 41, 52, 64, 215
Stein, E., 213
Stendhal, 233, 236
Stirner, M., 134, 143
Stoics, 190, 231
Straus, E., 73, 95
structuralism, 29, 32, 99
Stumpf, C., 73, 95
Suárez, F., 32, 36, 50–51, 64, 202

Taminiaux, J., 4, 27, 185
Tanner, K., 61, 64
Taube, J., 199
Tengelyi, L., 27–31
Teresa of Avila, St., 233
Tertullian, 220–21
Thao, T., 24, 26, 38
Thomas of Erfurt, 213
Thor, J., 143
Tilliette, X., 197, 210
Tokyo, Japan, 53
Travis, C., 13, 102, 111, 116
Troeltsch, E., 38
Twardowski, K., 187

Uhl, M., 143
Université catholique de Louvain, 117, 119
University of Freiburg, 177, 187
University of Louvain, 185
University of Lyon 1 and 2, 174
University of Nanterre, 45, 177
University of Paris 1 Panthéon–Sorbonne, 63, 116, 174, 186
University of Paris IV–Sorbonne, 24, 41–43, 62–64, 175, 177–78, 193, 210
University of Paris VIII (Vincennes), 145, 174
University of Poitiers, 44
University of Strasbourg, 177
University of Virginia, 208

Valentians, 220
Valéry, P., 93, 96
Vaschalde, R., 143
Vasquez, G., 51, 64
Vezin, F., 42, 63
Vienna Circle, 65, 67, 83, 87–89, 92, 102
Vincennes. *See* University of Paris VIII
Vioulac, J., 59
Vries, H. de, 6, 22, 239
Vrin, 46

Waldenfels, B., 27
Wardley, K. J., 209
Weiss, J., 199
Weizsäcker, V. von, 73, 95
Wells, A., 226
Western phenomenology, 127
Western philosophy, thought, 5, 7, 21, 36, 121, 124–26, 129, 177, 179, 182, 184–86, 199, 206–7
Windelband, W., 38
Wittgenstein, L., 12–14, 61, 63, 67, 69–70, 74, 77, 83, 89, 92–93, 95–96, 99, 102, 104, 108
Wolfson, H., 32, 39
Woolf, V., 236

Zahavi, D., 210
Zähringen seminar, 180
Zeus, 231

Perspectives in Continental Philosophy

John D. Caputo, series editor

John D. Caputo, ed., *Deconstruction in a Nutshell: A Conversation with Jacques Derrida.*

Michael Strawser, *Both/And: Reading Kierkegaard—From Irony to Edification.*

Michael D. Barber, *Ethical Hermeneutics: Rationality in Enrique Dussel's Philosophy of Liberation.*

James H. Olthuis, ed., *Knowing Other-wise: Philosophy at the Threshold of Spirituality.*

James Swindal, *Reflection Revisited: Jürgen Habermas's Discursive Theory of Truth.*

Richard Kearney, *Poetics of Imagining: Modern and Postmodern.* Second edition.

Thomas W. Busch, *Circulating Being: From Embodiment to Incorporation—Essays on Late Existentialism.*

Edith Wyschogrod, *Emmanuel Levinas: The Problem of Ethical Metaphysics.* Second edition.

Francis J. Ambrosio, ed., *The Question of Christian Philosophy Today.*

Jeffrey Bloechl, ed., *The Face of the Other and the Trace of God: Essays on the Philosophy of Emmanuel Levinas.*

Ilse N. Bulhof and Laurens ten Kate, eds., *Flight of the Gods: Philosophical Perspectives on Negative Theology.*

Trish Glazebrook, *Heidegger's Philosophy of Science.*

Kevin Hart, *The Trespass of the Sign: Deconstruction, Theology, and Philosophy.*

Mark C. Taylor, *Journeys to Selfhood: Hegel and Kierkegaard.* Second edition.

Dominique Janicaud, Jean-François Courtine, Jean-Louis Chrétien, Michel Henry, Jean-Luc Marion, and Paul Ricoeur, *Phenomenology and the "Theological Turn": The French Debate.*

Karl Jaspers, *The Question of German Guilt*. Introduction by Joseph W. Koterski, S.J.

Jean-Luc Marion, *The Idol and Distance: Five Studies*. Translated with an introduction by Thomas A. Carlson.

Jeffrey Dudiak, *The Intrigue of Ethics: A Reading of the Idea of Discourse in the Thought of Emmanuel Levinas*.

Robyn Horner, *Rethinking God as Gift: Marion, Derrida, and the Limits of Phenomenology*.

Mark Dooley, *The Politics of Exodus: Søren Kierkegaard's Ethics of Responsibility*.

Merold Westphal, *Overcoming Onto-Theology: Toward a Postmodern Christian Faith*.

Edith Wyschogrod, Jean-Joseph Goux, and Eric Boynton, eds., *The Enigma of Gift and Sacrifice*.

Stanislas Breton, *The Word and the Cross*. Translated with an introduction by Jacquelyn Porter.

Jean-Luc Marion, *Prolegomena to Charity*. Translated by Stephen E. Lewis.

Peter H. Spader, *Scheler's Ethical Personalism: Its Logic, Development, and Promise*.

Jean-Louis Chrétien, *The Unforgettable and the Unhoped For*. Translated by Jeffrey Bloechl.

Don Cupitt, *Is Nothing Sacred? The Non-Realist Philosophy of Religion: Selected Essays*.

Jean-Luc Marion, *In Excess: Studies of Saturated Phenomena*. Translated by Robyn Horner and Vincent Berraud.

Phillip Goodchild, *Rethinking Philosophy of Religion: Approaches from Continental Philosophy*.

William J. Richardson, S.J., *Heidegger: Through Phenomenology to Thought*.

Jeffrey Andrew Barash, *Martin Heidegger and the Problem of Historical Meaning*.

Jean-Louis Chrétien, *Hand to Hand: Listening to the Work of Art*. Translated by Stephen E. Lewis.

Jean-Louis Chrétien, *The Call and the Response*. Translated with an introduction by Anne Davenport.

D. C. Schindler, *Han Urs von Balthasar and the Dramatic Structure of Truth: A Philosophical Investigation*.

Julian Wolfreys, ed., *Thinking Difference: Critics in Conversation*.

Allen Scult, *Being Jewish/Reading Heidegger: An Ontological Encounter*.

Richard Kearney, *Debates in Continental Philosophy: Conversations with Contemporary Thinkers*.

Jennifer Anna Gosetti-Ferencei, *Heidegger, Hölderlin, and the Subject of Poetic Language: Toward a New Poetics of Dasein*.

Jolita Pons, *Stealing a Gift: Kierkegaard's Pseudonyms and the Bible*.

Jean-Yves Lacoste, *Experience and the Absolute: Disputed Questions on the Humanity of Man*. Translated by Mark Raftery-Skehan.

Charles P. Bigger, *Between* Chora *and the Good: Metaphor's Metaphysical Neighborhood*.

Dominique Janicaud, *Phenomenology "Wide Open": After the French Debate.* Translated by Charles N. Cabral.
Ian Leask and Eoin Cassidy, eds., *Givenness and God: Questions of Jean-Luc Marion.*
Jacques Derrida, *Sovereignties in Question: The Poetics of Paul Celan.* Edited by Thomas Dutoit and Outi Pasanen.
William Desmond, *Is There a Sabbath for Thought? Between Religion and Philosophy.*
Bruce Ellis Benson and Norman Wirzba, eds., *The Phenomenology of Prayer.*
S. Clark Buckner and Matthew Statler, eds., *Styles of Piety: Practicing Philosophy after the Death of God.*
Kevin Hart and Barbara Wall, eds., *The Experience of God: A Postmodern Response.*
John Panteleimon Manoussakis, *After God: Richard Kearney and the Religious Turn in Continental Philosophy.*
John Martis, *Philippe Lacoue-Labarthe: Representation and the Loss of the Subject.*
Jean-Luc Nancy, *The Ground of the Image.*
Edith Wyschogrod, *Crossover Queries: Dwelling with Negatives, Embodying Philosophy's Others.*
Gerald Bruns, *On the Anarchy of Poetry and Philosophy: A Guide for the Unruly.*
Brian Treanor, *Aspects of Alterity: Levinas, Marcel, and the Contemporary Debate.*
Simon Morgan Wortham, *Counter-Institutions: Jacques Derrida and the Question of the University.*
Leonard Lawlor, *The Implications of Immanence: Toward a New Concept of Life.*
Clayton Crockett, *Interstices of the Sublime: Theology and Psychoanalytic Theory.*
Bettina Bergo, Joseph Cohen, and Raphael Zagury-Orly, eds., *Judeities: Questions for Jacques Derrida.* Translated by Bettina Bergo and Michael B. Smith.
Jean-Luc Marion, *On the Ego and on God: Further Cartesian Questions.* Translated by Christina M. Gschwandtner.
Jean-Luc Nancy, *Philosophical Chronicles.* Translated by Franson Manjali.
Jean-Luc Nancy, *Dis-Enclosure: The Deconstruction of Christianity.* Translated by Bettina Bergo, Gabriel Malenfant, and Michael B. Smith.
Andrea Hurst, *Derrida Vis-à-vis Lacan: Interweaving Deconstruction and Psychoanalysis.*
Jean-Luc Nancy, *Noli me tangere: On the Raising of the Body.* Translated by Sarah Clift, Pascale-Anne Brault, and Michael Naas.
Jacques Derrida, *The Animal That Therefore I Am.* Edited by Marie-Louise Mallet, translated by David Wills.
Jean-Luc Marion, *The Visible and the Revealed.* Translated by Christina M. Gschwandtner and others.
Michel Henry, *Material Phenomenology.* Translated by Scott Davidson.
Jean-Luc Nancy, *Corpus.* Translated by Richard A. Rand.
Joshua Kates, *Fielding Derrida.*
Michael Naas, *Derrida From Now On.*

Shannon Sullivan and Dennis J. Schmidt, eds., *Difficulties of Ethical Life.*

Catherine Malabou, *What Should We Do with Our Brain?* Translated by Sebastian Rand, Introduction by Marc Jeannerod.

Claude Romano, *Event and World.* Translated by Shane Mackinlay.

Vanessa Lemm, *Nietzsche's Animal Philosophy: Culture, Politics, and the Animality of the Human Being.*

B. Keith Putt, ed., *Gazing Through a Prism Darkly: Reflections on Merold Westphal's Hermeneutical Epistemology.*

Eric Boynton and Martin Kavka, eds., *Saintly Influence: Edith Wyschogrod and the Possibilities of Philosophy of Religion.*

Shane Mackinlay, *Interpreting Excess: Jean-Luc Marion, Saturated Phenomena, and Hermeneutics.*

Kevin Hart and Michael A. Signer, eds., *The Exorbitant: Emmanuel Levinas Between Jews and Christians.*

Bruce Ellis Benson and Norman Wirzba, eds., *Words of Life: New Theological Turns in French Phenomenology.*

William Robert, *Trials: Of Antigone and Jesus.*

Brian Treanor and Henry Isaac Venema, eds., *A Passion for the Possible: Thinking with Paul Ricoeur.*

Kas Saghafi, *Apparitions—Of Derrida's Other.*

Nick Mansfield, *The God Who Deconstructs Himself: Sovereignty and Subjectivity Between Freud, Bataille, and Derrida.*

Don Ihde, *Heidegger's Technologies: Postphenomenological Perspectives.*

Suzi Adams, *Castoriadis's Ontology: Being and Creation.*

Richard Kearney and Kascha Semonovitch, eds., *Phenomenologies of the Stranger: Between Hostility and Hospitality.*

Michael Naas, *Miracle and Machine: Jacques Derrida and the Two Sources of Religion, Science, and the Media.*

Alena Alexandrova, Ignaas Devisch, Laurens ten Kate, and Aukje van Rooden, *Re-treating Religion: Deconstructing Christianity with Jean-Luc Nancy.* Preamble by Jean-Luc Nancy.

Emmanuel Falque, *The Metamorphosis of Finitude: An Essay on Birth and Resurrection.* Translated by George Hughes.

Scott M. Campbell, *The Early Heidegger's Philosophy of Life: Facticity, Being, and Language.*

Françoise Dastur, *How Are We to Confront Death? An Introduction to Philosophy.* Translated by Robert Vallier. Foreword by David Farrell Krell.

Christina M. Gschwandtner, *Postmodern Apologetics? Arguments for God in Contemporary Philosophy.*

Ben Morgan, *On Becoming God: Late Medieval Mysticism and the Modern Western Self.*

Neal DeRoo, *Futurity in Phenomenology: Promise and Method in Husserl, Levinas, and Derrida.*

Sarah LaChance Adams and Caroline R. Lundquist, eds., *Coming to Life: Philosophies of Pregnancy, Childbirth, and Mothering.*

Thomas Claviez, ed., *The Conditions of Hospitality: Ethics, Politics, and Aesthetics on the Threshold of the Possible.*

Roland Faber and Jeremy Fackenthal, eds., *Theopoetic Folds: Philosophizing Multifariousness.*

Jean-Luc Marion, *The Essential Writings*. Edited by Kevin Hart.

Adam S. Miller, *Speculative Grace: Bruno Latour and Object-Oriented Theology.* Foreword by Levi R. Bryant.

Jean-Luc Nancy, *Corpus II: Writings on Sexuality.*

David Nowell Smith, *Sounding/Silence: Martin Heidegger at the Limits of Poetics.*

Gregory C. Stallings, Manuel Asensi, and Carl Good, eds., *Material Spirit: Religion and Literature Intranscendent.*

Claude Romano, *Event and Time*. Translated by Stephen E. Lewis.

Frank Chouraqui, *Ambiguity and the Absolute: Nietzsche and Merleau-Ponty on the Question of Truth.*

Noëlle Vahanian, *The Rebellious No: Variations on a Secular Theology of Language.*

Michael Naas, *The End of the World and Other Teachable Moments: Jacques Derrida's Final Seminar.*

Jean-Louis Chrétien, *Under the Gaze of the Bible*. Translated by John Marson Dunaway.

Edward Baring and Peter E. Gordon, eds., *The Trace of God: Derrida and Religion.*

Vanessa Lemm, ed., *Nietzsche and the Becoming of Life.*

Aaron T. Looney, *Vladimir Jankélévitch: The Time of Forgiveness.*

Robert Mugerauer, *Responding to Loss: Heideggerian Reflections on Literature, Architecture, and Film.*

Tarek R. Dika and W. Chris Hackett, *Quiet Powers of the Possible: Interviews in Contemporary French Phenomenology*. Foreword by Richard Kearney.

Jeremy Biles and Kent L. Brintnall, eds., *Negative Ecstasies: Georges Bataille and the Study of Religion.*

Richard Kearney and Brian Treanor, eds., *Carnal Hermeneutics.*